Naipaul's Strangers

DAGMAR BARNOUW

Naipaul's Strangers

INDIANA
University Press
Bloomington & Indianapolis

This book is a publication of

Indiana University Press
601 North Morton Street
Bloomington, IN 47404-3797 USA

http://iupress.indiana.edu

Telephone orders   800-842-6796
Fax orders   812-855-7931
Orders by e-mail   iuporder@indiana.edu

The paper used in this publication meets the minimum requirements of American National Standard for Information Sciences—Permanence of Paper for Printed Library Materials, ANSI Z39.48-1984.

Manufactured in the United States of America

Library of Congress Cataloging-in-Publication Data

Barnouw, Dagmar.
   Naipaul's strangers / Dagmar Barnouw.
      p.   cm.
Includes index.
   ISBN 0-253-34207-4 (cloth : alk. paper) — ISBN 0-253-21579-X (pbk. : alk. paper)
   1. Naipaul, V. S. (Vidiadhar Surajprasad), date—Criticism and interpretation. 2. Naipaul, V. S. (Vidiadhar Surajprasad), date—Journeys. 3. Trinidadians—Foreign countries—History—20th century. 4. Travelers' writings—History and criticism. 5. Pluralism (Social sciences) in literature. 6. Intercultural communication in literature. 7. Islamic countries—In literature. 8. Pakistan—In literature. 9. Strangers in literature. 10. Iran—In literature. 11. Islam in literature. I. Title.
   PR9272.9.N32 Z57 2003
   823'.914—dc21
2002014599

1 2 3 4 5   08 07 06 05 04 03

Dedication

For our grandson Nicholas Chen Barnouw.

Contents

Introduction: Cultural Plurality and Cultural Value

This study of Naipaul's writing focuses on the documentary interests and approaches in both his fiction and his travelogues. Present from the beginning, they have become increasingly visible over the course of a long writing career that demonstrates the author's growing attentiveness to a multitude of other voices. Quintessentially a traveler, Naipaul has inhabited a large part of the world, looking at its amazing variety and trying to imagine the strangeness of people in different places and times. The experience of cultural plurality moved him to seek out others' stories, and the symbiosis of recording and writing found already in his early texts reflects the responsibilities of writing out of others' articulated experiences, of transforming something already formed. These transformations underlie the composition of novels as different as *A House for Mr Biswas, Guerrillas,* and *A Bend in the River.* They also inform the narrational shaping of documentaries such as *Among the Believers, A Turn in the South,* and *Beyond Belief* and the imaginative interweaving of actual and fictional histories and memories in *Finding the Center, The Enigma of Arrival,* and *A Way in the World.*

The large and varied body of Naipaul's work exhibits, along with the writer's growing awareness of the complexities and difficulties of cultural difference, a growing sense of incomplete, uncertain knowledge that has led to his expanding and fusing the modes of the documentary and of fiction. Tracing these developments, I am interested in Naipaul's sophisticated literary strategies and experimentations primarily in their relation to the meanings of his cultural critique. He has worked hard on learning to write well because the craft, the "profession" of writing, was from the beginning intimately connected with his enterprise of learning about and documenting the enduring strangeness of large parts of our world. It was this deliberately combined process that created the peculiar accessibility and persuasiveness of his arguments for the "common reader." Among professional readers, reviewers of Naipaul's work in newspapers and general cultural journals have been much more perceptive and appreciative of its literary and intellectual qualities than have academic postcolonialist critics, especially those trained in literary studies. It seems that the former have been better equipped to deal with the timeliness of Naipaul's critical observations over many decades.

My study comes into a curiously divided context: the ultimate general Western affirmation of Naipaul's work by his being awarded the Nobel Prize in literature and an intensified questioning of Western modernity in the aftermath of the recent traumatic terrorist attacks on the U.S. The current Western intellectual climate encourages mistrust in the heritage of the European Enlightenment and "global" denunciation of "colonialism." In the effort to understand different civilizations, Naipaul has insisted on a differentiating historiography of colonial rule and on the value of Enlightenment achievements, notably the secular affirmation of modern complexity, mobility, and diversity. Understanding is shaped by the when and where, the historicity of the observer. As long as the observer relates to the observed in the context of larger social and political concerns that direct his interest in them, understanding will not be value-neutral. Naipaul has always pointed to his focus on the particular in the terms of its broader, "universal" meanings, and he has been very open about finding some societies and some cultural conventions more conducive to a reasonably good life than others. This is true also for his critical excursions into fundamentalist Islam in *Among the Believers* (1981) and *Beyond Belief* (1998). Understanding here means eliciting and retelling the stories of individual believers to gain some degree of access to the variety of religious experience within the sameness of the pure faith, and to learn more about the conditions under which belief systems have become powerful political tools. Naipaul has been curious about the believers and is often moved by their experiences but is also consistently critical of the religio-political symbiosis in Islamic fundamentalism that has impeded the development of functioning political institutions. He would be the last to call for a radical reconsideration of Western modernity in the light of recent traumatic events of terrorism; he would be the first to claim the developed countries' co-responsibility for these events—as he analyzed it explicitly in these two books and in many of his other critical explorations of the difficulties experienced by developing countries.

The problems of accelerated modern technological developments in the experience of different populations have exacerbated existing difficulties of cultural difference and anxieties of contact. Naipaul's view of cultural plurality has been of successes but also profound frustrations, of sharing and divisiveness, of gradual openings and abrupt closures: the emergence of restrictive "traditionalisms" set against perceived threats of globalization. There are instructive parallels in intellectual debates on cultural plurality more than two centuries ago, whose concerns are remarkably contemporary to the beginning of the twenty-first century and on which I will draw repeatedly. The second half of the eighteenth century was a period of extraordinary progress in many fields of knowledge because it saw the beginning of globalization by exploration rather than conquest. It is true that the two cannot always be cleanly separated and that exploration, requiring contact between groups of different degrees and with different concepts of cultural complexity, has frequently done damage to the contacted. Enlightenment intellectuals were well aware of that danger, among them the "philosophical traveler" Georg Forster, later the mentor of Alexander von Humboldt and his model for the traveler's intense attentiveness and concentration. As young man, Forster had accompanied his father, a research biologist, on Captain Cook's second circumnavigation and documented the experience in *A Voyage around the World* (1777).

Writing what would become a classic of European literature out of his father's materials, the young Forster was remarkably clear about the perspectival limitations of observation and the composite nature of evidence. Like many of their European intellectual contemporaries, Kant and Herder were avid readers of travelogues, with their fascinating new information about different ways of being human. But traveling in their armchairs, as Forster noted, they argued from positions that were not developed in the process of experiencing the realities of human diversity but were defined by preestablished, speculative assumptions. "The philosophers of the present age," Forster wrote in the preface to *Voyage,* have relied too much on certain authorities, which prevented them from looking at the world in its newly documented variety: "Without being competent judges of the subject, they have assumed a few circumstances as facts; and wresting even those to suit their own systems, have built a superstructure which pleases at a distance, but upon nearer examination partakes of the illusive nature of a dream."[1] (Ironically, the authorities invoked by postcolonialist theorists more than two centuries later include some of Herder's most speculative assumptions, which are based on much less information than is available now.) Forster's concern was the rigid eclecticism of the "philosophers'" perspective, their narrow understanding not only of the world "out there" but also of the dynamics of observation. Such "superstructures," he pointed out, obscured the fact that "two travellers seldom saw the same object in the same manner, and each reported the fact differently, according to his sensations, and his peculiar mode of thinking" (p. 13). The readers of his *Voyage,* he insisted, needed to know "the colour of the glass" through which he had looked, if they wanted to make sense of, to judge his observations (pp. 13–14).

Forster also explained that the discoveries made by Captain Cook and his team of researchers had not happened by chance alone, spontaneously. New facts were found on the basis of existing information to which they added, and they aided in the formation of general views which, pointing to "the proper objects of farther investigation," would in turn enable more discoveries. But this process was inevitably filtered through the individual researcher's acculturated temperament which, though nurtured and enlarged by it, would also control it (p. 14). Arguably, it was the amazing novelty of information, its wealth and diversity, that made Forster aware of the hermeneutic circle: it is inescapable in terms of the observer's limited or qualified objectivity *and* essential in terms of the accessibility to him of the object. The very selectiveness of the observer's perspective, his "colored glass," enables and drives observation, and the reader as observer of these acts of observation needs to be aware of this circle as much as the narrator of the observation. In competition with Cook's official account of the circumnavigation, Forster affirmed his authorship of *A Voyage around the World* by pointing out the "questionable" documentary authority of his book: he claimed the authority of his experience both for the intended accuracy of his account *and* for its recognized peculiar limitations, his, the observer's, complexly acculturated perception.

In the Enlightenment spirit of tolerance, Forster explicitly wished to exempt from such inevitable (European) selectiveness racial and cultural prejudice.[2] This is an issue we are still struggling with more than two centuries later and which cannot be easily resolved by current Western ideological multiculturalism. A document of the Enlightenment, the *Voyage* was written "with a retrospect to our general improvement and welfare" (p. 14). Forster's spontaneous reactions of delight and repulsed pity, most clearly expressed in the cases of the (almost) paradisiacally happy people of O-Taheitee and the fearfully "wretched" inhabitants of Tierra del Fuego, have to be judged in the light of this intention. More subdued, more skeptical, more anxious about the enduring obvious distress and seeming "superfluity" of many populations in many parts of the world, this intention has also been Naipaul's: his work is not therefore less "dark" but more relevant. In Forster's observation, the Fuegan "character" was the "strangest" and most oppressive "compound of stupidity, indifference and inactivity," preventing this people from living "more comfortably and happily" (p. 616). In relative terms they could have done so, even in an environment as hostile as Tierra del Fuego. Another people, whom Cook had encountered on his first voyage at nearby Success Bay, had managed much better: "Their stature was taller; they had contrived buskins which secured their feet; they appeared to be sensible of the excellence of several European goods, and to set a value upon them; lastly, they were more communicative, and had ideas of ceremony or civility" (p. 617). Forster described the physical discomfort of the other group: almost naked, barefoot in the cold weather, they were always shivering, "from their nose there was a constant discharge of *mucus* into their ugly open mouth. The whole assemblage of their features formed the most loathsome picture of misery and wretchedness to which human nature can possibly be reduced" (pp. 615–16). What had made this group so much less alert and competent than the other one? For Forster their misery emphasized the fallacies of a nostalgic perspective on the noble savage that would redeem European complexity: "Till it can be proved, that a man in continual pain, from the rigour of climate, is happy, I shall give no credit to the eloquence of philosophers, who have either had no opportunity of contemplating human nature under all its modifications, or who have not felt what they have seen" (p. 618).

In his encounter with human beings whose strangeness he cannot begin to understand, the traveler will still have to "contemplate" them and bring to this act of looking attentively his knowledge of humanity. He then cannot but "feel" what he observes because he will have imagined himself in the place of the observed. Within the parameters of an always limited, relational objectivity, Forster presented his felt observations as facts: the people he saw *suffered* from the cold; the smell, taste, and condition of their food *was* repulsive. It is true that a diet offensive to Europeans can signify cultural adjustment to a natural environment, in this case producing the body heat needed to survive in the unrelenting cold. But the Fuegans' particular diet seemed much more a natural necessity than a cultural choice modifying such necessity. If Forster, his teammates, and the sailors were simply limited to their acculturated sensibilities when they abhorred the putrid seal flesh, why, then, did they adore the also largely unfamiliar vegetarian diet of the Tahitians? The issue of choice, that is, of value judgments concerning cultural arrangements that are different in different ways, cannot be circumvented that easily.

The "brutishness" of the Fuegans was the passivity of their wretchedness; their ugliness was derived from their being acted upon rather than acting, empty of thought rather than thoughtfully responding to their environment. When Forster referred to them as "loathsome" (p. 616), he expressed the European's feeling of being weighed down by so much misery—too much to be human. In his *Ideas for a Philosophy of the History of Mankind* (1785) Herder drew on information available in Forster's *Voyage* to argue a more diffuse concept of happiness and wretchedness. He insisted that the "contentment" of the Tahitians, an admirable cultural achievement in Forster's eyes, was not different in kind from that of the "poor Fuegans." Yet, quoting from Forster's descriptions of their physical distress, he also praised the generosity of "nature itself," restricting human settlement in this inhumanly harsh environment. Herder's argument from climate in book 8 of *Ideas* culminates in section 5 with a Rousseauean praise of simplicity. But *Ideas,* now a quarry of quotes for postcolonialist theorizing, is shot through with ambivalences, ambiguities, and contradictions reflecting the cognitive obscurities of the bewildering wealth of new anthropological information. Herder presented his idea of earthly happiness in terms of the individual's culturally mediated ability to respond to the accident of having been born into this or that environment. At the same time, he explicitly based his abstinence from judgments of cultural value on the authority of divine intervention: God created us happy as Europeans and the Fuegans happy as Fuegans. For Forster, the cultural achievement of human happiness carried its own authority, a value established by judgment and choice. The Fuegans' human, that is, cultural, condition was different in kind from that of the Tahitians, because their distress was real in *any* human's (higher mammal's) terms.

Critical of European complexity and mobility, Herder saw happiness as a profoundly simple sensation of being, shared by all humans in all situations, especially by all savages. It was rooted in emotional enrichment rather than the power of reason. Forster's ideas of happiness were based not on ideology but experience: he had been happy on O-Taheitee because its inhabitants had made a good life for themselves that included him—for a time. European "contentment" required greater mobility and complexity, going on with the voyage and writing about it. Time traveling into the twenty-first century and accused of Eurocentrism, Forster would have told Herder's postcolonialist admirers that his celebration of non-Western simplicity, of heart over mind, of soul over intellect, was based more on principled acceptance of the otherness of the other than on his own experience and understanding of it. Trying to understand strangers, Forster had learned about the documentarist's challenge to understand what it felt like to be that stranger—as Naipaul would learn. Accepting the challenge, they both knew that they had to depend, at least partially, on an acculturated perception which would be distorting to a degree. Yet the questions they needed to ask concerned not so much the fact itself of that distortion but its relational nature: Distorted in relation to what situation? What event? What act or actor? What observer? There is a broad spectrum of positions between principled embracing and rejecting of observed otherness, the various strange modes of cultural behavior, and these positions are defined, to varying degrees, by the experiential involvement of the observer. Without it, no judgment is possible; with it, the judgment is always tainted.

For Forster, the Enlightenment curiosity about what is different that informed his remarkably self-questioning observation was the key to understanding strangers: a partial, provisional, temporal process of knowledge. This process is echoed in Naipaul's self-perception as "traveler and looker" who has learned to recognize and use to advantage its uncertainties and incompleteness. But where Forster was still at the beginning of making—and reflecting about—contact between vastly different civilizations, Naipaul is the product of this process. Forster's intellectual position was European, even where he was aware of and analyzed his and other travelers' (by necessity) "Eurocentric" perspective. Naipaul's position is that of the "inquiline" moving between civilizations, bridging the colonial and postcolonial experience. Though it made him vulnerable to hostile and on occasion stunningly thoughtless attacks by postcolonialist critics from Said to Homi K. Bhabha and Derek Walcott, there are clearly great advantages to this position. It helped Naipaul to develop a particular kind of mobile social intelligence that allowed him to see with the problems also the benefits of colonial rule, and with the positive also the negative aspects of the "postcolonial condition." In the multiculturalist West he is an eminently contemporary, emblematic figure arguing the fallacies of late-modern cultural co-temporality and co-locality—the Western "moral" illusionary achievement of having done away, once and for all, with the strangeness of difference. But he also understands the easy seductions of this assumption for some groups and its serious, much needed promises for others. His in-between position sharpened his understanding of social and political power, namely his level-headed acceptance of its reality and his apprehensive concern with its implications. As a colonial, he came from a place he thought had no history because his reference point was British history. Yet British history also taught him to develop the disciplined curiosity and the skills needed to reconstruct the multiple histories of places like his own. More, it taught him that he could never take for granted the modern insight into the historicity of understanding, the importance of knowing when and where we are in the world. If today's postcolonialists easily denounce "the" European Enlightenment, they tend to forget that for the people who lived at that time the importance of finding their way in the world was self-evident since they were in real terms much more likely to get lost; so are many people now who do not live in the proverbially well-lit developed countries.

All of Naipaul's stories, whether invented or recorded, are true stories in that the author is a documentarist, responsible to a shared life-world. The weight of true stories is their time and place, to which the documentarist has to pay intense attention, trying to understand where he is in the world at any given moment. Naipaul's recording over many decades the enormous changes brought about by what he once called the "mixing of continents" in the second half of the twentieth century is an important and in some ways unique achievement. Yet no matter how thoughtfully conceived, lucidly argued, and densely written, his recording shares with journalism the lure of the particular and temporal rather than the reassurance of the universal and timeless. His work is a difficult fit for cultural canons: it is too varied in its responses to the immense variety of the world. Attempting truthfulness, it is too truthfully intense, impure, and incomplete.

Naipaul's Strangers

1   Understanding Strangers

There is perhaps no significant contemporary writer whose work has been shaped as profoundly by his cultural background and who, in learning to write about it, has made its disorienting strangeness as intelligible. A traveler and looker, moving away from his origins but never leaving them behind, V. S. Naipaul has learned to pose questions that go to the core of cultural (ethnic) plurality, the most important and difficult challenge to late modernity. Ever more sophisticated technologies and their globalizing energies have brought into sharp focus the fact that many populations seem unable to sustain functioning societies. For better or worse, questions of functionality have been central to technological modernity, increasingly so in the last half of the twentieth century, when technocracy has established itself more and more clearly as the one-party system in Western culture. This fact may have contributed to the current reluctance among intellectuals concerned about Western political and cultural "imperialism" to pose questions of functionality and competence to troubled non-Western societies. Naipaul is not one of them, and his independence, though provocative and irritating to his many critics, has also been useful to many readers because it has accommodated a dissonant plurality of voices not heard otherwise.

Critical readings of Naipaul's work have generally been divided into two groups: a strongly focused postcolonialist critique of his indebtedness to Western cultural values that does not deal with textual complexity, and literary studies of his fictional and nonfictional texts that do not deal with representational complexity, the texts' connectedness to social and political realities. The first kind of reading, increasingly common, is usually presented courtesy of a Western (mostly U.S.) university setting. To readers of this group, the single most shocking aspect of Naipaul's work has been the "metacolonial" tentativeness of his observational position: the traveler on unknown territory who, seeing the unfamiliar, does not yet know what it is that he is looking at. In the eyes of many critics committed to postcolonialist theory, Naipaul's modern understanding of truth as processual trust in evidence shared with others is a priori suspect. And so is his declared interest in the particular rather than the general, his insistence on individual over collective responsibility, and his skeptical insights into the approximate, obscurely composite nature of cultural identity.

A British-educated West Indian, Naipaul has tried to understand and document the difficulties of other cultures through his difficulties at understanding his own multiethnic background. But if he explicitly accepts the modern accountability for the presence of others, he has also been anxious about where it might lead him, intrigued and apprehensive about the "enigma of arrival." He has been concerned about the precarious knowledge of difference in a complexly diverse world, where desires are increasingly public and fears intimate and veiled. In his later, more openly autobiographical texts, the traveler's mobility has become metaphorical, a strategy for his documentary narration that circles around ever more subtle redefinitions of observational position.[1] Straining to overcome his own group's cultural self-delusions caused by multiple displacements, Naipaul has sought out the obscurities of his origin so that he might escape their troubling strangeness. His intense, even fearful dislike of that strangeness has its source in his fear of an imposed, alien cultural identity. Naipaul's anxieties are concrete: he is appalled *for* others in their Third World desolation, because out of his own experience he can imagine them fully. In his "Prologue to an Autobiography," an account of "my literary beginnings and the imaginative promptings of my many-sided background," memories emerge of past "feeling of dirt and poverty and empty days" which have sharpened the adult observer's awareness of the superfluousness of people, both natural and cultural.[2] For the boy growing up in "multicultural" Trinidad, "the other" was not a stimulus to understand himself in cultural terms. Rather, this "other" was the constant reminder that for him there were no such terms and that he had to go it alone by becoming "a writer." The "Prologue" ends with his understanding, after he listened to his family's stories and learned more about his history, what his father had left him: the "vocation" of writing out of "his fear of extinction." It was his father's "subsidiary gift" to him, fueling his "panic about failing to be what I should be, rather than simple ambition" ("Prologue," p. 72).

Driven by his determination not to become extinguished, he made it to Oxford and he learned with some difficulty to be a writer. European intellectual and literary culture proved indispensable for the successes of his ongoing learning process, particularly the well organized London culture business: the BBC Caribbean Service, for which he worked for a while and where other journalists helped him with his writing, the publishing houses, the critics, the booksellers, and the literary prizes.[3] Only after he had published his first two "real" books in England did he "begin to go back" to the Third Worlds of Trinidad, India, South America, and Africa ("Prologue," p. 72). He needed the affirmation of his "vocation" by a functioning, complex literary culture to make sure that experiences which confirmed rather than mitigated the anxieties and frustrations of his youth would not go "beyond writing," that is, overwhelm him. And to be able to write he had to "compose," to steady himself with the cultural "apparatus of order" that he had found in London.[4] Going back to Trinidad had been difficult enough, but traveling in India, recounted in *An Area of Darkness* (1964) and in *India: A Wounded Civilization* (1977), was and continued to be a "shock." Naipaul had thought of India as the "very old and civilized land" of his ancestors, taking it for granted as his "real" origin and expecting it to be able to "grow" into a new, modern civilization. It was his sharp disappointment with the "triviality of Indian thought" and the "poverty of its leadership" that made him say in 1981 that "India has nothing to contribute to the world, is contributing nothing at the moment."[5] He has tended to be "provocative" in interviews, not always usefully. Categorical statements of this kind have to be taken with caution because they generalize unfairly and, above all, simplify Naipaul's own elusive ambivalences.[6] But he seems to have been badly shaken by the Indian experience, admitting at the end of *An Area of Darkness* to "facing his own emptiness" and the realization "how close in the past year I had been to the Indian negation." Yet his vulnerability to these feelings, frequently misinterpreted as lamentable "pessimism" and "nihilism," has been an indispensable dimension of his peculiarly clear-sighted cultural critique.[7]

Naipaul has found variations of this "negation" in many other "areas of darkness" on this planet, and increasingly in the rise of fundamentalist Islam, which he explored first in his documentary *Among the Believers: An Islamic Journey* (1981). Fear has been a more powerful motivation for his writing than hope, releasing greater efforts of intellect and imagination. The father's lesson that fear of extinction can only be combated by self-assertion through the "vocation" of the writer shaped the son's development, but in ways that were unimaginable to the father. The family's past, Naipaul writes in "Prologue to an Autobiography," was "like our idea of India, a dream." What the son learned about family events was as "dateless" as the events of his "own confused childhood." Only much later did he think to ask for a "more connected narrative," urging the father to write an autobiography, "to encourage him as a writer," as the father had encouraged the son (p. 49). He wanted him to go to materials he had never used, not the familiar "story of ritual and reconciliation"; but some "deep hurt or shame" had kept the father from doing it, as the son would find out much later (pp. 49–50). In Port of Spain in 1938, when Naipaul first understood that his father was a journalist, he did not understand what that meant for a man with very little education in a small agricultural colony. It took years before he was able to appreciate the achievement and even longer to puzzle out how it might have come about.

About 1880 his father's grandmother had come to Trinidad from an ancient Indian town in the United Provinces, a young girl with her probably illegitimate baby, since she had been willing to travel that far all alone. But she managed to realize her ambition for her son to become a pundit, and with luck she found him a bride from a suitable clan. Her son the pundit, a hard, avaricious, caste proud man, would die young. The family was scattered, but the younger son, Naipaul's father, was spared for school, and working in his relatives' shop late into the night he dreamed of becoming a writer, a "version of the pundit's vocation" ("Prologue," pp. 52–54). In the pundit tradition he found his guru, the managing editor of the *Trinidad Guardian* from 1929 to 1934, Gault MacGowan, brought in on the recommendation of the *Times* to modernize the deeply provincial paper. He was quite successful with his mix of international and local reporting that included exotic stories about French fugitives from Devil's Island, voodoo in Negro backyards, and Venezuelan vampire bats. Signing his columns "The Pundit," Naipaul's father began to write for the paper from a reformist Hindu position, helped at first by MacGowan, as his son would later be helped with his writing by his more experienced fellow journalists at the BBC. But by the time he was finding his own voice reporting on daily life in Trinidad, MacGowan had to leave. The local directors of the paper thought his investigative journalism damaging to their business interests and did not renew his contract. Naipaul's father could have left Trinidad with the enterprising MacGowan, who had procured a passport for him, but he was unable to trust himself to a larger, unfamiliar, unpredictable world. Staying behind, jobless, he became depressed and dependent on his wife's family, a great humiliation. It took four years for him to get back his job at the *Guardian*, though under much less encouraging conditions, and to move his wife and children into a house in Port of Spain, away from the suffocating pressures of her family compound in Chaguanas. His son, whose first real memories of his father are from that time, has repeatedly spoken of this period as "the serenest," "richest" time of his childhood.[8]

The relative peace and order of that more intimately articulated life was broken up after only two years when they had to join the mother's extended family on a cocoa estate in the hills northwest of Port of Spain. The forceful grandmother had bought the house with the intention to have them all live communally in a big estate house and work the beautiful land. But the family, now even more of a "totalitarian organization" (p. 64) than in the Chaguanas compound of separate dwellings, soon became too crowded and too isolated. Naipaul's memories of this situation are important for understanding the complexities of similarity and difference in his father's failed and his own relatively successful quest for a humanly rational, contestable, flexible order. Such order would be a guiding principle, and searching for it would be an ongoing process. But both father and son understood the central importance of this process to the modern experience of mobility, orientation, distinctness, and transformation on which is predicated the ability to find one's "way in the world." Their quest led both of them away from their overpowering, paralyzing, extinguishing Hindu family. The father "raged" against it ineffectively (p. 62); the son would leave it for England to realize his "vocation" as a writer.

Breaking away, he and other sons and daughters like him also took with them traces of an old cultural order that would prove important to their successful modern transformations. In the Chaguanas compound, the mother's family had drawn on a network of "Hindu reverences" involved in communal activities, but on the isolated country estate their own "internal reverences" began to break down. The child watched the constant quarreling and shifting of alliances, sensing that nobody, nothing could be relied on. It was a feeling of abandonment and panic that the adult writer would later evoke with uncanny precision. Finally the "neutered" men and "oppressed and cantankerous women" would break away (pp. 26–27), stirred out of their passivity by the disintegration of their private Hindu world.[9] Despite their postponed education, many of his fifty cousins became professionals, and some immigrated to "more demanding" lands" (p. 44)—a move his father had not been able to make. Yet their remaking themselves, for Naipaul an extraordinary, admirable achievement, had in some important way also drawn on the life of the clan they were leaving behind.[10]

Despite its physical and emotional chaos, it had allowed the development of a protective "caste certainty, a high sense of the self" (p. 44). His father, however, had been overwhelmed by the chaos. When Naipaul, already an acclaimed writer, asked his mother much later, "what form did my father's madness take?" she said, "He looked in the mirror one day and couldn't see himself. And he began to scream" (p. 70).

In his scathing review of *Among the Believers: An Islamic Journey*, Edward Said observed that "Naipaul the writer" had become "the celebrated sensibility on tour" exhibiting an "unexamined reverence for the colonial order." He found "a deep emptiness in Naipaul the writer," which caused the celebrity Naipaul "to promote an attitude of distant concern and moral superiority in the reader."[11] For Said, the upper-class Palestinian-American academic, Naipaul's fearful reaction to Indian "negation" in *An Area of Darkness* is not only inaccessible but also inadmissible: it is profoundly lacking in "compassion."[12] It is true that Naipaul has never thought much of the intellectuals' principled, "literary" compassion for the anonymous downtrodden.[13] But such compassion does have the great advantage of being much safer than Naipaul's own appalled pity for the people from whom he came—"immemorially poor, immemorially without a voice"[14]—and from whose obscurity and superfluousness he had to distance himself to be able to see and document them more clearly.[15] In all their extraordinary variousness, Naipaul's texts have been fully accessible to the "common reader," one of the reasons why the nonacademic reception of his work as reflected in newspaper reviews has been much more favorable than the academic postcolonialist readings. Said's assessment of Naipaul's impact on his readers seems farfetched and condescending. If Naipaul has "promoted" anything in his readers, it might be greater openness to a wider variety of social and political problems and more curiosity. There is also the pleasure of his intelligence, his ability to make sense of obscure, entrenched situations by looking at them in new, surprising ways.

In its physical vastness and cultural and political variousness, India has looked very different to different travelers, depending on their position of observation. Paul Theroux begins one of his chapters in *The Great Railway Bazaar* with a quote from *An Area of Darkness*: "It was at a railway station in Bombay that Naipaul panicked and fled, fearing that he 'might sink without a trace into that Indian crowd.'"[16] Theroux did not find Bombay Central "especially scarifying": "The hurrying daytime crowds might have frightened me more if they had been idly prowling, but in their mass there was no sense of aimlessness" (p. 120). Naipaul, in contrast, had seen their aimless, circular flow in its essential "Indianness" and it had frightened him; he had taken it personally. Unlike Theroux, he never wished to present himself as the seasoned traveler, surveying the world with cosmopolitan ease. Inside the pushing Indian crowds Naipaul was one of them, immersed; he did not stand out.[17] Theroux was the tall, handsome stranger assured of his position of distinctness, traveling for the adventure of the good story, the striking anecdote.[18] With his eye for the comical and the pleasure of the story, Naipaul has traveled to understand how cultures work, looking for the deeper, more universal meanings of specific flaws and successes.[19] To Theroux travel in foreign cultures has meant new material for his writing, which in recent years has become more narrowly focused on playing with multiple fictional refractions of the self. In contrast, Naipaul's imaginative use of the documentary mode has become more capacious the more he has seen of the world. The reasons for their different perspectives lie in their different backgrounds, as these have shaped their different temperaments and talents. In the past, Theroux respected that difference and let it be, granting Naipaul his own experience, not only because he admired the work of a friend and fellow writer, but also because he could be surprised and intrigued to change the direction of his travel: in his earlier travel books, Theroux shared with Naipaul the traveler's disciplined spontaneity.[20]

If travel has been indispensable for Naipaul to "release" his imagination from the "deadening" familiar, he has also distinguished his kind of travel from that of writers like Graham Greene. Their world has been "made safe for them by empire," and so, traveling "for the picturesque," they are free to "imagine the Europeanness of their characters against the native background." It is a freedom that he, "*desperately* concerned" about the places he visits, does not have because they are part of him in ways which he cannot control; their difficulties are all too familiar. They are real and ought not be "romanticized," one of the greatest sins of Western intellectuals. His opinion offered in many interviews that "people must do things for themselves"[21] has been rejected by critics for its "ruthlessness," but it was the result of his "direct looking" that strips away false pieties.[22] There can be no functioning cultures in modernity without intelligent endeavor and the capacity for transformation—a view that comes close to breaking one of the few remaining Western taboos. Naipaul has been especially hard on India, arguing that its ancient civilization has shut itself off from the future, making it unable to develop a modern concept of history, a sense of events happening in a certain way in a certain place at a certain time, being distinct and datable. To one of his interviewers Naipaul explained impatiently that Hindu history is "bizarre" because "Hindu civilization stopped growing a long time ago. Nothing has been happening except plunder, war, decimation."[23] But how should the history of the Third World be written? Not from a position of unquestioning advocacy for the victims of imperialism. Since history is "built around achievement and creation," India does not have a history because for the longest time it has not achieved and created.[24]

Naipaul would later reverse himself in *India: A Million Mutinies Now* (1990), where he praised what he then saw as a host of positive intellectual and political developments—to the displeasure of some critics, who thought he had become too "soft," hoping for a knighthood. But there would always be expressions of his frustration with troubled postcolonial societies that made him vulnerable to accusations of an enduring sympathy for colonialism. Yet he has been one of the most thoughtful, shrewd critics of colonial infantilization, pointing out that dependence on authority outside the individual and the community prevents the development of a sense of responsibility. Naipaul told an interviewer in 1971 that "as a colonial" one had to first distance oneself from the familiar and focus on personal achievement before one could assume responsibility for others. The writer's cultural responsibility was his "honest" dialogue with his own "undeveloped society," but his steady, unsentimental dissection of colonial and postcolonial irrationalisms has never been easy to take.[25] When asked in 1994 whether the gentler, more searching imagination for the delusions of Third World characters in A Way in the World (1994) might have been a "response to the critics who had over-simplified his work," Naipaul suggested angrily that his critics should rather ask why he was able to see the problems so clearly, and he would tell them that it is "very easy to see the flaws in movements if you abolish sentimentality and you question everything that bothers you." He could not lie even for the best of causes: "I've never served a cause. A cause always corrupts."[26]

Yet the Western intellectual environment has been shaped by alliances with causes and the resulting unquestioned certainty of speech and action. "Mere" analysis if it does not contain the hopeful seeds of intervention is easily suspected of negativism or nihilism, an accusation brought against Naipaul habitually. Irving Howe, a commonsense socialist, was impressed by A Bend in the River (1979), the brilliantly unsettling novel about a small East Indian businessman in Africa trying to survive that continent's violent, treacherous conflicts. In his review, "A Dark Vision," he praised the book for being "free of any romantic moonshine about the moral charms of primitives or the glories of blood-stained dictators" and for its lack of "Western condescension or nostalgia for colonialism." He also stated reservations about Naipaul's pessimism, which, he thought, might indicate some insufficiency, some lack of social energy in the writer himself.[27] Yet the expectations that informed Howe's judgment of Naipaul's composite diagnostic perspective are too Western utopianist and in that too parochial. Valuing cultural activity and transformation over stagnation and sameness, and the importance of the future over the past, Naipaul is still profoundly uncertain, apprehensive about possible different futures for the social and political conflicts represented so powerfully in his narration. Howe did not consider his own lack of familiarity with both the societies analyzed by Naipaul and the cultural genesis of his critical perspective. Coming from the proverbially "other country," Naipaul cannot be expected to share the American intellectual's vision of cultural critique as cultural "activism," because he cannot share its certainties. His "direct looking," too "violent" for some readers, comes out of an observational detachment and a patience hurried, as it were, by a quick analytical irony.[28] Finding much that makes sense in this dark and comical novel, Howe seems to mind that he cannot be quite sure of it.

One of the sources of Naipaul's composite perspective is Hinduism: "speculative and probably also pessimistic," not in the sense of "things turning out badly, but a pessimistic view about existence; that men just end. It is the feeling that life is an illusion. I've entered it more and more as I've got older."[29] This feeling is not contradicted by the fact that Naipaul's writing has been based on imaginative transformation of observation rather than on invention, and that narration has meant for him ongoing processes of exploring the world.[30] If it feels like an illusion, he still has the responsibility to make sense of it. Fictional characters serve as tools in this process, and increasingly the novel is stretched to accommodate more and more documentary (historical) materials and reflections. Naipaul explicitly includes his documentary travelogues when he speaks of the openness of the writing process that changes the writer's original intentions: "There's always something more than you've set out to do. And I suppose, with some, there's always something less. People give themselves away completely in their fiction."[31] Spontaneity *and* control: as a writer Naipaul has sought out and yielded to the surprising reality of other people's self-perceptions and self-creations, but it was *he* who sought out and *he* who yielded. Understanding more, or less, than he had thought he might have depends on the kind of encounter, the unexpected stories and ideas it releases. This is why the most interesting books for him "have a certain instability," traveling as they do "in a new direction." Their authors (including himself) have "some sense of what is, wasn't always, has been made, and is about to change again and become something else."[32] Yet it is easier to gain access to an "enclosed world," a relatively stable society: "To write about a world which is much more shattered, and exploding, and varied, write about it in fiction, is very difficult."[33]

Laboring and lamenting, the writer Naipaul has thrived on these difficulties. The increasing "instability" of his narration has derived, in part, from looking at cultural variety and disorder: what he saw, he saw clearly, but he did not know its meanings since he had "nothing to fit it into."[34] If his vision of diminished people in self-destructing societies has been too sharply focused, he also saw "that there is more to people than their distress. That they are real people. And unless you understand that everyone has cause for self-esteem, you make a terrible political error."[35] Many Third World intellectuals, often living in the U.S., speak summarily and predictably for "the people" as nothing but victims of imperialism and U.S. aggression. Not unlike the proverbial colonial victimizers, they deny "the people" their own voices and self-perceptions. Naipaul has identified fiercely with the experience of being denied this way because it goes directly to his own fear of loss of individuation, of extinction. Memories of the combined instability and rigidity of his Hindu family have made him deeply uneasy: life within a constantly shifting immigrant society in the "atmosphere of a camp" where people are randomly, casually thrown together, and his family's reaction of panicked preoccupation with outside "contamination" that would threaten their caste distinction and thereby their sense of selfhood.[36] Asked to explain the phenomenon of "untouchability," Naipaul emphasized the impossibility of escape from the slavery maintained on one meal a day, the seemingly absolute power of conventions upheld by families, villages, ancestors: "One-fourth of the population—contaminated. Living in an unending contamination."[37] Since it is time honored, Indians of other castes do not feel guilty about this (to the outsider) fantastically literal practice of exclusion; more likely they feel "terror" of being contaminated.

Naipaul escaped the terror of his family's fears with his own fear of extinction intact, the source, as he has often said, of his productivity.[38] His mother was "a perfect Asiatic" with no experience of emotions "particular to *her*" but only as "ritual moments." He partly attributes his own fear of "being reduced to nothing, of feeling crushed" to the "old colonial anxiety of having one's individuality destroyed," but to a much greater degree to his Indian extended family, a "microcosm of the authoritarian state, where power is all-important."[39] By the age of fourteen he had learned all the "worst things" about human behavior; at the end of 1946, when his father finally managed to buy their own house, his childhood was over: "I was fully made."[40] These experiences were formative but they did not diminish his desire for escape into a larger world, nor his ability to find his way in it.[41]

Once he had found the cultural "apparatus of order" in England that enabled him to become a writer, Naipaul began traveling all over the world. He has often been portrayed as the archetypical homeless intellectual, the eternal wanderer, the "ultimate exile," suggesting the profound insights of marginality.[42] But the challenges he had to cope with were less harmless; he could not have afforded this essentially Western neo-Romantic sensibility. Given his background and intellectual temperament, his need to make sense of himself in the world meant a concrete need for orientation, and more than anything else it was the energy of this need that shaped his work. *A Bend in the River*, Naipaul's most intimately and complexly disturbing book and also "one of the century's great political novels," is a narrative of disorientation in the most literal way: going in the wrong direction, reading the danger signs but unable to make use of them, to turn back.[43] Here his protagonists travel for him; the dangers that threaten them are his only in the imagination. But they are also firmly based on observation, their reality extending beyond the limited territory, the "reservation" of the text, and they are shared by many other people. Submitting himself to the risks and hardships of travel in order to find, observe, and imagine this reality, Naipaul also has to remain separate from it. The disorienting shocks and pleasures of new encounters that open up new directions are only productive to the extent that they can be controlled: traveling has to be well planned, orderly, and "quite secure." Acquiring these skills went together with becoming a better writer, and that, in turn, enlarged his "discovery of the way the world is organized."[44] His growing security as a writer enabled him to make better use of the contingencies of travel: looking and listening, he learned to learn more.[45]

This process began in a period of great political and social change, when the young writer expected of the postcolonial future a more humanly rational "reorganization of the world."[46] The motivation for much of his traveling and writing has been a better understanding of why this did not happen: why are certain groups more vulnerable to exploitation and abuse than others? To externalize this experience as based on others' hostile intentions and acts prevents understanding its root causes: "Flaws might be within, in the limitations of particular peoples, the limitations of their civilization or their culture."[47] This is an important observation, already hotly debated in the eighteenth century, but unfortunately it has become taboo in late-twentieth-century multiculturalist critique, especially in its politically potent postcolonialist version, which, in Naipaul's view, "romanticizes" all formerly colonized cultures in a "doctrinaire" manner. Long before the official advent of ideological multiculturalism, Naipaul had pointed out this problem in his 1967 essay "What's Wrong with Being a Snob?" He noted here that "sympathizing with the oppressed" has turned into "exalting their values," anticipating critically the preoccupation three decades later with the celebration of cultural identity on the basis of former oppression.[48] Such simple reversal is dishonest and condescending, since it assumes that populations in postcolonial situations always have been and always will be helpless, and all of them always in the same manner. With their exclusively painful memories of the colonial experience, they cannot but still be victims of Western aggression, and improvement of their situation is entirely the responsibility of the former oppressor. Thinking this argument harmful to the people whose lives had indeed been difficult in many particular, different ways, if not to the intellectuals who presume to construct for them a generalizing sameness of suffering, Naipaul sees change for the better as dependent on "a two-way process": "the oppressed have their responsibility as well."[49] As an observer he is "not interested in attributing *fault*" but in the successes and failures of individual civilizations.[50] The responsibility of "the West" for the difficulties experienced by Third World countries needs to be explored from case to case, in the context of specific, detailed historical, social, and political analyses.

This view of interdependencies contrasts starkly with postcolonialist scenarios of collective Western guilt versus collective celebration of Third World cultural values, no matter how worthless or even damaging these may have proved to the lives of real people.[51] Taking Said's "seminal" *Orientalism* as their point of departure, postcolonialist critics have portrayed Naipaul as a traitor to the cause of the victims of colonialism with whom he ought to feel solidarity. Instead, his distancing perspective, they argue, has affirmed Western readers in their colonialist distance from the powerless. The Swiss-educated Indian-American writer Bharati Mukherjee had in some of her earlier novels explored quite shrewdly the transformations undergone by immigrants from a Third World country. Now teaching at Berkeley, she congratulates herself on having "put down roots," "writing with affection and sympathy" about her heritage.[52] She would not touch now the "kind of morbid and self-protective irony" inherent in Naipaul's focus on "expatriation, which implies a distancing from the subject."[53] A firmly convinced postcolonialist, she is certain that he travels only "to confirm his Eurocentric prejudices."[54] Many writers of Asian and African descent have been remarkably emotional in their rejection of what they see as Naipaul's "professional pessimism" regarding Third World countries.[55] With his focus on the flaws of troubled societies to better understand their difficulties, Naipaul appears profoundly flawed himself, a moral failure: Is not his deepest desire to "pass for" white? Is he not playing up to the oppressor? Naipaul seems to bring out the worst in his enemies: Jamaica Kincaid has been "violently" annoyed by him, assuming that "the only people who'll say good things about him are Western people, right-wing people. I don't want to say 'white.'"[56] Why not? Her equation "Western" and "right-wing" equal "white" is quite clear. Ishmael Reed sees Naipaul playing to the "white insecurities market," confirming his readers' "fears and superstitions" about people of color and reassuring them that "the West is best." Reed understands Naipaul's texts and his readers' responses as a "last, desperate attempt by white liberals to stem the surging tide of multiculturalism."[57] This is a strange assertion, coming from a writer who has thrived on the principled "multiculturalism" of "white," "Western" intellectuals. There is also the more serious issue of his disregard for the fact that Western academic multiculturalists of all colors are far removed from the often dangerous difficulties of ethnic plurality as they are experienced by many Third World populations, difficulties to be found increasingly in American inner cities.

The self-righteous parochialism of these attacks simply denies the conflicts, contradictions, and ironies of the postcolonial situation. Naipaul's appreciation for the importance to Western culture of "intelligence and endeavor and enterprise," which is indeed central to the development of his critical perspective, can then be seen as original sin.[58] Writers like Kincaid and Reed have been served well by their membership in the intellectual elite of a pluralistic cultural environment where they could draw on and contribute to the inclusive "endeavor and enterprise" of the business of culture. Unlike Naipaul, they have embraced the position of minority writer from which they can then make negative generalizations about other groups, an activity strictly taboo for "white liberals." And it is in a curious way logical that, having procured that position, they would think it their right to denounce Naipaul for not joining them in this privilege. He, in turn, has "nothing to say" to them: "I would find it impertinent to talk about individuals who are colleagues in the writing business."[59] That "business" has been a "vocation" for Naipaul, who has worked hard to become simply the best *writer* he could.[60] As Boyers put it sensibly: "There's something grotesque about demanding of a world-class writer that he hew to a party line or an ethnic perspective. He's been very frankly associated with Western values and he's used *that* perspective to criticize what's happening in the Third World."[61] More important, Naipaul's association with Western values originated in his difficulties with the values of his background that in his experience hindered rather than supported the development of independent, rational thought.[62]

Naipaul's critique of the Third World has been focused on the politics of redemption, whether racial, ethnic, or cultural; it has become more nuanced and searching over the years but not less incisive. In the eighties he thought that *The Middle Passage* (1962) had been "too romantic" about the politics of racial redemption on which severely undereducated blacks in postcolonial South America and the West Indies had set such high hopes. Even more saddened now by their regress, he points to the cultural chaos in these areas: the lack of institutions and of deference to the law, to the public good, and to human rights. Disagreeing sharply with Naipaul, Mukherjee professes to be "amazed" by the "confidence" of his pessimism, though she cannot deny the correctness of his predictions.[63] But "pessimism" is only one ingredient of Naipaul's critical perspective, and it has changed with his experience, over time and in different places: the probing reflections on observational perspective in *The Enigma of Arrival* (1987); the hopeful documentation of promising developments in *India: A Million Mutinies Now*; the melancholic exploration of lostness and delusion in *A Way in the World*; and the narrator's retreating behind other voices in *Beyond Belief.*

Still, despite the various new directions taken here, these texts also reflect the continuity of Naipaul's core concern with the comparative analysis of civilizations. Postcolonialist disregard for the various responses in different places and at different times to different kinds of colonial power has produced a master scenario where all colonials were absolutely oppressed and victimized by absolutely evil colonial power. Overuse of terms like "compassion," "racism," "oppression," and "victimization" has led to vast, politically exploitable generalizations; more important, it has effectively obscured the uncomfortable (to some) yet unavoidable questions of cultural value. At issue is the competence of societies to sustain, through their institutions and laws, mutual responsibility among their members and to the larger world. "Self-forgiveness" in dysfunctional groups is destructive because it represses the symptoms of maladies in need of a proper diagnosis so that they can be cured.[64] But who would have the authority to make that diagnosis? Independence of judgment seems to be indispensable, but it is also true that the quality of such judgment depends on the judgment of others—in Naipaul's case his readers. His books will "have to look after themselves, and they will be around as long as people will find that they are illuminating," Naipaul said sensibly.[65] Interviewed on NPR on the occasion of the Nobel Prize, he said that the most important aspect of the award was that his books would now have a second life. They probably will, judging from the general reactions to the event. But will this mean greater tolerance for his diagnosis of postcolonial malaise among his postcolonialist critics, who so far have been remarkably unanimous in their refusal to consider it and in their disregard for the fact that as a documentarist he also has had to look "inward" to understand "why one is weak, why a culture like mine or like the one in India" has been "so without protection in the world."[66]

There may now be some changes in attitude in that camp too, but the temptations of knowing more about the faults of the other (enemy) group than of one's own are formidable. To the poet and critic Robert Hass, Naipaul has been the "supreme writer of disenchantment," a debunker of delusions: "He dislikes privileged people who are sentimental about primitivism in the Third World, and he dislikes the posturing of Third World people whose only tactic is to blame their oppressor, and he is *pitiless* towards the fantasies of the helpless, which is what people don't like about him. But nobody makes more sense of what's gone on in the world at large than he does."[67] Yet Hass had no use for

Guerrillas (1975), the first of Naipaul's books to be a critical and commercial success in the U.S. The book's more enlightened readers, Hass maintains, have all been troubled by its "racist," "misogynist," and "tremendously *reactionary*" aspects. He thinks it Naipaul's "worst, most repellant book"; and, the most heinous of sins, the author has visited on his black character "all of his own self-loathing as a colonial. The black revolutionary writer has a white upper-class groupie-journalist girl-friend. He rapes her in the beginning of the book and sodomizes and kills her at the end of it."[68]

Disliking the book so much, Hass also gets it remarkably wrong: the "black character" Jimmy is Afro-Chinese, and his revolutionary black identity has been forged by his white handlers in England, who are playing media games with the politics of racial redemption. Writing the occasional paragraph of "revolutionary" mumbo jumbo does not make him a "revolutionary writer." A mentally disturbed sociopath of mixed race who has never made his own decisions, he is literally nothing and therefore very dangerous, hardly the stuff to suggest his author's colonial "self-loathing." These are particular characters in a particular postcolonial situation; moreover, we see them through different perspectives. Jimmy's mutually exploitative affair with a white middle-class woman who has no professional skills, little intelligence, and less imagination ends with her getting herself killed; by then he is quite out of his mind with fear and rage and she has taken irrational risks. (The character Hass refers to is Jimmy's former political handler in London, a very different kind of woman who would not allow herself to be killed that way.) This violent and disturbing novel is certainly Naipaul's most risk-taking, most powerfully desolate fiction. But its very repulsiveness is also illuminating because its source is the indeed pitiless exploration of the weakness that comes from being without protection, truly lost in the world.

What kind of sense Naipaul makes depends on the person who reads him. Most of his writing made sense to Hass when he was interviewed by Winokur in 1991, with the exception of *Guerrillas,* whose "weakness as a novel" was also connected by him and others to its commercial success in the U.S. in 1975. A quarter-century later, Naipaul's publisher, Knopf, now much more rigorously interested in large sales and therefore exquisitely attuned to the right kind of mythmaking, might not even have considered a book that punishes delusions so harshly. To the current Western intellectual preoccupation with guilt and cultural humility and the non-Western focus on victimization, Naipaul's skeptical perspective has suggested rootless, coldly self-centered hubris. In the eyes of both Western and non-Western anti–former oppression activists it has amounted to treason. Naipaul's view of cultural plurality has been of successes but also profound frustrations, of sharing and divisiveness, of gradual openings and abrupt closures. It has alerted him to the emergence of restrictive, explosive "traditionalisms" against perceived threats of globalization as he presented them in his apprehensive dissection of the power of belief systems, especially fundamentalist Islam.

Naipaul's particular experience and political intelligence have prevented him from embracing Western ideological multiculturalism. They have also made him vulnerable to massive accusations of prejudicial Eurocentrism by readers invested in the cultural politics and rhetoric ("theorizing") of academic post-colonialism.[69] In their eyes he is the outsider determined to become the unquestioned, therefore unquestioning, insider, the former colonial turned colonialist. A less orthodox observer might see that Naipaul's experience of the reflections in Western culture of Enlightenment tolerance for human diversity and temporality enabled him to go on changing and redefining the relation between outsider and insider. Yet precisely such flexible openness has been deeply suspicious to many postcolonialist critics, as one can see in Fawzia Mustafa's "authoritative" volume on Naipaul for the Cambridge Studies in African and Caribbean Literature series. I will focus on her readings of Naipaul as emblematic of the effects of postcolonialist discourse: how its application leaves texts disfigured, frequently unrecognizable; how the most intellectually complex and compositionally sturdy texts are defenseless against its ideological and rhetorical single-mindedness.

In unhesitating acts of revelatory "deconstruction," Mustafa constructs Naipaul's writing career as the sameness of the "existentialist" outsider's "formalist," "dehistoricizing" predictability, and notes the "reiterative," "linear" quality of his work.[70] A traveler and looker in many parts of the world over many years, Naipaul has not learned anything but has stayed comfortably with the status quo affirmed by his knighthood (1990) and candidacy for the Nobel Prize. Mustafa simply asserts that the decade from the mid-eighties to the mid-nineties has brought nothing from Naipaul but "gestures of return and reconciliation," since her hegemonic reading strategies blocked her view of the variegated texts produced during that period.[71] Uninterested in Naipaul's development toward fusing different modes of representation, expanding the concept "novel,"[72] she reduces the intricate historical fictions of A Way in the World to a "comfortable re-settlement" of characters from earlier texts.[73] This "deconstructivist" reconstruction of Naipaul's "linear" nondevelopment not only pushes aside all questions of textual complexity but is also remarkably anachronistic in its complete disregard for the temporal contexts of texts. Mustafa quotes Naipaul from the early "Trinidad," "'Living in a borrowed culture, the West Indian, more than most, needs writers to tell him who he is and where he stands,'" so that she can accuse him, more than thirty years later, of having "long positioned himself closer to the heart of the 'borrowed culture' than at the brink of any 'new' identity-formations."[74] Mustafa draws here on the authority of Homi K. Bhabha's reading of an "Idea of Order based solely upon itself," a "belief" in the universal rather than the particular, into Naipaul's essay "Conrad's Darkness" (1974).[75] This interpretation, implausible for the common reader, enables Bhabha to present Naipaul as profoundly impressed by "the triumph of the colonialist moment" in Conrad's "texts of the civilizing mission," as transforming "the despair of postcolonial history into an appeal for the autonomy of art."[76]

From this Mustafa concludes that "if a particular 'civility' and the 'autonomy of art' are indeed the grids whereby Naipaul constructs his narratives of the Caribbean and the greater Third World, then his relation to history is aesthetic rather than historiographical, and predetermined rather than explorative."[77] Naipaul has failed to "historicize" the Caribbean experience since he has not seen it through the "transformative lens of colonialism," as has Fanon.[78] After finding in Naipaul's texts an "almost complete" reliance on his "belief in a system of preordained hierarchy and order," he has to be indicted for noninvolvement in "the process of 'decolonizing the mind,' where the alienation fostered by colonization becomes the site from which writers posit a 'liberation.'"[79]

The purple academese and uninformed utopianism of much of postcolonialist discourse (if not the stunning distortions of his texts) may seem irrelevant to Naipaul, but it has kept his texts from being taught both on the graduate and undergraduate level, and that is a shame.[80] Looking at Third World societies in rapid and often dangerous transition, he understands that they need concrete, detailed documentation and well reasoned analysis of their present and historical problems rather than postcolonialist theorizing. But since Mustafa has it on Bhabha's authority that "Naipaul's investment in the 'Novel' is deeply rooted in anxiety about 'Cultural' rather than historical authenticity," he simply has to be mired in his "canonical investments" (Conrad's texts)—the better to castigate him for not being able to "break away" from them.[81]

Naipaul has never had such "investments," neither in Art ("the 'Novel'") nor in "authenticity," and his statements about the meanings of Conrad's fiction for his own work are entirely clear on this point. Instructively, Mustafa blames Naipaul for writing out of self-declared "'incomplete knowledge'" where he could have had the certainties of postcolonialist orthodoxy.[82] The quoted phrase is taken from "Prologue to an Autobiography," where he explains the process of writing as providing new and surprising information: "the book before always turned out to have been written by a man with incomplete knowledge."[83] Awareness of his own particular incomplete knowledge had informed Naipaul's essay "Conrad's Darkness," where he tried to clarify some of the central problems of his own work without finding the "incompleteness" much diminished.[84] In contrast, as Mustafa informs us, Bhabha's "theory" of the colonial subject "utilizes Naipaul's work as the exemplary texts upon which his theoretical investigations are realized";[85] deconstructing and psychoanalyzing the author, Bhabha shows that Naipaul works with a colonial concept of difference: his writing *is* colonial.[86] And Mustafa, referring to Edward Said's authority,[87] maintains that "coupled with the intentionality of his manufacture of 'lived experience' in his travels and sojourns, Naipaul's 'bookishness' can with justification be read as Orientalist."[88] Her next move is to warn darkly that his work is vulnerable "to an indictment, the charge of which is political and, by extension, one which not only explores the issue of a writer's 'authority,' but also that of the *ethics* of writing and reading about non-western worlds."[89] Naipaul's unethical work, then, calls for "utilization" by critics in "their efforts to theorize, and problematize, the discourse of colonialism and the construction of the colonial subject" because his particular approach to history and his own personal history "allow for an examination of the discursive complications that exist in an *a priori* relation to postcolonial enunciations as a whole."[90] How could Naipaul or his non-postcolonialist reader possibly take on the densely entwined and contorted "postcolonialist enunciations as a whole"?[91] It would be lovely to just laugh them off but this is no simple matter, given the considerable political and economic power of academia, where postcolonialist studies thrive.

A long passage in "Conrad's Darkness" does indeed contain one of the most important self-assessments of Naipaul the writer. It starts with an evocation of a scene from *Heart of Darkness:* the steamer going up river to meet Kurtz, a hut on the bank empty but for one book, *An Inquiry into Some Points of Seamanship.* Tattered from use, it seems important to the narrator "in the midst of nightmare" because of its "honest concern for the right way of going to work." This scene particularly spoke to Naipaul when he first read it, perhaps because it addressed the "political panic" he began to feel traveling in newly independent Africa:

> To be a colonial was to know a kind of security; it was to inhabit a fixed world. . . . But in the new world I felt the ground move below me. The new politics, the curious reliance of men on institutions they were yet working to undermine, the simplicity of beliefs and the hideous simplicity of actions, the corruption of causes, half-made societies that seemed doomed to remain half-made: these were the things that began to preoccupy me. They were not things from which I could detach myself.

He realized then that sixty years before Conrad had already been everywhere before him, offering "a vision of the world's half-made societies as places which continuously made and unmade themselves, where there was no goal and where always something inherent in the necessities of successful action . . . carried with it the moral degradation of the idea." It seemed "dismal, but deeply felt: a kind of truth and half a consolation. To understand Conrad, then, it was necessary to begin to match his experience."[92]

Mustafa quotes fragments of sentences from this passage to get quickly and smoothly to the allegedly arch-colonialist statements: "To be a colonial was to know a kind of security" and "to match his experience." "Naipaul's map" is then Conrad's work and not colonial history, and his quest is "canonical rather than historical."[93] But as he says explicitly in the pages preceding the quoted passage, he wrote this essay to understand better the particular importance for his own writing of Conrad's specific problems with a high-cultural literary canon. His reading of Conrad had changed over the years, partly because Conrad's "literary" difficulties were becoming more relevant for his own writing. At issue is the messy, inconclusive, incomplete experience of social political reality past or present that resists easy summarizing and often defeats conventionally polished, "literary" representation. Mustafa not only disregards those statements but deliberately eliminates from the quoted text the very clear references to the importance, for both Conrad's and Naipaul's writing, of social and political historical realities that present serious obstacles to autonomous artistic decisions.

Made insensitive by ideological blinders to the experiential boldness and complexity of their writing, Mustafa simply imposes on it a "theoretical model" of art versus history which, if anything, reveals the critic's incompetence both as a judge of art and a reader of history. Her aggressive "essentialism" toward both Naipaul and Conrad reveals stunning limitations as a reader. It is impossible for her (and here she stands for many postcolonialist critics) to understand, much less appreciate, the rich, apprehensive, truthful ambivalence of a text like *Heart of Darkness*, an ambivalence that is the source of the artful incompleteness of Conrad's writing so intriguingly congenial to Naipaul.

Conrad "meditated" on what would later be Naipaul's world in ways that made it still recognizable in the future, Naipaul's present. This achievement was made possible by Conrad's extraordinary "honesty," his "'scrupulous fidelity to the truth of my own sensation,'" which would hold up or deflect the smooth flow of beautiful writing.[94] Naipaul's writing shares in this documentary ethos; both writers record their own sensations of what they observe, and in their truthfulness to their own experience of the world around them they appear curiously unselfconscious, guileless, as if simply absorbing what can be seen.[95] Conrad stated explicitly that the exotic nature of his subject matter demanded such truthfulness: it focused, controlled his imagination rather than set it free.[96] Naipaul emphasizes this control because increasingly he has experienced it in his own writing and with it, some of the "difficulties" he has found in Conrad's writing. It is Conrad consumed by the struggle of writing with whom he empathizes and whom he uses for the process of understanding his own position: Conrad's determination to represent as fully as possible the puzzles of his experience of strangeness, not his presenting solutions to cultural conflicts.

Conrad is for Naipaul the rare writer whose imaginative fiction took on the real issues, the real difficulties—as he saw them, as Naipaul sees them. Both of them are outsiders, if in different ways, and Naipaul has learned much from Conrad's involvement in the writing process and from its coalescence in his myth. In the past, the myths of great writers referred to their work more than their lives, Naipaul observed; nowadays the opposite is true. The work has become "less obtrusive," writing more private. As a genre, the novel developed in the great societies of the nineteenth century no longer seems appropriate to contemporary concerns, but neither is literary experimentation for its own sake. The "novelist's purpose, in all ages" has been examination of the world we inhabit, creating a "sense of true wonder" for the surprises of its diversity.[97]

Since he entered, as a young "colonial," one of those great societies struggling to deal with (or conceal) its real difficulties, Naipaul has salvaged that sense of "true wonder" of being in a world whose very temporality makes it so eminently worth examining. Its amazing "newness" is located not only in its future, but for the older Naipaul increasingly also in its past, calling for a mode of narration that is not "pure" fiction but *documentary* fiction, namely invention guided and shaped by historical characters in their past actuality. *A Way in the World*, puzzling to many critics who did not know what to do with that strange "interloper," shows how Naipaul's perspective of temporal plurality has created its own curiously mixed discourse, combining historical and personal explorations, report, essay, and fiction. The historicity in Western culture of all observational and representational positions is perhaps best demonstrated by the changing perspectives on the meanings of human difference since the Enlightenment, and ideally this would signify the processual, multiperspectival nature of understanding self and other. At the turn of the millennium, however, the emotional and cognitive distances between differently acculturated groups have not diminished with the shrinking of spatial distances. Rather, in the current multiculturalist, postcolonialist scenario, globalization has tended to arrest fluid, ongoing processes of negotiation between familiarity and strangeness by static constructions, claimed or imposed, of significant identity in difference. Naipaul's mature work has not only acknowledged but focused on the dangers inherent in such stylization of self and other. As a writer of fictions he has kept in mind the responsibilities of writing history. Attentive to spatial and temporal differences, such writing has been shaped by the challenges of cultural (social) authentication rather than by the liberties of artistic self-authorization. Ironically, in view of their arguments, these liberties have been freely taken by many of Naipaul's postcolonialist critics, who have fabricated a massively homogeneous colonial identity as the foundation myth of postcolonialism. It was precisely Naipaul's specific "colonial" experience that caused him to grapple with cultural authentication of difference, that is, the attempt to accommodate the authority of other voices in their puzzling distinctness.

With all its flaws and fallacies and their sometimes tragic consequences, modern technological and scientific culture with its intellectual source in the European Enlightenment has proved irresistible—a situation that very much includes fundamentalist and traditionalist resistance to it. Long before the cultural ascent of multiculturalism Naipaul showed the futility of that position, precisely because it does not differentiate. Asserting in absolute terms the equal value of all cultures, Western intellectuals, including many postcolonialist critics, have been parochial and arrogant in their disregard for the wide spectrum of differences in the attitudes of "developing" countries toward the alluring if mixed blessings of Western organizational and technological development. It seems that of the many contradictions and ironies inherent in such principled one-way tolerance, the increasingly divisive conflict between "progressivism" and "traditionalism," between arguments for and against change, for going forward and going back, has been the most difficult to appreciate. Ideological multiculturalism charged by the energies of postcolonialist sentiments tends to embrace "traditionalisms," no matter how limiting and repressive their influence on particular groups and individuals, as a priori legitimate reactions to the indeed often considerable difficulties of globalization. The increase in fundamentalist terrorism, including the spectacularly fused new-archaic attacks of September 11th, has not really changed that. Yet this position has not contributed to a better understanding of the social and political genesis of radical fundamentalisms. Narratives in which concrete and often explosive multicultural differences and conflicts are instantaneously dissolved in the generalizing sameness of multiculturalism need to be complemented with a more open-ended critical examination of the different meanings at different times for different groups of cultural diversity. If anyone's approach to these crucially important questions has proved to be "ahistorical," it has not been Naipaul's but rather his postcolonialist, multiculturalist critics'. They, not he, have consistently neglected to consider the implications of their own historicity.

2 Postcoloniality and Historicity

Two writers who in the past had liked, even admired, Naipaul's work have come to attack Naipaul in ways which light up sharply the enduring difficulties of difference and point to his work as a lightning rod for misunderstandings and resentments caused by ethnic and racial separations: Theroux, in his bad-tempered *Sir Vidia's Shadow: A Friendship across Five Continents* (1998), and Derek Walcott, in his melodiously malicious review essay on *The Enigma of Arrival,* Naipaul's most complex and most intimate book.[1] Theroux's bitter memoir can be explained only partly by Naipaul's alleged betrayal of an old friend and fellow writer.[2] Theroux is to a degree insightful on the earlier years in Uganda and in London when he was benefiting from Naipaul's advice, but the later parts of the book are strangely fixated on what he now sees as Naipaul's repulsive Indianness. Vidia "was not in any sense English, not even Anglicized, but Indian to his core—caste conscious, race conscious, a food fanatic, precious in his fears from worrying about his body being 'tainted'" (p. 344). Arrogant and insecure because of his West Indian background, Naipaul was also completely wrong, confused about Africa in his "futile attempts" to validate *A Bend in the River.* In Theroux's view, the novel is all about Naipaul's "horror of the bush. But in the bush lay Africa's essence, which Vidia never understood was more benign than wild" (p. 344)—a curious assertion in view of the many exotically brutal conflicts in Africa over the last decades. Moreover, he had explicitly praised that novel earlier in the book and agreed with Naipaul's account of African landscape, people, and politics[3] (pp. 285–89). But now his dislike of his former mentor has become intense and strikingly physical: on their last chance encounter, the inspiration for the slanderous memoir, Naipaul appears as a small man prematurely aged, a black face, the rest of him gray, "striding, thrashing the pavement with a walking stick; he wore a fruity little hat, floppy brim and all, a tweed jacket, a turtleneck . . . a little old soldier marching madly north towards Hyde Park." When Naipaul does not immediately recognize Theroux and his son towering over him, he becomes a frightened "little Indian" fearful of Paki-bashers (p. 356)—a pitiful figure, a nothing, "the mimic man personified" whom Theroux can finally exorcise (p. 358). Is his perspective on Naipaul "racist"? This buzzword has become largely meaningless because it discourages differentiation; Theroux's book is clearly all about his own unease with the other writer's achievements, but he chose to air it by drawing a bitter caricature of Naipaul, reemphasizing a separateness that had been overcome in their former friendship.

Walcott's attack was much more serious because it came from a prominent black writer who would soon be awarded the ultimate proof of planetary approval, the Nobel Prize in literature. Born to an African mother and an English father on the West Indian island St. Lucia, later a resident of Trinidad, Walcott built his writerly identity on the celebration of his African inheritance and his multiracial, multiethnic island paradise. In a sense emblematic of the enduring bitter conflict between Trinidad's blacks and Indians, his accusations against Naipaul establish a Manichean scenario of irreconcilable opposites, an instructive arrangement of postcolonialist self-definitions on the occasion of Naipaul's work. At the time, Naipaul was the much better-known writer, which might explain the acrimony of Walcott's complaints; in the meantime, the Noble Prize might have mellowed him, and, much noted and reported, he was "nice" to Naipaul at the Nobel ceremony, despite the fact that Naipaul passed over Trinidad in his acceptance speech.

One of Walcott's earlier poems, "Laventille," was dedicated to Naipaul, who liked his work and had encouraged Theroux to read it. But where Naipaul sees poverty as debilitating, frightening, a call for intervention, Walcott constructs a self-sufficient, stark beauty of poverty which becomes a recurring theme in his poetry and poetic prose. Maurice, the bitter, sensitive aging protagonist of the 1985 "Café Martinique: A Story," remembers the beauty of the island's poor women: glaring eyes and teeth "white as paper" in their "high-boned, smouldering faces," "the blank severity of ebony masks. . . . Their element was poverty." Marketing poverty to tourists as "an idea, a poetic truth," Maurice may not speak for the author, but the author speaks with him in this smoothly glamorizing description that supports rather than questions the colorful clichés.[4]

The sharp attack on Naipaul, as Theroux remembers gleefully, was completely unexpected and all the more hurtful because it concerned Naipaul's most tender and vulnerable book. Though he praises some of the writing in *The Enigma of Arrival*, Walcott dismisses its author as a traitor to the island, a racist to the core, a self-serving liar, and an unjust and unfair observer. A seemingly endless litany of complaints, his essay circles around these accusations, beginning with the "author's lie" in the young Naipaul's first experience of New York's splendor, its "enchantment of the light." The "lie" is Naipaul's disloyalty to Trinidad in praising the light or heat of other places. Walcott literally asks how Naipaul could find any heat "preferable or more magical than the dry heat of the Caribbean, which always has the startling benediction of breeze and shade? Why is this heat magical in Greece or in the desert, and just heat in Trinidad?" It is so only to a traitor to the island, who will then also find " 'racial obsessions' " among Trinidad's blacks and Indians. Walcott chose to overlook these notorious, enduring tensions and to concentrate instead on Naipaul's explanation of how his childhood " 'fear of being swallowed up or extinguished by the simplicity of one side or the other, my side or the side that wasn't mine,' " had " 'awakened' " his curiosity and desire for a larger world that would make him a writer. This statement signifies Naipaul's ignoring a multitude of gifted Caribbean writers so that he could deny that "what he felt in his youth was held to be felt in common by thousands of young Asian, African, Canadian, Australian writers from all the former provinces of the empire."[5] In Walcott's scenario, they all, including Naipaul, would have felt and written the same, regardless of the great differences concerning the writers' colonial situations and temperaments, not to mention talents. To expose Naipaul as a traitor to the Third World, Walcott has to argue that it is not that particular writer's talent of observation and recording developed in a particular environment that makes for a greater accessibility of the world but a fictitious commonality of the "colonial experience."

At issue is the importance of unquestioning solidarity to the politics of identity based on the memory of previous persecution. Walcott's absolutist rejection of Naipaul's work suggests his inability to tolerate a native island writer to differ so much from Walcott himself, whose writing has been focused exclusively and literally on the "magic" of the island. The very fact of this difference questions that magic and thereby betrays it.[6] Such rigorous demands for loyalty to one's "own" group are common in the current climate of postcolonialist pieties but they are not therefore less absurd. Absurdly, too, some postcolonialist critics found a reprehensible "Eurocentric viewpoint" in Walcott's epic *Omeros,* his casting of Caribbean themes in a "Greek mould." Others have defended him, pointing out that his Odysseus has a "multiplicity of identities and is finally Proteus," that Walcott has "redeployed" Homer to fit and thereby celebrate the Caribbean.[7] Naipaul's approach is not as easily adaptable since he is looking at societies in the terms of their own difference, their own history—perhaps one of the reasons why he did not think it his business to tell others how to look at the world, much less to "celebrate" their own, and only their own, part of it.

Walcott the poet thinks otherwise. The themes of his work are few and redundant: charged with the energies of renewal and rejuvenation, poetry is more powerful than history; nature is more powerfully real than culture; the oral mode is more authentic than the written word; and Trinidad is eternally writing its own poetry. All these themes come to together in his Nobel Prize acceptance speech, "The Antilles," which is indeed the sort of poem that the Antilles themselves might write: meandering, on occasion strikingly formulated poetic ruminations around thought images that evoke rather than clarify his theme conceptually.[8] There is a tendency to make large cultural claims that then serve to reject other views: "Visual surprise is natural in the Caribbean; it comes with the landscape, and faced with its beauty, the sigh of History dissolves" (p. 68). He, the Antilles, has rejected Naipaul for his commonsense, his lack of poetry, his belief in order and history. In Walcott's scenario, history freezes the anger of the victim and the remorse of the victimizer that are set free in his poetry; in Naipaul's view, history puts power relations into perspective, questions, revisits, revises them, begins the process of understanding.

Walcott celebrates the strength of "the Antillan experience," the Port of Spain of blacks, indentured Indians, English convicts, Sephardic Jews, and Chinese and Lebanese merchants, that benevolent "Babel," "a writer's heaven" (pp. 70–71).[9] It can be that as long as the writer is there temporarily, like Walcott on summer vacation from his university position in the U.S., content with his subjective impressions, disregarding the fissures. If there are few books on the island, there is much commemoration in oral recitation of poetry: "There can be virtues in deprivation, and certainly one virtue is salvation from a cascade of high mediocrity, since books are now not so much created as remade" (p. 73). Would their authors agree? For the Real Poet, nothing short of Original Creation will do, yet its seduction for his largely academic, intellectual audiences lies in its combined pre- and postmodernist resonances.[10] Reciting, Walcott speaks in *his* voice for every poet and all Caribbean people but wishes not to be asked more closely about the meanings of his words. Melodious echoes of the self-writing enchanted island world, they are redundant and opaque, indifferent to the realities of difficult lives.

In his celebration of "the local," untouched by (Western) history, Walcott glamorizes the eclectically globalized provincial, misunderstanding Naipaul's different perspective as "virulent contempt towards the island of his origin." If the seasonal resident Walcott claims that Trinidad's "forgiving" "earth" will not reject him who has rejected "his own soil, his own phantoms," the traveler Naipaul has learned that "the earth" cannot be separated from manmade phantoms.[11] In nature he has to look for culture, and then he cannot but see the differentiations, the always changing concerns of place that are obscured in Walcott's perspective. In "The Antilles" Walcott defines the traveler as the person who "cannot love, since love is stasis and travel is motion." Only stasis enables the resident's concentration on his part of the earth. Constructing his "native" identity, he has to discredit the traveler's mobility and curiosity because he is afraid of betrayal: "So many people say they 'love the Caribbean,' meaning that someday they mean to return for a visit but could never live there, the usual benign insult of the traveler, the tourist."[12]

It may seem petty to question Walcott's texts so closely because they clearly are not made for that. But it is important to show how his neo-Romantic preoccupation with permanence and sameness underlying the demand for postcolonialist solidarity makes it impossible for him to tolerate, much less understand differences: a love of place that acknowledges impermanence, motion, changes in time, as Naipaul's love for the English countryside in *The Enigma of Arrival*. To be a "native" means for Walcott to be outside time and history, in the state of unchanging innocence: the paradise of Trinidad which he has embraced without questions, reservations, regrets. His relentless celebration of who and where he is, his "authentic," unchanging identity, plays on this innocence. The celebrated simplicity and authenticity of "the native," before abstract concepts, reading and writing, not to speak of modern technology, is just one more variation on Rousseau's critique of the new complexities of eighteenth-century cultural modernity. But the enfant terrible of the European Enlightenment, embraced by generous intellectuals like Diderot and Hume for his intriguing contrariness, never deliberately misrepresented, much less slandered the position of other writers: arguing against them, he was very much interested in their ideas. When Walcott laments the writer's solitude in the English countryside while he could have benefited from the multicultural "writer's heaven" of Trinidad, he accuses Naipaul of profound vanity, worse, of "something alarmingly venal." Naipaul's "truth" is his "prejudice" against Trinidad's blacks, his "attitude towards Negroes, with its nasty little sneers." If it "was turned on Jews, for example, how many people would praise him for his frankness? Who would have exalted that 'honesty' for which he is praised as our only incorruptible writer from the Third World?"[13] Walcott has no rationally accessible documentation for this as for his other accusations. Where Naipaul's Third World background has been an issue, the important aspect of his work has been its disturbingly incisive social and political intelligence, not a sanctimonious "incorruptibility." For most readers, he has been a sophisticated, world-class writer, and it is this fact above all that caused Walcott's unhappiness.

It is a "glorious" fact for Walcott that "the provincial, the colonial, can never civilize himself beyond his province" no matter how much he gets absorbed into "what is envied," be it immuring oneself "in the woods of a villa outside Rome or in the leafy lanes of Edwardian England" (p. 131). In his efforts to enforce a leveling solidarity and sameness of Third World writers and present his own work as exemplary, Walcott has been emblematically suspicious of history, conceptual complexity, and a fluid identity, of change, curiosity, skepticism, ambiguity, and uncertainty. And so he cannot understand that the proverbial colonial living in a villa outside Rome could and did become fully "civilized," a new citizen, often more powerful than the "natives" precisely because there was a distinction between "imperial" and "colonial" that went with a levelheaded attitude toward the mixed negative and positive "gifts" of colonization. To a certain extent British colonialization shared in this mix, a situation appreciated by Naipaul, who managed to leave Trinidad behind once he was able to go to England to find a larger, more various world. His departure has "betrayed" the "descendants of indentured worker and slave," worse, his "lying" about Trinidad's lack of (high) culture has been "unfair" and "unjust" at the "obscene" cost of "those who do not have his eloquence, his style" and who were given "neither Art nor Culture, neither flower gardens nor venerable elms."[14]

These intemperate complaints are also inconsistent: the British educational system, the libraries, the landscaped colonial architecture liked by the adolescent Naipaul are pure negativity for Walcott. The issue is that multiethnic Trinidad had not developed a culture that would have nourished the young Naipaul's particular ambition to become a writer. This ambition was different from Walcott's for a number of reasons explored in the first chapter: it was not local and it required change. Leaving Trinidad behind, Naipaul would not be, did not have to be permanently at home anywhere. England would prove invaluable precisely because it taught him to be a writer and traveler: to be at home, provisionally and for a time, in many different places, among many different people. More important, it also helped him to understand that even if he had come to acknowledge the quintessentially human (not therefore less difficult) experience of temporality, he still could not assume to know its meanings. Sometimes he seemed closer to it, as when he wrote in the foreword to *Finding the Center* about his contentment with being a traveler and a looker, having "learned to look in my own way."[15] But then he had to admit again in *The Enigma of Arrival*: "I saw what I saw very clearly. But I didn't know what I was looking at. I had nothing to fit it into."[16] Preoccupied with the redemption of Trinidad from its colonial history, Walcott cannot bear this modern uncertainty; everything he looks at fits into the grid of postcolonialist grievances.[17]

Postcolonialist grievances are derived from complexly layered colonial pasts, and they tend to disregard connections with the periods before colonial rule. Where the grievances are clear, shaped by transparent current cultural and political power dynamics, those "bad" pasts, though constantly invoked, are opaque. Postcolonialist "theory," with its conceptually lenient literary strategies and moral certainties, has been more attractive than coherent historical research, especially work in archives requiring skills, for example, knowledge of languages. The cutting-edge deconstructionist compassionism of postcolonialist theorizing—a brilliantly invented double whammy authority—purports to have all the glamorously phrased answers. Laboriously retrieved fragments of difficult and often contradictory pasts seem to have little to add. At the risk of being misunderstood: academic postcolonialist studies, especially outside of history departments, has been greatly energized by growing numbers of non-Western graduate students and academics coming to U.S. universities to "theorize" their colonial pasts. Precisely the authority of their authentic (if vicarious) colonial suffering and focus on the "discourse" rather than historical research of colonial rule have made them attractive to Western institutions of higher learning. Together with this fact, the reorientation of disciplines like anthropology and the rise of fuzzily defined but academically influential "cultural studies" may have made it more difficult to resist this problematic trend toward dehistorization.

There is some recent and welcome dissent by historians: applauding the contributions made to the historiography of nineteenth- and twentieth-century India by the project *Subaltern Studies,* Richard M. Eaton also lamented its increasing openness to postcolonialist theory. Launched in Calcutta in 1982, it was dedicated to the historical documentation of India's peasants, industrial workers, tribals, and women and at first revitalized Indian history by unearthing a wealth of new historical materials.[18] At issue is not only the historical agency of non-elites but also the methodological question of arguing from the materials rather than a preestablished explanatory model that tends to suppress questions of perspective and plausibility. The written sources from the time before the British period preserved in the archives established under British rule document a much greater plurality of voices than most postcolonialist constructs of the "Colonial Discourse" will acknowledge.

The first volume of *Subaltern Studies* promised to deal with these problems, but by the fourth volume an "invasion" of postmodernist postcolonialism started a change in direction, away from the original position of empiricist historiography.[19] Eaton is not alone in his dislike of the new obscurantism and slippery bombast of postcolonialist theorizing by historically uninformed "cultural critics" who "claim to be speaking for global cultures or transnational discourse."[20] A nice example is Gayatri Spivak's argument in "Subaltern Studies: Deconstructing Historiography." She criticizes subalternist historians for "essentializing" the subaltern classes and advises them to proceed with "a *strategic* use of positivist essentialism in a scrupulously visible political interest"— linguistic opacity accompanied by correct political transparency.[21] Postcolonialist readings of historical records are notorious for offering selective interpretations that need no authority other than the formulaic announcement that the interpreter has read "against the grain." True to form, Spivak does the same with historiographical texts: "I read *Subaltern Studies* against the grain and suggest that its own subalternity in claiming a *positive* subject-position for the subaltern might be reinscribed as a strategy for our times."[22] It is the manner rather than the fact of reading "against the grain" that counts here. Underlying the cultural encouragement for strategies of "reinscribing" social and political identity is a Western intellectual anxiety about globalization and an ambivalent attempt to distinguish it from colonization: the fascination with both the victims of colonialism and the new fundamentalist victimizers. Known for her contributions to the growth of Derridaism in American literary studies, Spivak committed to postcolonialism at a later stage of her career, when younger Indian intellectuals came to U.S. universities expecting their postcolonial identity to authorize automatically their generalizing critique of colonialism. They quickly grasped the value of deconstruction, especially in combination with intellectual politics of high morality.

The mix proved fatal to the original mission of *Subaltern Studies,* which, however, had been vulnerable from the beginning because of the centrality given to the "inadequacy," the "historic failure" of Indian populations to fight colonial rule.[23] Since there was a perceived need to account for a "heroic" but nevertheless "failed" political resistance to colonial power, deconstruction seemed useful as a tool to focus on the co-optive power of colonial *discourse.* This interpretative strategy could deconstruct the discourse of colonial rule by constructing it as more pervasively, more irresistibly powerful than administrative political domination, and thus it became increasingly attractive also to beleaguered leftist intellectuals.[24] The issue has been power, since the interpretative strategies of academic literary criticism used in postcolonialist arguments had themselves been a reaction to the overwhelming cultural dominance of the sciences and technology, whose powerful presence could then simply be "de- or re-inscribed" out of existence. With respect to colonial India, discourse studies could go beyond finding excuses for the subalterns' failures by focusing entirely on the British as the only and then overwhelmingly powerful authors of discourses of colonial domination, erasing all other questions.[25]

Postcolonial phenomena, like the rise of the new Islamic or Hindu fundamentalisms, have led to some skepticism regarding the usefulness of ideological postcolonialism, especially in its postmodernist variation. Particularly troubling in the Indian context was the destruction on 6 December 1992 of Baburi Masjid, a sixteenth-century mosque in eastern Uttar Pradesh built by the Muslim Mughal emperor Babur. It was attacked by Hindu mobs, who claimed that it had been constructed—an act of violence never to be forgotten—on the site of the birthplace of the Hindu god Rama. The larger, dangerous implications of this ostensibly religious eruption were immediately clear, given the strong political connections of Hindu fundamentalism. It then seemed more important to understand the historical development of the explosive politicization of religious tensions between Muslims and Hindus than to offer yet another theory of colonial rule extracted from its "discourse."[26] The limitations of Said's "totalizing," profoundly ahistorical construction of a colonialist European "Orientalism" are now pointed out more frequently.[27] Followed religiously by a generation of postcolonialists, this wholesale condemnation of European "essentialist" perspective of "the Orient" in fact "essentialized" all European thought as an all-pervasive, all-powerful "Orientalist" discourse.

Yet the influence of Said's thesis continues even in the current climate of anxiety about fundamentalist terror precisely because of the unabashed eclecticism and disinterest in historical information that underlie Said's disregard for the rich and varied cultural meanings of the work of eighteenth- through twentieth-century Western scholars of non-Western cultures. European "Orientalism" and "essentialism" still has biblical authority in postcolonialist fundamentalism; no graduate paper or thesis would or will pass without reference to it. This mindless imitation is of course not Said's fault, but his irresponsible approach to the history of scholarship, the life work of other talented and devoted men and women over several centuries, enabled his followers to call on his authority to do the same. Kwame Anthony Appiah has realistically described the believers' "postcoloniality" as the "condition of what we might ungenerously call a comprador intelligentsia: of a relatively small, Western-style, Western-trained, group of writers and thinkers who mediate the trade in cultural commodities of world capitalism at the periphery."[28] Self-styled "diasporic" intellectuals, they came invested in ideas of cultural authenticity which would make them attractive to the new, well-funded identity studies curricula especially at U.S. universities demanded by growing numbers of competing immigrant groups. Whether deeply felt or not, "Otherness" has become an asset in the rapidly globalizing business of culture. Celebrating the recovery from British colonialism of an enduring, significant Indian community also proved to be helpful in promoting an intriguing symbiosis of existential exile and cultural rootedness—irresistible, it seems, to many Western intellectuals, who, like their "diasporic" counterparts, tend to forget the meanings of their membership in the professional elites.[29]

As Said's and his followers' argument of European "essentialism" is itself essentialist, so the postcolonialist construct of absolute difference between Europe and India (Asia, Africa) is itself neocolonial. Postcoloniality works with a linear periodization that organizes Indian time in reference to the British imperial period—precolonial, colonial, postcolonial—as if there had not been empires in India before British rule.[30] This may seem an obvious observation, but its implications are rarely explored. Indian time does pose difficult questions, and these are not addressed in the postcolonialist scenario of an all-powerful colonial discourse creating Indian history *ex nihilo* as a conceptually organized construct and thereby erasing it.[31] But they are also not addressed in an analysis of the fallacies of this position. If it is true as Eaton and others have argued convincingly that a notoriously undifferentiated postcolonialist perspective has removed the whole Indian precolonial period from history, it is also true that the concepts of time, historical memory, and critical historiography central to Western modernity have differed from that of non-Western cultures. This difference has been an important aspect of colonial power and should, as Naipaul has done, be seen in the terms of history, preserving its complexities and contradictions, its combined destructive and constructive influences.

Ironically, the neocolonialist aspects of postcolonialist discourse are largely derived from its inability to do so. In the postcolonialist scenario, all colonial power is absolute, therefore evil and guilty; all colonial impotence is absolute, therefore good and innocent. Such Manichean scenarios are common after traumatic large-scale changes in power structures; they are also counterproductive, because their hindsight perspective is uncommonly anachronistic and allows a historically unreflected transfer of power. In the condition of postcoloniality, the imputed guilt and bad conscience of colonial power automatically becomes the inherent innocence and good conscience of postcolonial power. The political and social responsibility of colonial rule for the culture of the colonized is absolute because it was "produced by the colonial encounter, the concept [of culture] itself was invented because of it."[32] If one accepts Dirks's proposition that "culture is a colonial formation," all cultural structures, including the centrally important caste system, can then be seen as "more a product of rule than a predecessor of it": "Caste became the essence of Indian culture and civilization through historical process, under colonial rule."[33] Dirks offers some details regarding this "success of colonial discourse," using census, landholding, and law to give certain Indian groups a share in the power derived from "new formulations and assumptions about caste." But more important, these were then "canonized in the theoretical construction of caste by anthropology, first in the hands of colonial administrators," a reminder that "Western scholarship has consistently been part of the problem rather than the solution." We cannot, Dirks asserts, study colonial rule without referring explicitly or implicitly to the charge made in Said's "pathbreaking" Orientalism that "not only our sources but also our basic categories and assumptions have been shaped by colonial rule." Including, one has to assume, our modern understanding of historicity— despite the fact that two pages earlier in that same text Dirks had warned his readers of "the risk of denying the fundamental historicity of colonialism."[34] If Eaton argues persuasively that indigenous structures like caste, gender, or class are "ancient Indian institutions that had experienced enormous transformations during the many centuries preceding the advent of British rule," not "inventions of the Raj," he does so in a position already weakened by the decline of empirical historical fieldwork to which the rise of postcolonialism has arguably contributed.[35] Over the last two decades there have been fewer and fewer researchers not only in Indian district archives, local libraries, and private collections but also in the more easily accessible national or state archives and even in London. The habit of limiting themselves to already published materials written in English has arguably not helped postcolonialist historians to learn how to look for new materials and how to use them critically and creatively, particularly where it concerns the Indian past before colonial rule.[36] Instead they produced the redundancies of "armchair theorizing," the result of relying so exclusively on already known and much worked-over materials and the ready-made authority of "seminal" studies like *Orientalism.*[37]

Supported by a growing community in the U.S. of "diasporic" scholars of non-Western cultures, postcoloniality has encouraged disregarding the issue of historicity. An absolute separation from the colonial past makes it possible to blame it for all postcolonial difficulties and to affirm cultural and political identity on the basis of an unquestioned and unquestionable memory of oppression. By necessity, this perspective will deny not only all potentially useful aspects of colonial rule but also all potentially troubling aspects of precolonial periods. In India this would concern the problems of caste and gender hierarchies which were addressed under British rule, if from an outsider perspective and for reasons of political self-interest. This should not a priori devalue British modernizing efforts to mitigate some particularly harsh aspects of ancient social structures. But like the complex and messy reality of power, the issue of self-interest politics is prejudged by all-too-innocent, namely uninformed postcolonialist consciousness.

The question remains, how much and in what ways we can actually obtain historical knowledge of ancient, all-important institutions like caste?[38] Naipaul, the British-educated ex-colonial, has been as sharply aware of his own historicity as of the fact that where the Indian past is concerned, "on its own terms" could not be the terms of modern historiography. Access to the rich and complex traditions during the long periods preceding the British Raj has depended to a high degree on British cultural habits of gathering and preserving records, establishing archives, supporting scholarship, and setting up research protocols. This is what Naipaul meant when he referred to the Trinidad of his childhood as sadly without history—to him; it was blissfully so to Walcott. Or when he pointed out that the great sixteenth- and seventeenth-century Mughal architecture was better protected in British India than in other places. The Hindu mobs that destroyed Baburi Masjid, built more than four centuries ago, did not invoke the time of history but of myth as the source of collective memory. So did the suicide pilots of September 11th, 2001, transforming their planes into bombs. Myth unifies and activates; history distinguishes and reconsiders. Naipaul may indeed be unique among contemporary writers in the ways in which he documents the modern necessity of history by exploring the ancient, ageless, and often destructive seductions of myth.

3   Stories of Other Lives: Novels

In *A House for Mr Biswas* (1961) Naipaul drew on his memories of the world
he had left behind and his father's stories about it—writings that were crucially
important to the success of the book because they refreshed the already receding
sounds and shapes of that world. The recently published correspondence with
s family while he was at Oxford makes very clear the conflict between the need
be connected, "please keep me alive with letters," and the need to break away,
Trinidad, as you know, has nothing to offer me." To his father, who since his
heart attack in early 1953 had been increasingly anxious about the survival of
the family, Naipaul wrote on 8 October 1953: "I know and can understand your
wish for me to settle in Trinidad. But let me explain why, if I did so, I shall die
from intellectual starvation" and "Never before have I felt so urgently that I
must write." His father would never read that letter; Naipaul cabled two days
later: "He was the best man I knew. Everything I owe to him be brave my loves
trust me=Vido."[1] They had to be brave, and they could of course not trust his
promises to take care of them. The father, speaking for the family, had asked
him shortly before his death not to get married but to concentrate on helping
his younger siblings.[2] Later Naipaul would ask his older sister, now the only supporter of the family and unable to realize her own marriage plans, for two more
years in England, the only place where he could write. Promising that he would
then relieve her, he admits that he has kept news about his marriage from them,
fearing their resentment. He is working hard, "not having it easy," worrying
about his responsibilities, feeling "ashamed"; everything will change when his
book is accepted. Two months later a cable announces "novel accepted," then
months of silence while he is hectically working on the next book. He is not
coming home; he is not settling down to a job; writing is his profession.[3]

It is the familiar story of the talented individual's assertion of his "calling":
the first book is published, others will follow; finally there will be the Nobel
Prize in literature. But Naipaul's dedication to the writer's profession has been
complete to the point of complete self-absorption—notwithstanding the fact
that his writing has been outward-bound in its fascination with the observed
and recorded lives of many others.[4] At the end of his introduction, the editor
of the letters ironically expressed his gratitude to Naipaul "for his understandably disengaged approval of the project. It entertains me to reflect that this is a
book he will never read." Interviewed for the *Lehrer Newshour* on PBS (3 March
2000), Naipaul confirmed that he had nothing to do with the edition, did not
wish to write an introduction, had not read the letters again. It would have been
"too painful" because the voices from the past would have spoken to him directly, without the writer's selecting and shaping, his mitigating mediation.

Repeatedly, over many decades, Naipaul has tried to explain the complications of not "really" belonging to the world he was born into by accident and yet feeling he had to write about because it was all he had—as a writer. The life he reconstructed in his early novels could not be the "true nature" of *his* life because, growing up in that world, he had not felt it was his.[5] But it *was* his father's, his extended family's, and this was how he recorded it. Conciliatory and intimate, the third-person narration of *A House for Mr Biswas* does not, as one critic sees it, balance the "sympathetic 'inside' and evaluative 'outside' views of the main character" and resolve "provisionally" the tension between Naipaul's Trinidad past and his London present.[6] On one level the novel is driven by the son's fear of what would have happened to him had he not managed to leave: the father's (Biswas's) unfinished manuscript "Escape" signifies not only his own unrealized desire to become a writer but also the son's anxiety about this achievement. Writing out of the experience of not belonging in order to deal with it applies equally to father and son. The important issue is not that the son, having managed to escape, will become what the father could not, a writer.[7] If Naipaul was able to write a successful book about his father's failure, he could do so because it was "very much my father's book. It was written out of his journalism and stories, out of his knowledge, knowledge he had got from the way of looking MacGowan had trained him in. It was written out of his writing."[8] There were the early articles for the *Trinidad Guardian* cut out and pasted in a big ledger that had been an important "book" for the child, but also some stories that the father, with some help from his family, had published himself. Four of them celebrated the "fairy-tale" idyll of Indian village life, but one long comical story dealt seriously with ambition and cruelty in a small village setting. Writing and rewriting, the father made new typescripts as the story grew, and the boy read all of them, "every new bit," "every little variation." This story, more complex, less reconciling than the others, became his "private epic," and his involvement in its slow making became the "greatest imaginative experience" of his childhood ("Prologue," p. 30).

The father, then, did practice writing as a vocation, as would the son. As writers they differed in temperament and talent but perhaps most of all in the situation in which they wrote. *A House for Mr Biswas* follows closely the father's story and would not have been possible without the son's full access to his narration that kept the voices of Trinidad alive and distinct.[9] Writing *Biswas* out of the father's writing, the son shaped that story with the help of the father's "gift" of fear to him ("Prologue," p. 72)—a gift that would prove as important for his becoming a (good) writer as would his father's love, which was inseparable from his fear. Much later, Naipaul tried to describe to an interviewer this "very curious kind of love" which made the child feel responsible for the father. The father's loving admiration for the child was "a great thing" because it gave him "an idea" of himself—and of the vulnerability caused by such premature responsibility.[10]

To be housed permanently, one's privacy and dignity safeguarded, would become the largely elusive goal that drives Mr Biswas. He finally does manage to acquire "his house" after several unsuccessful attempts, but here, too, without noticing its many obvious problems. It would have been terrible for Mr Biswas to die without "his house," amid the "squalor" of his wife's "large, disintegrating and indifferent family," even worse, "without any attempting to lay claim to one's portion of the earth; to have lived and died as one had been born, unnecessary and unaccommodated"—superfluous as no human being should be.[11] Yet the house for Mr Biswas does not redeem this terrible and ordinary fate. For a while he was successful as a journalist, but his career, like that of Naipaul's father, was prematurely ended by the loss of his mentor. His one story, "Escape," remains a fragment, and his son will not be able to draw on his father's writing. Biswas, in contrast to Naipaul's father, will not have "his book."

Like all of Naipaul's fictions, *A House for Mr Biswas* is to a large extent a true story, and, like all true stories, it is not fully known to the author; more, in certain important ways it is precisely his ignorance that enables him to tell it.[12] Repeatedly but in vain, Naipaul had urged his father to compose the materials he would later use for *Biswas* into a "connected" autobiographical narrative. The experience of "disorder within, disorder without" shared by father and son in Trinidad could only be overcome by the sequential connectedness achieved in writing: the son's reconstructing the jumbled past in the prologue to his own autobiography ("Prologue," p. 27).[13] Many years after the publication of *A House for Mr Biswas,* Naipaul discovered the reason for his father's failure. A journalist acquaintance sent him a clipping from the *New York Herald Tribune* of 24 June 1933, "Reporter Sacrifices Goat to Mollify Hindu Goddess: Writer Kowtows to Kali to Escape Black Magic Death." Reporting on cattle disease made worse by Hindu farmers' following the ancient rites of the goddess Kali rather than government regulations based on expert veterinary advice, his father had been threatened with Kali's revenge, sudden death by poison. At the urging of family and friends he offered the required sacrifice of a goat. Naipaul had never heard of the incident, though he knew of his father's abhorrence of the Kali cult practiced also in his mother's family. So he thought at first that this might have been one of "MacGowan's joke stories, with my father trying to make himself his own news"—the father's tendency to exaggerate and embellish ("Prologue," p. 61). But two years later, researching the history of Trinidad, he found in the *Guardian* file in the Port of Spain newspaper library the evidence for the truth of "the story of a great humiliation." It had happened just when the father's "vocation" as writer began to seem more possible, and it intensified his despair over MacGowan's departure. Knowing about his father's long nervous illness, Naipaul had not known what he now thought "its origins": "My own ambitions had been seeded in something less than half knowledge of my father's early writing life" ("Prologue," pp. 61–62).

In a sense, then, it was the incompleteness of his knowledge that enabled him to write *his* successful book about his father's life. The ambiguities of Biswas's desires and frustrations, successes and defeats, have their source in the interdependencies of his cultural environment and his individual temperament. He was not Naipaul's father, but Naipaul created him out of his father's writing about such interdependencies as he had experienced them. He had not wanted his son to know this particular instant: to be forced back into the darkness of that cult as punishment for his attempts to be a rational professional with a certain degree of control over his life signified ultimate defeat. With MacGowan's encouragement he had attempted to claim his place in the world, to contribute something useful, to be "somebody." Agreeing to the sacrifice, he had allowed himself to be pushed back into the vast, undifferentiated multitude of the "unnecessary and unaccommodated."

For the father, the contrast between being able to speak rationally of one's fears and desires and being irrationally silenced was so stark that it might have shattered the precarious emotional balance of the son's book; for the son, the underlying threat of superfluity and annihilation might have been overpowering. Over many decades Naipaul would refer to *A House for Mr Biswas* as a special achievement reflecting, in the narration of its qualified reconciliations, a curiously innocent kindliness. Not knowing the father's story fully had indeed meant here the son's luck in writing it. The meanings of incomplete knowledge in the retelling of true stories would change for the writer as he came to know more and more of them. But the symbiotic relationship between recording and writing, the responsibilities of writing out of others' experiences, of transforming something already formed, their life stories, would not. These transformations, the composition of novels like *A House for Mr Biswas* as well as *Guerrillas* or *A Bend in the River,* the narrational selection and shape of documentaries like *Among the Believers* or *Beyond Belief,* have been informed by the son's and the father's anxious experience of cultural vulnerability.

Guerrillas (1975) and *A Bend in the River* (1979) are formally conventional novels and also essays in political analysis drawing on contemporary events.[14] In contrast to his documentary texts, Naipaul's voice in response to the voices of the characters created by him is implicit rather than explicit. Consequently, the play of his emotional and intellectual concerns is more refracted in the representation of the intellectual and psychological interplay of the characters, which is more tolerant of ambiguities. But in these fictional texts, too, narrative strategies serve to underline the issue of responsible cultural (political) judgment—most clearly because most fearfully in *Guerrillas*. It is Naipaul's darkest, most uninhibited, but also most tightly structured account of postcolonial difficulties and the ensuing self-delusions. Yet despite the narrational control, the dangerous moral and political uncertainties of life suspended in a post-independence vacuum appear to be not fully known to the third-person narrator. There is only partial guidance for the reader in tracing and unraveling the complex of relations between the groping, "floating" characters in their often hostile environment on a small, barren Caribbean island. Their interaction clearly reflects the danger posed by political conflicts and intrigues, but since these are never fully explained the characters' behavior remains in important ways unpredictable. There are obvious connections between *Guerrillas* and the title story of *In a Free State* (1971), with its powerfully somatic description of black-on-white physical and mental aggression. Timothy Weiss sees an equation here of Black Power in the Caribbean and in Africa "not with a profound empowerment of the people, but with racism and regression, with a return to a kind of mentality of the tribe."[15] But this is too simplistic; in both cases, Naipaul's "reading" of the situation does not choose between a celebration of black "empowerment" and a denunciation of black racist regression. He describes black and white regressive racism released by a black empowerment for which whites are responsible in different ways and on different levels. This intertwining of co-responsibilities makes for the surreally distinct, brilliantly evoked presence of fear and the uncertain meanings of the situation in both cases.

In the official report of the Black Power killings in Trinidad on which Naipaul drew for *Guerrillas*,[16] a young white groupie of a Black Power commune was stabbed nine times on 2 January 1972 and buried while still alive in a four-foot hole on the edge of a ravine (*REP*, p. 69).[16] Naipaul was intrigued with the literariness of the killing: shortly before her murder, the victim had received a letter from her father quoting a Lamartine poem that eerily foreshadowed her death, fulfilling the self-deluding fantasies of Black Power (*REP*, p. 75). The deliberately perspectival narration of *Guerrillas* prevents such explicit premonition: here the white groupie Jane is unable to see the danger and, more important, does not care, convinced that she can always come, have a look and a thrill, and leave (*Guerrillas*, pp. 170–71).

Fear dominates the novel to the point that it becomes a negatively exhilarating energy which, like the heat and the desolation of the place, wears out the protagonists and makes them vulnerable to irrational decisions.[17] The ominous appears as if reflected from the "derelict" surroundings, marked by shacks, rags, corrugated iron roofs, junked vehicles, and the scars of drought and bushfires: something that the former anti-apartheid activist Peter Roche senses but does not fully understand. Now a public relations consultant hired by a wealthy island firm once involved in slave trade, he is involved in one of their socially responsible projects, an agricultural commune for "difficult" young black men. It is run by the black-Chinese Jimmy Leung from an island working-class family, who was trained in England to be a black leader and came back confused and violently resentful. Roche is aware of that highly combustible situation, but his wife, Jane, just arrived from London, is fascinated rather than alarmed. His response to her excitement is allusions rather than explanations of the dangerous entwinement of reality and illusion underlying the power games on the island. Ostensibly working for the benefit of the "native," mostly poor, mostly black population, whites deliberately embrace Difference. Jimmy, in Roche's view, is of course "absurd in nearly every way" but he "somehow" gets things done, and this pleases his firm, intent on maintaining a cost-effective progressivist image. The work farm will turn out to be a cover for recruiting guerrillas. But what, in that situation, is the meaning of "cover" or of "guerrilla"? Roche knows that most people on the island accept strange, unsettling, dangerous behavior, engaging in their own little wars, uniting momentarily when things "really" get out of hand—in the view of whoever has the power at that moment. He "laughed, and Jane saw his molars: widely spaced, black at the roots, the gum high: like a glimpse of the skull'" (pp. 6–7).[18] Jane, not Roche, is the one who will die, killed by Jimmy, to whom she is attracted precisely because he is so profoundly alien.[19] But there is an all-enveloping threat of mortality that rules this most elaborately violent of Naipaul's books.[20]

The threat is both physical and cultural: the white, dizzying, shimmering, hissing heat that assaults all the senses contributes to the physical, emotional, and mental displacement of the characters. Nothing is what it presents itself to be, and people's self-presentations yield no clues. Arriving at Jimmy's farm, Roche and Jane see a big cleared area, the furrows full of weeds, the brown ridges dry as bone, an abandoned looking tractor. The desolation is seen through Jane's eyes: the tangled forest, the already overgrown clearings, the fields that are wasteland, the glaring incompetence. It could be Jane or the narrator stating that "neither Roche nor Jimmy appeared surprised" (p. 15). But Jane does not seem troubled by Jimmy's "wildness," his irrational, "crazed" exclusion from culture as a shared nurturing, enabling enterprise. The long hut built of concrete blocks that houses the young men who sullenly and desultorily work "the land" appears "alone" in the empty silence, its roof of corrugated iron radiating the heat instead of casting a shadow: "There was no wind; the forest wall, dead green, was still; the asphalt road was soft below the gravel. . . . The stripped land baked. Jane wanted shade; and the only shade lay within the dark, almost black, doorway of the long hut" (pp. 7–8).

This is the place where she will eventually be murdered; her self-absorption lets her be drawn so naively to Jimmy's hyperactive strangeness and yield to her contempt for Roche's passivity. Naipaul constructs this triangle to show the relation between understanding and passivity on one side, not understanding and activity on the other, and delusion and self-deception on both. In the political reality that Roche and Jimmy have accidentally come to share and that Roche, up to a point, understands and Jimmy enacts, there is no good or bad, only an anarchic struggle that seems unstoppable to Roche. In contrast to him, Jane has never been in real danger, and her selective, distorting view of the situation reinforces her dangerous illusion that she will always have the option of escape. If Jimmy is "unreadable," that makes him all the more exciting (p. 10).

The hesitations and detours of the exchange between Roche and Jimmy about the still nonfunctioning tractor are skillfully staged: Jimmy answers Roche's questions unwillingly and ambiguously, and Roche, as one does with a recalcitrant child, is busy pretending not to notice. Deferring to Roche as "massa," Jimmy both assumes and rejects the status of victim. Had Jane looked and listened differently, she might have understood better Jimmy's attempts to both stay in *his* world and to exploit the world of white power. But she is focused on a poster that shows Jimmy as she had envisioned him from Roche's stories, more "negroid," more like the proud warrior of Black Power. When Roche comes up to the farm after she has been murdered and sees Jimmy posturing in person and on the poster, he senses something dangerously awful, the scene of a slaughter (pp. 243–44), and he immediately removes himself from it. Jane, tempted by the completeness of the alien as she sees it from her outsider position, is excited rather than alarmed by the danger. Like Jimmy, she is deluded by illusions of control: not understanding it at all, the unfamiliar remains whole and therefore seems magically manageable.

The interdependencies of controlling and being controlled, of victimizing and being the victim are developed with great care in the differing perspectives of Roche and Jane. To both of them Jimmy appears dangerous and pitiful in his self-delusion, but they respond differently. Shortly before she is murdered Jane accuses Roche of playing with Jimmy, but so does she; moreover, as Roche rightly points out, Jimmy is the major contributor to that process. Is Roche responsible for Jimmy? Is Jane? Her social and sexual control feeding on her increasingly self-absorbed distance from the world around her will drive Jimmy over the edge and separate her from Roche, who in the end will manage to leave the island without reporting her murder. Naipaul's women characters are often sexually self-absorbed and controlling, indicating his perhaps in some way flawed view of women, but the writer has put this personal limitation to good use. In one scene a shocked Roche is watching Jane flinging her empty tampon box against the wall. They have moved apart, and he sees that distance expressed in her changing sense of her body: "it was as though she didn't belong to her body, as though there was some spirit within her that was at odds with the body which she yet cherished and whose needs she thought to satisfy" (p. 123). This conflict will make her more vulnerable to Jimmy's physical aggression (pp. 232–34, 238–39); but if Roche has a sense of her being in danger, he does not act on it. Like Jimmy, watching, smelling her body, he sees her clearly and mercilessly without really knowing what he is looking at. The novel turns on the political activist's fear of the lawlessness, the unpredictability of particular people in a particular situation. Roche has shown considerable courage in the past when the danger, the position of the enemy, was clear. Now things are muddled and his fear is somatic, not so much overpowering as sharply present, self-evident and at the same time inarticulate. Jane's experience and her relationship with Roche are too limited to allow her to focus on his fear in this changed situation. The announcement of her love affair with Jimmy is defiantly self-assertive: she is not caught in the oppressive power games of the place as is Roche; her sympathies are with its victims (p. 219); he has failed her.

There is no way for the characters to sort out the tangle of fears and desires that motivates them; the narration suggests that this tangle in which they are all caught together at a certain time and in a certain place is their truth—for the time being. Roche sees Jane as a person without memory and coherence and therefore protected from experience, indifferent to the contradictions between what she perceives and who she thinks she is (p. 18). Only when she allows Jimmy to take control is her "innocence" finally broken. He sodomizes her and then has her killed by his abused, crazed young black lover (pp. 233–34). Roche has been profoundly irritated by her simple dismissal of the difficulties of post-independence reconstruction and her refusal to see that Jimmy's "madness" is real, that different people fear and use this madness differently. The survivor of many treacherous situations, he can appreciate these differences, up to a point. Jane in her peculiarly tainted innocence cannot, and her "playing" with the roles of controlled and controller is in Roche's experience of that postindependence world the most dangerously self-deluding game. Yet his complacent "working with what's there" is too self-protective and in that also dangerous to others, as the black politician Meredith rightly complains. They are all responsible for Jimmy's murderous rage, for the botched "revolution."

In England, where he was a minor celebrity with his book about his activist past, Roche had seemed to Jane "a doer," giving her a "vision of the world of real events and real action" with clear political battle lines (p. 44). But on the island those lines are no longer clear: despite its provinciality and remoteness, the conflict of interests is more complex, as Naipaul demonstrates in several sets of intricately staged, tense conversations. Used to the large and fuzzy "vision" of London's political junkies, Jane does not see them for what they are, dangerous political battles. Roche, in her eyes, is no longer capable of passion, political and otherwise; the "motor of action" has stopped (p. 48). Out of her own need she has constructed an inviolable activist persona for him that he cannot but fail. Asking him about surviving in the African jail, she is surprised by his answer that he had always "accepted authority": "It probably has to do with the kind of school I went to" (p. 49). It is unclear to her and perhaps to himself whether this is a virtue or a weakness, but he refers to it once more when he defends the depth of his fear of the island's "madness" (p. 218). His early acceptance of authority was the precondition for the general fearlessness and physical and mental endurance needed for his kind of political activism. In that sense it was a virtue, though it did not make him invulnerable; he was wounded mentally and physically in the process. Jane is unable to appreciate the connections between his generally fearless, daring activism, and his self-protective instinct to remove himself from particular dangers: the death threat delivered to him in London, the slaughter scene at Jimmy's work farm, the island's lawlessness which would engulf all of them.

The processual, refracted uncovering of Jane's and Roche's interwoven fears and desires includes Jimmy as well as Meredith Herbert. A member of the black professional and political island elite, he refers to himself as a "political dropout" (p. 129), having exchanged his post of minister for that of host of a popular weekly radio program. At first Roche sees him as a "restful man" amidst the "hysteria" of the elite, taking in stride the increasing breakdown of institutions on the island and finding pleasure in his family, his law practice, and his radio work. In all of this he seems to Roche oddly but reassuringly certain that he would continue to be settled in the place he had made for himself. Jane has no patience for Meredith's fascination with political alliances and strategies and finds him too "suburban," too "domesticated and settled" (p. 130). Roche criticizes her "trivial," "lazy" reactions (here his perspective is indistinguishable from the author-narrator's: p. 131); but gradually he, too, begins to judge Meredith differently, looking at his domesticity as a deliberate disguise for the "rages, deprivations, and unappeased ambition" he shares with the island elite. Roche becomes wary of Meredith's preference for their mutual friend Harry de Tunja, a funny, shrewd, generous East Indian businessman with no political ambitions who loves the island, hates to leave it, and talks openly about having to do so before they all get killed (p. 131).[21] However, Meredith's unsettling opacity and Harry's reassuring transparence are partly constructs of Roche's perspective, the result of his culturally "unnatural" situation: he is a stranger on the island, and its increasing political chaos causes him to hide this fact from himself.

So are Jane's condescending views on Meredith as a boring, black middle-class professional the product of her particular, limited perspective. Accusations of Naipaul's "racism" reflected in this character are based on careless reading; both Meredith and Roche are flawed, Roche probably more so than Meredith. We know them only in their interaction, through each other's perspectives, incompletely; but it is clear that Roche has failed to help build a better life for the island population. Knowing beforehand what "they" want, seeing their needs in his rather than their own terms, he has remained a self-centered stranger and inevitably disappointed their hopes. The book's most disturbing message—much more so than the extreme alienness of Jimmy's violence—concerns the omnipresence of this self-centeredness in the politics of the island: Meredith can deliver the most painfully lucid analysis of Roche's political failure because he shares in it. This fact has not been lost on Roche but it may not be clear to Meredith, a psychologically realistic rather than "racist" constellation, since Roche's involvement in the politics of race in a variety of situations has led him to comparison and to a certain degree of introspection that Meredith may or may not have. Meredith's character, the most intriguing in the novel, is also the most elaborately constructed: we see him mostly through the eyes of others, whose views are shaped by their own fears and reflect back on him.

The last meeting for Sunday brunch at Harry's beach house lights up sharply the differences of opinion and temperament (pp. 134–45). Harry, the most sociable, balanced character and also the most openly concerned about the volatility of "the people," talks about their irrational habits and "mad" explosive anger, which he understands and tries to appease with individual acts of kindness, fearful of the government's incompetence and corruption. Meredith summarily dismisses Roche's comments on the situation; unlike Jane, Meredith fears that danger, and unlike Roche, he knows what he is looking at. He knew Jimmy before he had become the "black radical" interviewed for the BBC by Meredith in London: the nobody mixed-breed son of a Chinese grocer. Meredith, the "real Negro," watched how this void was being shaped into somebody important by Jimmy's white postcolonialist handlers. Eminently suggestible, Jimmy Leung could be programmed to do anything. The backwater project of revolution based on "the land" still points to London programming: a sexual and political postcolonial time bomb, Jimmy will duly explode in violent aggression. Roche does not agree with this scenario, at least not outwardly; Harry does, and his clearheadedness based on cautious self-restriction is supported by the narrator. Playing the game of "one wish," Harry wants not to want anything, Roche, to have "the most enormous sexual powers," Jane, "lots and lots of money," and Meredith, the capacity to "express" himself "fully" (p. 140). Apart from Harry, who would love his life on the island to continue, their wishes are subterfuges: everybody playing to the other person. Asked to describe for the second part of the game their "perfect day," the four agree that not having to make real decisions now would be perfect: " 'Release,' Meredith said, and at that moment was like a friend again. 'That would be lovely. Just to be oneself. That's how I see it too' " (pp. 144–45).

There is of course no perfect environment in which to be "oneself" in the postlapsarian human condition of which the postcolonial situation is a particularly striking, complexly ambiguous example. In their differing ways they are all aware of it. Jane does not want to project a "perfect day," since this would mean loss of control over her options. Meredith, shrewd psychologist and connoisseur of control, understands: women tend to include men in their wishful projections, which multiplies the possibilities. She can be anything; anything can happen to her. Alluding to her self-delusive, dangerous suggestibility he remarks: "I often think that if I were a woman I would be very frightened" (pp. 142–43). In this subtly and cleverly composed interaction of the four characters on their last "perfect day," Meredith appears androgynous both in his effortless games of control and in his momentary amiable, pliable openness, which makes Harry fear that he will be "chewed up" by the ever more irrational politics on the island. Like Jane the political groupie, the practicing politician may have too many possibilities and too few real options.

Roche takes away from this conversation the enormous advantage of his position: a stranger, he is free to leave; Meredith cannot but be resentful since he does not have the privilege of escape. This makes Roche more vulnerable to Meredith's attacks during their last confrontation, an interview for his radio program. It is a most painful public rejection of the white intellectual and political activist who stopped paying attention and lost his way in the politics of the island. Meredith's questions are judgments, turning Roche's answers against him: selling out to business interests, he has betrayed the people who trusted him; thriving on the conspiracy of the British liberal establishment that groomed "political leaders" like Jimmy, he is now abandoning the islanders to the chaos created by the self-serving politics of liberation; his anti-apartheid activism was without direction, ineffectual; taking large risks for very little, he did great damage to many others. His experience, his much touted bravery, did not help him to see that Jimmy's commune was a cover for the guerillas (pp. 205–208). Roche is literally gasping for air under the blows; the interview takes place in a dusty, dimly lit, very hot room in an atmosphere of extreme physical discomfort and nervous anxiety. It is one of Naipaul's recurring evocations of the somatic violence of fear, the third presence in that room, enveloping and palpable to both the torturer and the tortured. Meredith may have turned off the air conditioner on purpose to better control Roche. He has forced him to leave; it is no longer his choice; nor is it Meredith's choice to stay.

In that they are even. But the violation of Roche's sense of self causes him to turn, running away into the achievement of escape. Getting away from the "slaughterground" of Jimmy's place unharmed is "the bravest thing" he has ever done, and erasing Jane is literal and alarmingly easy (p. 244–48). Even Jimmy can be dealt with; when he demands that Roche come back to the commune to help him with the young men's madness, he counters, "'Who do you think you're talking to?'" (p. 248). This question is central to the novel and to much of Naipaul's writing: how can one know the person to whom one is trying to talk? The issue is not Jimmy's "victimization" by Roche's inattentiveness, but Roche's failure to recognize Jimmy's potential murderous aggression and to protect others from it. His escape means leaving the others "alone," Jane in death and Jimmy in a situation which he may very well not survive. It would have been Roche's responsibility to deal in some way with Jimmy's playacting and delusions and their fatal attraction for Jane. But thinking that he knew what "they" wanted—Jimmy, Jane, Meredith—he deluded himself about his own ability to control the situation.

Oscillating between the familiar and the strange and unable to avoid self-deception, Roche's relations to Jane are as ambiguous and strained as is his attitude toward the oppressed, to whose cause he has dedicated much of his life. His failure is easily summed up by the black politician Meredith, who retells the white activist's banal and paradoxical story in the terms of his own political ambitions and frustrations and thereby assumes control. Jane, failing her husband, is unable to understand the significance for him and for her of that reversal of power. Narrated through the perspective of each other's desires and anxieties, the ideas and visions of the protagonists become tainted, even discredited. Naipaul's interest is not in the characters themselves, but in their dissonant relations which reflect the larger cultural issues—issues that have not changed much at the turn of the millennium. Imagined within treacherously obscure situations, they cannot become fully known, especially in the case of Roche, whose half-hearted self-questioning seems to increase his remoteness.

Naipaul has come back repeatedly to the character of the older political activist, still not at home in the world as he found it but now unable to envision, much less desire, its radical change.[22] The sharp contrast between past certainties, vitality, courage, decisiveness and present uncertainties, exhaustion, fears, lostness is also a sharp reminder of time passing and change passing him by where he had hoped to bring it about. Roche's book about his activist past has not taught him anything about his mistakes, and so his past fails him in his dealings with Jimmy. The failure is incomplete self-knowledge of the wrong kind: the connections between the unquestioned self of the revolutionary hero before and the self-doubting, failed progressivist social organizer after are tentative, speculative; Roche's historical agency has not taught him historical awareness. Meredith can easily uncover his self-delusions in particular and the fallacies of radical political intervention by outsiders in general; he can even make Roche disappear from the island. And yet, narrating the barrenness of Roche's disappointments, Naipaul also gives it the eerie reality of fear that comes out of his own experience on that other island—Roche's growing sense of being insubstantial, a shadow that people can walk through.

Ostensibly empathizing with the local people drawn to the complexity of city life rather than the simplicity of rural communes, Roche dismisses the relevance of their desire. He knows what "they" want and that most cannot have it, will "miss out," and that he had to "work with what was there" (p. 133), with "what they said they wanted" (p. 200).[23] But this excuse denies the danger of misunderstanding "their" stated wishes and of misreading "what was there." In the local politician's view supported by the narration, Roche has remained a stranger disastrously blind to the implications of his position, one of the radically progressivist Western intellectuals whose lack of information and political realism can only add to the trouble. As we encounter them in Naipaul's documentary and fictional texts, they are out of their depth in dangerous situations made more dangerous by their unwillingness to consider the responsibilities of their Western acculturation: if "what is there" signifies chaos and violence, it has to remain unacceptable, unworkable. Its diagnosis requires skills, intelligence, and informed decisions, and *Guerrillas* is mercilessly clear in its dissection of yet another version of postcolonial racial and ethnic confusion and betrayal. The most disturbing scene in the book is not the sexual killing of the white woman by a violent, racially mixed black man, though its description is a virtuoso performance. It is rather the uncanny deliberateness with which the white, anti-apartheid activist-writer and former guerilla Roche becomes his wife's second murderer. Leaving the island he is truly without options, without a sense of self.

Guerrillas is the darkest, most frightening of Naipaul's texts because it is focused so single-mindedly on the threat of annihilation. This threat is more diffuse, as if refracted by multiple layers of strangeness, in *A Bend in the River,* a still disturbingly contemporary political novel about the eruption at independence of African "madness," fear, and rage against Europeans, Arabs, Indians, and other Africans. Set in an unnamed town on an unnamed river in an unnamed country in central Africa (postcolonial Congo), the events are narrated by the East Indian merchant Salim, who sums up his experiences in the opening sentence: "The world is what it is; men who are nothing, who allow themselves to become nothing, have no place in it." The novel ends with the image of myriads of moths and insects visible in the searchlight of the last steamer to leave the battle-torn town where Salim has run his small business. For a moment it also lights up a barge overcrowded with more passengers frantic to escape that has been tied to the steamer. Presently the searchlight is turned off, and the steamer moves into the dark, away from the gunshots, and the moths have become invisible, nothing. So have the unfortunate people on the barge, cut off in an attempted takeover. Temporarily safe on the steamer, Salim watches without comment their final abandonment to superfluity.[24] Separated from the static, "antiquated" life of his Indian community on the east coast before he ever left it, he has always observed from the distance of not "really" belonging. He remembers learning how to see familiar African scenes and objects by looking at the British stamps that depicted them beautifully and thereby drew attention to them. His perception shaped by European attention to what is different and noteworthy, he "developed the habit of looking, detaching myself from a familiar scene and trying to consider it as from a distance. It was from this habit of looking that the idea came to me that as a community we had fallen behind. And that was the beginning of my insecurity" (*A Bend in the River,* pp. 15–16).

Like Naipaul's, Salim's insecurity and pessimism is to an extent temperamental but is intensified by the negative effects of rapid political change for large populations. In this perspective, the Europeans have been better equipped to deal with the end of colonial Africa than the Indians because they were able to act in changing political situations, "preparing to get out, or to fight, or to meet the Africans halfway. We continued to live as we had always done, blindly" (p. 17). Theroux recounts how on his visit to Kampala Naipaul had been "browbeating" the local Indians with his apprehensive predictions that their days in Uganda were numbered and had "nagged" them about contingency plans. His questioning them sternly on what they would do "when the crunch comes" was resented and achieved nothing. Five years later Idi Amin came to power and threatened to expel all Indians.[25] Such vindication of his pessimistic assessment of African developments would not give Naipaul pleasure, but it also would not change the assertive impatience of his warnings.

Sharing certain aspects of Naipaul's background and social intelligence, Salim is also in important ways different: a shrewd observer, he appreciates European future-oriented complexity, but his author has denied him the ability to make use of it.[26] It is not a question of European colonial immorality, which is too simplistic in Naipaul's experience and irrelevant in Salim's. Like everybody else, Europeans have wanted gold and slaves, material and energy resources, but unlike Africans and African Indians they have been able to "express both sides of their civilization," domination and progressivity (p. 17). Coming from a traditional Muslim merchant family, Salim has had little education and few options, in contrast to his childhood friend Indar, whose wealthy Hindu family sent him to England to study. Indar is the one to bring up the precarious situation of their community, and his contempt and irritation help Salim to break away. But deciding "to make good" instead of simply being "good in the ways of our tradition" (p. 20), Salim knows that he has only the African trading skills of his family. The business he buys in this mood of anxiety is located in a town in the center of Africa at the bend of the great river, the end of the old Arab trading routes. He will not go any further, and his hopes will be restricted to a future that is nothing but a future past.

The limitations of Salim's perspective are crucial to the success of this political novel: his observations are based on his dealing with people in a town built and administered by Europeans and now taken over by Africans. As a small businessman he gets to know their reality because he is part of it, the participating observer attentive to the reactions to him of the people he watches. As he tells it, his story is inevitably shaped by the growing conflict between the new technocratic Africa and the old Africa of the bush in the life of the town, the source of its ambiguities and opacities. On his first drive from the east coast to the center, Salim could still follow the old trade route, talking and bribing himself through from one new frontier post to the next. In the meantime this route has been made impassable by many bloody uprisings, but on his first drive penetrating deeper and deeper into Africa had already seemed "madness," "going in the wrong direction." He remembers the slaves going the opposite direction, away from their tribal areas and terrified by ever more strange Africans on the way till they arrived on the coast in such a state of shock that they willingly boarded the boats: "to be taken to safe homes across the sea. Like the slave far from home, I became anxious only to arrive" (pp. 3–4).

He arrives at a place of constant political conflict between different African groups. Rebels destroyed the town at independence, only to become angered by the destruction and then angrily afraid when the town started to grow. Coming out of the bush, having suffered so much and brought so much suffering on themselves, these people seem half-crazed to Salim. Feeble and hungry, they need the town, but, like a natural force, their rage cannot be assuaged by reasonable talk or action. And so the war has started up again (p. 67). The African president's army has been recruited from the warrior tribe, used by the Arabs as slave hunters and by the colonial government as soldiers, and is kept under tight control. They are careful not to provoke their traditional enemy and prey, the bush people, and they uphold order, which is good for business. In a moment of feeling particularly unsettled Salim identifies with "the ragged Africans who were so abject in the town we served" (p. 107). But they are also the major cause for his unease, equipped with their rage, their weapons, and their belief in the magic protection by all the spirits of the forest and the river. Salim knows from experience that deeper than all other fears is the "African terror of strange Africans" (p. 71); rumors of the president's soldiers running away with bent guns may or may not indicate an army in retreat but certainly an imminent uprising in town (p. 69).

Salim also knows that carrying on is his only option. Africa has been home to his people for centuries as it has been to Arabs, Persians, and Portuguese, but their trade orientation has been to the East, "true Africa" at their back. And yet they have felt like Africans, living like the generations before them, never asking "why," never "recording" their lives (p. 11). Like Naipaul, Salim had to learn about his people's and the region's history from books written by Europeans. The early achievements of Arabs and Indians "formed no part of our knowledge or pride. Without Europeans, I feel, all our past would have been washed away, like the scuff marks of fishermen on the beach outside our town" (p. 12). The past does not anchor him, and the African trouble intensifies his sense of transience. Naipaul has burdened Salim with his own shocked reaction to the poverty and squalor, the ignorance of the village Africans: without plans and determination, futureless, they seem to be drifting in an indefinitely chaotic present. And yet, Africans from the bush have proved to be better equipped for bad times than anybody else. Suffering terribly from the war, they would go back to their villages and tribes: "They could run away again to their secret worlds and become lost in those worlds, as they had done before" (p. 71).

Salim notes that Father Huismans, the Belgian headmaster of the town's surviving Lycée and a collector of African art, does not seem interested in the material condition of the destitute bush dwellers. The beauty of their masks and carvings lies for him in the fact that every one of them has spiritual authenticity and uniqueness, each created for a specific religious purpose. Salim is a good listener, considering his responses carefully. The Christian priest's high regard for the religious dimension of African art seems odd to him, but his presence in the town is "comforting": "His attitude, his interests, his knowledge, added something to the place, made it less barren" (p. 62). Salim takes in stride the priest's absorption in his collection, which sends him on frequent trips into the bush and generally separates him from people around him. He appreciates Huismans's enthusiasm—"his Africa was a wonderful place full of new things" (p. 62)—and his lack of bitterness about the destruction by African rebels of the town that his countrymen had built. Huismans, Salim understands, sees this as "only a temporary setback. Such things happened when something big and new was being set up, when the course of history was being altered" (p. 63).

Both puzzled and oddly reassured by Huismans's view of the town as part of that sweeping scenario of history on the march, Salim thinks about his translation of the Latin inscription on the monument near the dock gate where the steamer stops, the motto of the town: "He approves of the mingling of people and their bonds of union" (p. 62). Huismans told him that it was a line from a poem about the founder of Rome landing on the coast of Africa but having to move on and leave the local queen who loves him. The great Roman god who guided his travel to Italy might not approve of an African settlement that would bring about the mingling of peoples and a union between Africa and Rome. The quoted verse, then, containing several altered words, reverses the meaning of the original text. Huismans may not have told Salim the name of the poem, Virgil's *Aeneid,* but he has a sense of the age and weight of the original words and is troubled by the "twisting" of two-thousand-year-old words: "Rome was Rome. What was this place? To carve the words on a monument besides this African river was surely to invite the destruction of the town" (p. 63). And indeed, the monument is destroyed in an uprising almost immediately after its erection, its inscription "gibberish" to the people who are now camping in front of it, selling goats, hens in their cages, and monkeys as travel provision to the passengers on the steamer. At the same time Salim understands Huismans's acceptance of the alteration: it has helped him to see himself in Africa as "part of an immense flow of history. He was of Europe; he took the Latin words to refer to himself. . . . He had his own idea of Europe, his own idea of his civilization. It was that that lay between us" (p. 63). It also connected them because the priest, secure in his particular understanding of his European identity, did not make much of it, nor of his separateness from Africans. He collects African art out of gratitude for being able to witness the "true Africa" that is about to vanish (pp. 64–65). Some critics objected to Salim's uncommon thoughtfulness, but Naipaul needed his protagonist to be a perceptive observer aware of his incomplete understanding and able to match this knowledge imaginatively with his experience of political chaos and warfare, to be someone with social intelligence on which he draws for mental and physical survival.

After another uprising brutally put down, Father Huismans's mutilated body drifts down the river in a dugout, the head cut off and spiked. His murder does not attract much attention and he is buried in great haste. Recounting the event, Salim once more tries to sort out his feelings about the man who had become important to him because of the "purity" of his interest. The "idea" he had of his civilization had "sent him looking, inquiring; it had made him find human richness where the rest of us saw bush or had stopped seeing anything at all." Yet this idea was also "like his vanity. It had made him read too much in that mingling of peoples by our river and he had paid for it." Attempting to make sense of the events, Salim acknowledges futility: being "flesh and blood and mind," people will soon come out of their "questioning mood." What remains with him is a strong feeling that Huismans had "passed his time better than most of us" (p. 82). And yet he observes how the "ant-like" persistence of the people in town who knew nothing about the priest's "big views" brought about what he had said would happen: "After each setback, the civilization of Europe would become a little more secure at the bend in the river; the town would always start up again, and would grow a little more each time" (pp. 85–86).

It does, but so does the army, increasingly a mix of men from different regions and different tribes, equipped with more sophisticated weapons, and more arrogant and brutal. The town may continue to grow after each destruction but further away from civilization, back to what it had been centuries before the Europeans came, a trading center for a vast region. The president, a military man, builds "the Domain" where the rich European suburb had been, using European technology, materials, and manpower to create "a miracle that would astound the rest of the world," modern Africa. This seemed to fit Father Huismans's view of pure Africa retreating and the European "graft" becoming stronger. But the shiny new buildings of concrete and glass are badly built, the materials shoddy, and as they are shown to the ragged villagers bussed to town to admire the new Africa, Salim realizes that the European graft does not work. The president's Domain has simply bypassed the real, difficult Africa and finally becomes a university and research center for African studies. Salim does not condescend to the failure. It makes him see more sympathetically the "defeats and humiliations" of postcolonial desires, but he also finds them difficult to live with: "Old Africa, which seemed to absorb everything, was simple; this place kept you tense. What a strain it was, picking your way through stupidity and aggressiveness and pride and hurt" (pp. 100–101).

Salim's story is made of a host of distinct, fragmented memories, not of coherent remembrance. The events he narrates are selected according to their importance for him, but there is no unifying insight or purpose that gives shape to the narrative. He has no firm opinions about himself or the world, least of all how he should or might live in it differently. The "darkness" of Africa seems too dense; it has defeated better educated people than Salim, like the Belgian historian Raymond, who for too many years has been working on the biography of the African president. The more he collects, the more he becomes obsessed with the completeness of his documentation of the president's rise to power. He speaks wistfully about the "sadness" of the overwhelming absence of the "unrecorded" from historical memory, wondering if one would ever get to the "truth of what has happened in Africa in the last hundred or even fifty years? All the wars, all the rebellions, all the leaders, all the defeats?" (p. 130). The problem is not the inevitable selectiveness of historical memory but rather the circumstances in which history is written. The Belgian historian who once advised an ambitious African boy on his first steps toward becoming a great leader and was rewarded with influence and complete access to information finds it increasingly difficult to interpret, select, and structure the data he has amassed because he knows too much and too little.

Raymond is unable to provide a historical narrative that would accommodate the African president's ever changing politics of identity. By the time he chooses the currently correct portrait of the leader it will already be outdated: large numbers of photographs portraying the leader in the short-sleeved safari jacket of African military chic have been superseded by even larger numbers that show him as the clan's chief with the leopard-skin cap and carved stick of African tribal authenticity. Raymond finally realizes that he would be safer editing a selection of the president's speeches, tracing in his own words his development from the "simple" ideas of "unity, the colonial past, the need for peace" to the "extraordinarily complex and wonderful" thoughts "about Africa, government, the modern world" (p. 136). These thoughts are echoed in the discussions of African students in the Domain, whose verbal sophistication astonishes and confuses Salim. Had the young men whose halting thought and speech he clearly remembered learned so much in such a short time? Or were they just repeating slogans from the self-congratulatory African journals published in Europe at government expense and sent back into the country? Was the Domain a hoax or did it support real intellectual and political change (p. 124)?

Fascinated and apprehensive, Salim tries to sort out his confusions with the help of Indar, now a guest lecturer at the Domain and well acquainted with its cultural politics. Indar explains Raymond's role as "the Big Man's white man" who knows most about the country, yet he also seems to have doubts about the historian's effectiveness, which Salim is reluctant to judge. Raymond himself feels the need to explain the superabundance of the African photos with the president's insight that the people want to see themselves in the picture of their African ruler: "It takes an African to rule Africa—the colonial powers never truly understood that. However much the rest of us study Africa, however deep our sympathy, we will remain outsiders" (pp. 134–35). The Domain, in Raymond's reverent scenario, signifies the president's openness to new ideas and is also his shrine to the memory of the old Africa, whereas most of the other African leaders, wanting to forget the past, have simply superimposed skyscrapers on the bush.

From his in-between position, Indar sees the situation more clearly, as he explains it to Salim. Like Raymond, he is impressed with the president's ability to be everything to all people: a modernizer with hugely ambitious plans for his struggling country; a traditionalist cultivating his African soul. He also understands that this "mishmash" has worked for the president, who has been changing the details but holding on to his foundational narrative of the native son's rise to absolute power from the humblest beginnings and through the greatest of conflicts. Raymond's real predicament is that the Big Man is going his own way and has long since stopped reading the historian who knows too much about the past of the country to be useful to its leader who claims the future. Raymond himself states the professional dilemma of the African historian engaged in the larger historical narrative of his subject: where the great nineteenth-century European historians could be sure of the historical value of European cultural and political developments and therefore the achievement of writing their history, historians of Africa have no such assurance. They cannot say how the events they are chronicling will be seen in the future because they have "no idea where the continent is going. We can only carry on" (p. 137). In that, as Salim realizes, the European academic Raymond is not much different from the small Indian artisans and businessmen like himself, carrying on their "ant-like" work in town through all the cyclical destructions and reconstructions.

Salim learns from both Indar's and Raymond's self-deceptions about Africa. He has admired Indar for the British glamour reflected in his work in the Domain, and Raymond for his closeness to the African president, but he also understands that they are both in their own ways doomed to remain complete outsiders. Indar has redefined himself by his own "construct," the idea of the "true" African revolution through its young first-generation intellectuals. He has built a career on bringing this idea to places like the Domain, without any reflection on the consequences for the young Africans, whose identity he is helping to mold. He believes not in their revolution but in his own role in bringing it about, carrying the world within himself, thinking himself lucky not to have his choices limited, "a man without a side" (pp. 153–56). This in his view makes him destined for success in Africa, if not England. He acknowledges that room was made for him in England, admiring the European openness to other people and blaming his own acculturation, his own unsettledness, for his inability to make use of it. The European colonial enterprise does of course play a role in the making of Indar as of all the characters in the novel. But since they are all made to be who they have become in their vastly complicated, particular relatedness to particular others, blaming their postcolonial difficulties on a generalized "colonialism" does not seem useful to their author and his narrator. Indar blames his own group, at the same time putting a good spin on his failure, but Salim is able to see the East Indian intellectual's self-creation as a sign of weakness rather than strength. Indar, he realizes, has changed places with him; he has become "the man who needed to be led by the hand" (p. 156). He will leave abruptly at the end of the term, will find it more and more difficult to sell his African ideas to his rich American supporters, and will let himself drift into dreams of returning to a simpler state of being where all conflicts are resolved, an idyllic Hindu village—echoes of Naipaul's father.

Naipaul has constructed his political novel around the issue of self-invention that leads to an ever more rigid self-deception and prevents a gradual negotiation of strangeness as a process of approximate understanding. The character who brings into sharp focus both Indar's and Raymond's enduring isolation is the son of one of Salim's traders, a shrewd, tough woman of the African bush who comes and goes in her dugout, seemingly unaffected by the violent politics of the place. Salim has befriended the young man through the different stages of growing up in this African town: a slow, lonely pupil at the Lycée, an uncertain, arrogant student at the Domain who dislikes Indar's "complicated" ideas. When he leaves the Domain for an administrative cadetship in the capital, Salim sees him off in his first class cabin on the steamer, impressed with his "new unsurprised attitude to himself." Coming from his forest village, his tribally mixed parents, he has "leapt centuries," learning to accept the country as his and, knowing nothing beyond it, to expect everything from it: "He was at home in every setting, he accepted every situation; and he was himself everywhere" (p. 158). With this imperturbable self-confidence, he is destined to rise quickly to a position of authority—as was his president, tutored by Raymond. But when Salim sees him again some years later during a particularly bad uprising, the young man, now a rapidly grown-up commissioner, is profoundly shaken by the leader's increasingly totalitarian politics and brutal arbitrariness. Salim has been imprisoned by a minor official bent on squeezing more money out of him, and his former protégé comes to his rescue. His order to take the next steamer and leave this town, this country, will save Salim's life. The country is going to hell, he is told: wholesale killing, total cultural collapse, everyone frantic to make and keep his money and run away. But whereto? Even the African bush is no longer a refuge. The commissioner has toured the villages and describes the situation as a "nightmare": with the help of foreign companies the president has built up the bush with airfields; there is no safe place left (p. 272). The European graft has made everything worse, at least for the time being. Self-invented, the African president, like an evil and elusive god, reacts unintelligibly to the chaotic reactions to his rule. There is nothing to contain his absolute power; it will absorb all resistance and thrive on its self-generated energy.

The African "Third World" has become something worse, a peculiarly layered chaos, a fourth dimension of being lost, frozen in panic. In jail Salim watches the faces of the Africans rounded up in the bush for fear of insurrection and listens to the sounds of torture. Acutely aware of the vulnerability of his body, all he has now, he sees that the African prisoners have retreated far into themselves, unreachable to the wardens, whose brutality increases in proportion to their captives' remoteness. Indifferent to everything, those faces did yet not appear to him "vacant or passive or resigned"; he senses the "frenzy" of both the torturers and their prisoners, "active" in the first case, "internal" in the second. This frenzy had taken them "far beyond their cause or even knowledge of their cause, far beyond thought. They had prepared themselves for death not because they were martyrs; but because what they were and what they knew they were was all they had. They were people crazed with the idea of who they were. I never felt closer to them, or more far away" (p. 269).

Salim has learned some important things about the African country, because as observer and narrator he has also lived and worked there, involved with a great variety of people. Unlike the intellectuals Indar and Raymond, he could not afford to marginalize himself. Reading the Belgian historian's scholarly essays, heavy with quotes and cross-references to newspapers, letters, and missionary reports, Salim realizes that Raymond has never appreciated, much less understood, Africa's potential for dangerous surprises. A faithful chronicler, he lists events without fitting them into a conceptually organized, explanatory narrative. Having recorded so much, knowing so much, and completely absorbed by his work, he could not make Africa more intelligible because he could not respond, by acknowledging them, to the terrors and the wonders of its strangeness. Perhaps, Salim muses, he had made Africa his study because he had found himself there and, a scholar, had been intrigued simply by the wealth of new materials that shielded him from the African reality to the point of enabling him to remain almost completely ignorant about it (pp. 180–82). Salim's own narrative, in contrast, traces his difficult involvement with African strangeness and his failure to turn it into familiarity. Yet needing to find his way in that world he, like his author, allowed himself to be drawn into it, in time understanding better its terrors and its wonderful, if indeed dangerous, capacity to surprise.

4   Stories of Other Lives: Documentaries
Among the Believers: An Islamic Journey

Travel has meant understanding the world, if partly and provisionally, and in that it has been the core energy for Naipaul's writing. His comings and goings have had little to do with "the writer's" proverbial existential homelessness on the melancholic margins of the human condition. Instead, he has over many decades traveled to many places to meet with and listen to a great variety of people and to record what they had to say about their different cultural experiences. The young man's fear of becoming invisible in the crowded, myopic island community of Trinidad was of crucial importance for the formation of the writer, who made good use of the separation. Moving around, establishing points from where to look, and trying to understand what he was looking at, he developed a flexible observational distance, the source of his curious, precise regard. Over time he became more intrigued by the challenges of the documentary, particularly the interdependencies of representation and information, and writing clearly and accessibly rather than "beautifully" became a major concern. Trying to understand the other person means to "pay attention. Everything is here for a purpose."[1] His "place of birth committed" him to the documentary mode: "From that starting point I looked at the world."[2] Over many years of writing, he has come to think the cultural status of the documentary higher than that of the contemporary novel, which, as intimately imaginative transformations of experience, seems to him too narrow. Most contemporary fiction does not have the "smartness" (sweep, conceptual interests, social-psychological explorations) and general accessibility he has admired in the great nineteenth-century novels. His travelogues are not about him traveling but about the people whom he is among and whose stories he elicits and records. There is little room here for creative readings "against the grain," so dear to postmodernist postcolonialist critics. Naipaul is working hard to understand, as fully as possible, what he is told and to pass it on to his reader with as few distortions of the speakers' meanings as he can manage. Obviously, this is an area of easy self-deception and even easier fallacies: the circularity of understanding, already complicated in the situation of an interviewer who elicits and retells the statements of other speakers passing them on to his readers, is further complicated by the frequently considerable cultural differences between the observer (interviewer) and the observed (interviewed), not to mention the difficulties of translation.

Understanding depends on making judgments, and judgments concern valuation, that is, choice on the basis of preference, which also includes rejection. Questions of cultural value have become increasingly politicized with the migration of large populations beginning in the second half of the twentieth century. A result of cold war divisions, the end of empire, and technocratic globalization, these questions have emphasized dramatically the growing gap between technological "haves" and "have-nots" and contributed to the increasingly powerful politics of identity on the basis of memories of former repression or persecution. Often drawing on religious belief systems, these politics have in many different ways adapted Western technology to their own power systems. Naipaul has been interested precisely in the variety of such adaptations as he found them in different developing countries and could not but pose questions of cultural value if he wanted to understand them. His approach has often not been appreciated for its judiciousness but rejected as inappropriately judgmental. Quintessentially neo-Romantic in his playful stylistic self-absorption, the Indian writer Salman Rushdie has lamented, as have other critics, the "lovelessness" of Naipaul's "pessimism," his lack of "compassion," his reluctance to embrace "the other."[3] Naipaul has been more interested in understanding the various particularities of human conduct than in accepting them "as they are." Celebration of difference for its own sake is a luxury affordable only from the distance of "theory," after "the other" has been safely purged of historical agency. In contrast to its decorative harmlessness in Western academic discourse, real cultural diversity with its often destructive politics of identity—conflicts of political self-interest, competition for resources, and bloody ideological clashes—is something quite different. When Naipaul speaks about his attempts at understanding he refers to the other person not as an "Other" but as a social being, that is, complexly and conflictedly related to others, including himself, the observer. A late-twentieth-century shibboleth, the "Other" is constructed as enduringly distinct, paradisiacally inviolable, unable to talk back to the theorists of Otherness. It is a construct that will never challenge the theorists' unwillingness to ask, "Is that true?" "Was that true"? But these are precisely the questions that have driven Naipaul's writing. He has judged the truthfulness of his observations by their intelligibility, the degree to which they can be shared with his readers, assuming that they will ask, in the terms of *their* experience, "Is (was) that really true?" and he will have to convince them that, as far as he could tell from the evidence, it is (was). Yet the power of evidence can only be temporary, because there will most probably be more information in the future—a process of coming closer, seeing more clearly, for which the mobility of the traveler who arrives, leaves, and returns to have another look is a fitting allegory.

There is both modesty and arrogance in Naipaul's fascination with the traveler's observation and recording because it means his shifting from the non-assertive discourse of fiction to the at least partially assertive discourse of the documentary that may claim a *relative* truth but nevertheless some kind, a part of truth. Since Naipaul works explicitly with the modern (Enlightenment) concept of truth as a process of trusting evidence, the question how we come to trust, or mistrust, his descriptions, recordings, and commentaries is very important. A largely admiring interviewer, Charles Michener stated some mild reservations regarding Naipaul's observational objectivity when trying to document cultures that are dominated by belief systems profoundly alien to his own intellectual temperament. Naipaul insisted that he has, on the whole, realized his goal to see clearly and record truthfully. "*Nothing* was falsified," he said about *Among the Believers: An Islamic Journey* (1981). "I'm very, very scrupulous about that. And I have seldom been misled by people because in every new situation I'm always with the other man, I'm always looking at the world through *his eyes.*" He observed people shaped by what he thought "false hopes, political beliefs, tribal causes. People with causes inevitably turn themselves off intellectually."[4] But he tried to gain access to them through a great deal of research, a careful choice of informants, and meticulous recording of their voices. Several documentary texts later he would say that he has been "passionate" about accuracy: "[I] never alter a word that people spoke; I take it down by hand, and I don't change it."[5]

In a curiously literal sense, Naipaul has also "copied" from real life his fictional characters, not just in his early novels like *A House for Mr Biswas*, where he was "trying to remember words, gestures and expressions in correct sequence, to arrive at an understanding of people I had been with and the true meaning of what had been said."[6] But his lifelong working habit of "checking, checking"[7] has been particularly striking in his documentary "books of inquiry and exploration."[8] He prefers small notebooks to tape recorders, which he thinks undermine the concentration of a conversation: "One would not get the exercise of mind and memory that the need to write would give you."[9] His procedure reflects "a writer's appreciation of speech, the novelist's way of looking." He "shapes" the interview while he is conducting it and thinks that intense mental preparation sets him free for the "*encounter,* a free-wheeling inquiry." At night he organizes his notes by checking them with his informant in preparation for the process of writing the book.[10]

Naipaul quite openly speaks of his work as "a great *achievement,*" "a great intellectual labor" over a long period of time, pointing out the difficulties of writing about what he refers to as "the mixing of continents": "The books are varied, and the inquiry expands, and the vision expands, and the knowledge expands."[11] The weight of other lives is their time and place, to which the documentarist has to pay intense attention, trying to understand where he is in the world at any given moment. The truthfulness of their recordings needs to be judged by the "encounter" that enabled them—that is, by its combined spontaneity and careful constructing. Above all, our acts of judging will inevitably be motivated, in ways both obvious and hidden, by our own involvements with the there and then of the encounter: our doubts regarding the documentarist's stated goal of a high degree of accuracy and objectivity should be as carefully questioned as should be acceptance.[12] Naipaul's recording over many decades the enormous changes brought about by the "mixing of continents" in the second half of the twentieth century is an extraordinary achievement, and its aggressive denial by postcolonialist criticism is embarrassingly "academic." Yet no matter how thoughtfully conceived, meticulously executed, lucidly argued, and densely written, his recordings share with journalism the lure of the particular and temporal rather than the universal and timeless. Naipaul's work is a difficult fit for cultural canons: it is too varied in its responses to the immense variety of the world. Attempting truthfulness, it is too truthfully intense, impure, and incomplete.

Once he had established himself as a writer in England, Naipaul started traveling extensively, curious about the larger world because it was *there*. His motivation for leaving England was ostensibly to gain a better understanding of his origins, but the realization that he was free to come and go and to engage in this search on his own terms meant the "real" liberation: it freed him to go on traveling and looking for its own sake. In his first book about Naipaul's early novels and travelogues, Theroux rightly pointed out that for Naipaul creation "involves perception. The ability to assess oneself in one's setting is necessary if a person is to write well or to make anything new; detail must be seen, judgments questioned." [13] One of his interviewers remarks that there is the "charity" of seeing even in Naipaul's darkest books, that he "refuses not to see."[14]

For Naipaul, invisibility is the ultimate human abandonment because it means superfluity—the moths in the searchlight of the last steamer at the end of *A Bend in the River*. Though no known human culture seems to have managed to eliminate such superfluity, some have done better than others. Naipaul's perspective is useful precisely because it draws on his unmediated experience of cultural differences in that respect. If the remembered "feeling of dirt and poverty and empty days" did not make him identify with the "unneeded" and "cast out"—still the vast majority of the world's population—it did sharpen the adult observer's awareness of their cultural rather than existential predicament.[15] This is one of the reasons why he admires Conrad's ability to look at the non-European world "with the utmost seriousness. What an achievement! Can you imagine the pressure not to see it?" In Conrad he has found the "great effort of understanding, of sympathy" he hopes readers will find in *his* texts.[16] Conrad is not a "great" novelist in the European tradition, but he is for Naipaul an exceptionally valuable writer, as is Darwin: in both cases he is happily impressed by the quality of their intelligence in writing.[17]

Though he has taught himself considerable literary skills, Naipaul's natural inclination has been toward an intelligence both imaginative and analytical—in texts like *The Enigma of Arrival*, not unlike that of the Austrian writer Robert Musil in his *Man without Qualities* (whom he has probably never read and to whom, as far as I know, nobody has ever compared him). Naipaul has repeatedly described the panic of learning how to write, of not having a natural talent for creating something out of nothing;[18] he has never been "an inventor of material, always a transformer." This does not mean that he has not been—or has not seen himself to be—a gifted narrator. Narrative occurs all the time; there is narrative in every process of exploring of the world: "I don't know the world yet. I began to understand that quite late. I began to understand the full richness of the world that I was in the middle of and how to go about it."[19] Given that richness, pure invention is too arbitrary; it does not do justice to what is there to be seen in order to be made sense of.

Among the Believers: An Islamic Journey, Naipaul's first exploration of Islamic fundamentalism, was prompted by the Islamic revolution in Iran, the explosive clash between religious and political traditionalism and technocratic progressivism. He had dealt with this core conflict of many developing countries, most perceptively in the novel *The Bend in the River,* but also in earlier travelogues. In Iran he found the familiar tension between new and old, modern and archaic, change and sameness, linear and cyclical time, historicity and timelessness, mobility and stasis, but he also found that it had another dimension. Though he had grown up in Trinidad's mixed Hindu, Muslim, and Christian population, he had not been much interested in Islam as a civilization before because it had seemed to him impoverished in the present, unless it was fueled, and then problematically, by oil. But in Iran Islam proved more alien, literally more difficult "to read," since the tension was both more layered, rooted in the long, richly articulated history of the place and the people, and more explosive. He arrived into the chaos of a revolution back into the past. Watching and listening to medicine men selling their powders, roots, and minerals in the streets of Tehran, he is surprised when his guide tells him that their medical authorities are Avicenna and Galen, names he had associated with the European tradition but that refer back to the time when the power of Muslim civilization was a crucially important reality for the West.[20] His surprise becomes awe at that suddenly visible link to the riches of the past, and he understands that Iran's present simplifications will have to be seen in the light of its historical complexities—and the reader will have to follow him.

More than Naipaul's many other travelogues, *Among the Believers* and its follow-up, *Beyond Belief: Islamic Excursions among the Converted People,* almost two decades later are highly explicit about the great importance of guides and interpreters. As the stranger who needs to get to seemingly remote places and understand people whose judgments seem obscure, Naipaul is easily frustrated with incompetent guides but also relieved and appreciative when he finds intelligence and dependability. One may quarrel with his reactions, but decisions have to be made in a situation where faces, gestures, and acts (leading to mishaps) are difficult to read and he has to rely on hunches. He invites inspection of his decisions, which are guided by the both obvious and elusive interdependencies of temperament and experience. It is true, he tends to be apprehensive that things can and will go wrong—in the situation of the stranger that could mean prejudice but also shrewdness. His first guide in chaotic Tehran is described as "a small man on the rise," not much different from a peasant, though he had presented himself as being above that level: "there was a lot of the Iranian hysteria and confusion locked up in his smiling eyes" (pp. 8–9). Ingratiating, the smile conceals the man's incompetence, his inability to orient himself, to reason coherently. For the stranger who needs guidance in a literal sense, being misled

and misinformed is a serious matter, and Naipaul is anxious when his expectations of halfway rational conduct are not met. For his postcolonialist critics, in
most cases "armchair" travelers at Western universities, such expectations are
just another indication of his prejudices, of Western "linear" rationality and
predictability. Their own privileged position has made it impossible for them
to understand Naipaul's real fear, born out of his own experience, of the consequences of cultural irrationalism; more, how this fear has made him sensitive
to the different meanings of differently acculturated behavior. It is precisely
Naipaul's "mixed" perspective, Caribbean and European, that highlights the abstracting, simplistic fiction of "the Other." It has sharpened his awareness of
the instability of difference, shifting with the experience of other people in
their mutual strangeness.

When Naipaul is among the believers, looking at them, asking them questions, he cannot but interact with them on some level, even though, as he
knows very well, communication is highly mediated and information is filtered
through layers of possible misunderstanding. He notes their appearance, their
bodies, their clothes, the way they move, their voices, reacting to all the aspects
of their physical presence as they are to his. In each case these rapid and often
imperceptible notations will influence their understanding of his questions,
their answers, and his responses to them. This influence will be all the more
decisive if distinct emotions like fear, frustration, hatred, love, hope, despair enter the equation. One of Theroux's many complaints in *Sir Vidia's Shadow* is
that Naipaul, who had once amazed him with the observation that Columbus
never mentioned the blinding, dizzying Caribbean heat, had in his later work
become uninterested in the sensuous details that make good travelogues. He
finds Naipaul's books on Islam, but also *The Enigma of Arrival* and *A Way in
the World*, "odd and insufficient. He took down the laborious monologues of
people, and these lengthy interviews were presented as documentary almost
without intervention by Vidia."[21] Theroux is plainly wrong here: there is a great
deal of effective sensuous description in these books and also a great deal of
"intervention": the choice of the place and time of the interviews, of the interpreter and the interviewees, of the ways of looking and listening, of taking
notes and reworking them shortly after the interview and again later, when
composing them into a book. Each one of these choices had needed judgment
and decision and is reflected in the "laborious monologues" as we now read
them (contributing our own choices as we read). Still, obsessed with "getting
it right," Naipaul might have been intrigued by this assessment. Theroux, a
skilled, experienced writer who had learned a great deal from Naipaul's early
fiction, had "bought" the artfully constructed illusion of voices directly recorded without the interference of another consciousness: as if, going back to
them as they appear later in Naipaul's books, we could think that we "had" their
true voices now, access to the truth of the believers' past presence. Moreover,
that this truth, the dangerous seductive power of belief, could have been so
obvious—and therefore so manageable—without the recorder's intervention.

Yet for the documentarist Naipaul nothing is ever self-evident or can ever become fully understood, least of all the seemingly simple certainties of belief. In contrast to Theroux, whose focus has always been on himself as a traveler in exotic settings selected for their entertaining, colorful detail, Naipaul focuses on observing people within their cultural context, which in most cases eludes the ease of the exotic. The people with whom he speaks often remain remote, even where he explains them well: their lives are often difficult, even dangerous, and Naipaul does not encourage the reader to identify with them. Where he goes back into the past, understanding other people becomes even more difficult, since nothing separates more than time, and history is the best protected depository of difference and strangeness. Because the strangeness of differently acculturated people is real, Naipaul wants to make it accessible without fantasizing, domesticating, or prettifying. Theroux criticizes this perspective because it leaves no room for the self-inventions that have populated his recent travel writing, most densely in *My Other Life* (1996). Walcott resents above all Naipaul's "disloyalty" to their shared place of origin, the natural beauty and cultural richness of the islands to be found in *his* poetic imagination rather than in the sober, shared effort of history (the documentary). The issue here is not to weigh the comparative value of these different approaches but to point out that one might consider them to be in certain ways complementary and to remember that Naipaul never rejected either writer's work. It is true, Theroux's summary dismissal of Naipaul's later work is too skewed and personal to have the cultural weight of Walcott's harsh critique, particularly its accusations of racism. But both are intensely irritated by Naipaul's explorations of strangeness because they result in the *instability* of difference: something that changes in the process of looking and listening with the changing perspective of the stranger; something that is prettified and simplified in Theroux's travelogues and Walcott's poems; most important, something that questions the cultural politics of identity.

Behzad, Naipaul's second guide in Tehran, was younger, more educated, and without the other man's "nervousness and raw pride." To help the reader comprehend the kind of understanding between them that will be crucial to the success of the interviews, Naipaul describes how he learns to rely on Behzad's interpretation to make the city negotiable. With its chaotic traffic and obscure signification, Tehran forces him to depend "for his life" on his interpreter's intelligence, patient good sense, and kindliness (pp. 9–11). There is, however, the issue of his specific perspective and political intelligence. Behzad is unconcerned about his Iranian identity, disapproving of both the Shah's precipitous modernization and the Islamic revolution. Genuinely "confused," he has no agenda in this respect but also no irony, and his translations of the new Tehran are oddly literal. Puzzled by a pair of posters showing a small peasant group with archaic tools and a crowd with machine guns, Naipaul asks for a translation of their written message: "Twelfth Imam, we are waiting for you" (p. 13). It means what it says—but what does it say? Behzad knows that the Twelfth Imam, the last in the Iranian line of succession to the Prophet more than eleven hundred years ago, has been waiting to return to earth, and that the revolution is an offering to make him come. Not himself religious, he cannot help Naipaul to understand the revolution's emotional force. The communist son of a communist father, Behzad is a thoughtful political activist who knows little of the complicated history of Iranian Islam and is as unawed by its past power as by the greatness of pre-Islamic Persian antiquity claimed by the Shah to legitimate *his* rule.

Naipaul is intrigued by his iconoclasm and his sense of himself: "Was he Persian or Iranian in anything except his love of the Iranian people? Had his political faith washed him clean?" (p. 13). In a sense it had, and that was more than Naipaul could have hoped for in a guide in that situation. Later he will see—and repeatedly mention—that Behzad was the best guide he ever had traveling among believers because he supported efforts to understand them with translations that stopped short of interpretation. The important aspect of their relationship was a simultaneous dependence and independence, their shared interest in people and differently focused curiosity. Naipaul is puzzled by Behzad's acceptance of the failure of "his" (secular) revolution. When their leftist newspaper is closed down by the Islamic prosecutor in Tehran and Revolutionary Guards occupy the paper's offices, Behzad is not shattered but seems to see "in one popular movement the possibility and even the beginning of another" (p. 58). Is there for him, then, some connection between the Islamic and the communist revolution? Naipaul knows that Behzad is sustained by his loving identification with his people, though its meanings are largely inaccessible to Naipaul. Accepting the young Iranian's "ideal of the good and gentle worker," he does not seem troubled by the religious dimension of communism, the course of its eschatological history predetermined in the theological control of Marx's "all-powerful" doctrine by the Communist Party. It does not seem an issue where Behzad's political goals are concerned; to Naipaul's relief, he is different from the believers.

Naipaul decided to go to Iran in the winter of 1978, watching interviews with Iranians in the U.S. on American television that puzzled him. There was an Iranian intellectual wearing the obligatory tweed jacket, speaking the (at the time) obligatory turgid "Marxese" and praising the Islamic revolution, trying to impress his Western audience with his sophistication rather than help them understand what was going on. About the same time I watched an interview with a high ranking Iranian official, also in the reassuring tweed jacket, who explained the goals of the Islamic revolution and promised moderation. I remember my deep shock when I learned soon afterward of his execution. In my naïve perspective the man's death seemed particularly incongruent with his familiar appearance and civilized conduct: he had just been there, alive and, under the circumstances, remarkably rational, plausible. Naipaul's Iranian intellectual was quite different: a believer, uncompromising and yet intent on his credibility for American viewers. Watching, Naipaul also noted unhappily the Iranian woman with her head covered who praised Islam for giving dignity and security to women and the law school student who extolled the beauty of Islamic law. In all these interviews he saw a simultaneous attraction to the West—"it was more than a need for education and skills"—and unwillingness or inability to admit it: "in that attraction, too humiliating for an old and proud people to admit, there lay disturbance—expressed in dandyism, mimicry, boasting, and rejection" (p. 17). If the causes for the revolution were clear, the seemingly eager acceptance of the new Islamic fundamentalism by the elites was not.

Looking for clues, Naipaul thought that fiction might be more successful in this situation than political reporting: people can "hide behind direct statements; fiction, by its seeming indirections, can make hidden impulses clear" (p. 17). This statement has repeatedly been quoted by literary critics to emphasize the "constructedness" of Naipaul's observation in travelogues or to read more profundity into his cross-genre narration in partly autobiographical texts like *Finding the Center, The Enigma of Arrival,* and *A Way in the World.* But the contrast set up here does not concern fictional and nonfictional accounts of states of affairs or of mind in general. It concerns, rather, real-life, direct statements of belief in the monological voice of authenticity—subverted by the multitude of (recorded) voices in Naipaul's documentaries—and the (potentially) multivocal discourse of fictional narration that does not claim such authenticity. Nahid Rachlin's *Foreigner* (1978), published while the Shah was still in power, made clearer to Naipaul the fact and the power of Iranian confusion, precisely because of its indirect protest: "the political constriction drives the passion deeper; and the novel, with all its air of innocence, is a novel of violation, helplessness and defeat" (p. 17). I read the novel about the same time and remember clearly my irritation with this seemingly unmotivated fable of resignation, particularly its bloated self-righteousness. A U.S.–educated Iranian woman biologist in her early thirties, "blessed" (in my shallow view) with a good research job and a supportive American husband, decides on a visit with her family to stay in Iran to regain wholeness in her reclaimed Shia religion. In his office equipped with the latest Western medical technology, her U.S.–trained Iranian physician diagnoses a "Western" disease, an old ulcer, and advises her to give up her American life for the passive tranquility of renouncing all that hectic emptiness. Happiness is in languid visits to mosques and shrines, her Western clothes covered by the chador. Naipaul, appalled, calls relinquishing the "life of intellect and endeavor" an "Iranian Death pact," a disastrous retreat into the vacuities of spirituality that leaves technological and scientific productivity up to other groups: "That expectation—of others continuing to create, of the alien, necessary civilization going on—is implicit in the act of renunciation, and is its great flaw" (p. 19). It puts into question the concept itself of culture.

In Naipaul's strongly expressed view, the culture of belief is not viable because it is parasitic on Western scientific culture. Perhaps most urgently in this book, under the shock of the new phenomenon of a religious revolution, he poses the question of cultural value in the terms of Western secular modernity. The increasingly obvious implications of re-Islamization during the last two decades culminating in the events of September 11th have proved him right, despite massive Western self-deceptions about the cold war and now about the glories of globalization. It is precisely the global significance and power of Western science and technology—the core issue at the turn of the millennium—that benefits from Naipaul's negotiation between Western and non-Western perspectives: his realistic assessment of non-Western difficulties with globalization *and* of postcolonialist politics of "the Other." Attacks on Naipaul's critique of re-Islamization tend to be deaf to the variety of voices he recorded from his position *among* the believers. If he thinks certain aspects of their culture flawed, he still knows that they come in many different shapes which he cannot understand without their help. Looking at Pakistani "experiments" with re- Islamization, he realizes after a few days that by himself he "would see nothing" because, lacking some sort of frame or guidance, he cannot figure out what he is looking at (p. 98).

Behzad is the best interpreter he will find because by background and temperament he fits so well the profound cultural dissociation. If he fills in the details of the conflict between progressivism and traditionalism which seem less incongruous to him than they do to Naipaul, he still does so with a certain distance to what they both observe and also to Naipaul. Behzad especially, but also others who helped Naipaul to become less of a stranger among the believers, could not have been made up like the characters of *Guerrillas* and *A Bend in the River*. What they teach him is primarily a part of *their*, not of *his*, experience—an experience that depends on them and never becomes as clear, or clearly appropriated, as the Caribbean islands and the Africas of the novels. Importantly, puzzles of belief are stated as obvious but shown as intricate, because we encounter, again and again, a phenomenon of "negotiated" belief, a curiously tenacious collectivity in individuals that remains troubling to Naipaul and is perhaps the most important obstacle in our current hectic and panicked attempts to understand fundamentalist Islam.[22]

With all his secularism, Behzad will remain ultimately inaccessible because he too acts out of faith where Naipaul had not expected it. For the train trip back to Tehran from the holy city of Qom, he brings his communist girlfriend along, and the two become completely absorbed in a simple game of cards. Naipaul is struck by Behzad's hurt pride when a small young soldier orders them to stop their game—one of the many new rules. Himself shaken by the unexpected intrusion, he is bewildered by Behzad's explanation, a "dialectic" as dumbfounding as the Qom ayatollah's scholasticism they had just experienced: "The army always serves the upper-classes. That is why I call him an upper-class man" (p. 75). Demonstrating a power now rightfully belonging to the people, the young soldier had really objected to the young woman not wearing the chador. His interpreter's ideological love for "the people" made it difficult for Naipaul to know "who, in Iran, were now the people?" (p. 76).

He will know soon. Back in Tehran, Naipaul watches the preparations for battle: on one side the young Islamic revolutionary soldiers in camouflage battle dress with machine guns and sand bags, on the other, the young communists, looking more vulnerable in their open shirts.[23] There is no doubt that they will be defeated by the revolution. But both sides are united by "the same passion: justice, union, vengeance" (p. 78) and by their dependence on revealed truth, absolute faith, and the resulting eclectic misreading of historical events. The passions of adolescence in an old people have been a common cause for the political catastrophes of the twentieth century: what Naipaul found in Iran he could also have found in Weimar Germany. Young, attractive, intelligent, and full of good intentions, Behzad has become a prisoner of the death pact. Lined up for battle, he is already remote, as if he and Naipaul had never been friends, always strangers.

The strength of Naipaul's perspective is its focus on the behavior and the arguments of individual believers rather than on systems of belief. At the core of all these systems is the same religious dissociation from the ambiguities inherent in social reality, but it comes in a variety of forms, the variety of believers. At the airport, going to Pakistan, Naipaul found himself among crowds of Pakistani migrant workers who had done their shopping in Iran; in London the airport had been crowded with Iranians who had filled their bags in Europe and the U.S.: a hierarchy of cultural identities and desires.[24] The flight was delayed by American-made Iranian air force planes taking off for Kurdistan, on Khomeini's orders, to attack Kurdish rebels. Arriving in Pakistan they are told that two Phantoms had crashed, killing badly trained young believers, murderous perpetrators (p. 79). Political failure and religious fanaticism seem to go together everywhere; the reason for the decline of the state, Pakistanis tell him, has not been a flawed faith, but human failure to keep the faith pure (p. 87)—for Naipaul the most powerful indictment of cultures of belief. There is his conversation with a poet openly enraged by the condition of his country but still insisting on a history that shows Islam saving Muslims, not Muslims sustaining Islam. Where Naipaul argues the civilizing "conversion of ethical ideals into institutions" (p. 87), the poet asserts that the Muslim state should have developed out of the faith as if "naturally," independent of human intentions and agency. The true, the only issue has been its purity.

The poet's voice is one among others, and Naipaul is attentive to all of them, despite his almost somatic reaction to the suffocating sameness of the pure faith. Both descriptive and analytical, these recordings document and explain: attempting objectivity, they use narrative strategies to clarify obscure motivations. When Naipaul tells the government information officer in Karachi that he wants to see how Islam works in Pakistan, he is advised to focus on the Koran rather than on individual people: it is too hard to be a true Muslim. He is taken to observe prayers and a group of Mecca-bound pilgrims as "Islam in action," the official translation of his request. Though it explicitly claims the political realm, Islam does not signify political institutions and economic transactions, but rather religious activities governed by high standards of a faith controlled by seemingly infinite numbers of rules. Since Islam does not acknowledge secular needs, interests, and divisions, its politics is chaotic. Anything can be punished, explained, claimed, forgiven, or forgotten by invoking the authority of Islam. A good example is the interpreter assigned to Naipaul, a young female civil servant about to leave Pakistan, since her Muslim sect has been declared non-Muslim by Bhutto.[25] Nervous, discontent, and inattentive, she is also remarkably ignorant of the history of her sect. Without her official "excommunication" she would have been just another Pakistani believer. Noting how the "fever of the faith" coming in many forms "nearly always gave a phantasmagoric quality to an encounter," Naipaul is irritated by her seemingly deliberate incompetence: she promptly loses him in a crowd of people leaving for its pilgrimage to Mecca. But he is also troubled by the unhappy story of a life inexorably shaped by the irrational energies of faith. The most intriguing aspect of the event is the "layer upon layer of history" it signifies: sent off by the governor, who has brought with him a bagpipe band in tartan, the pilgrims are boarding a big, old, British built boat, the military style of their departure inherited from the British and superimposed on a religious journey that is older than Islam, going back to Arabian tribal worship (pp. 102–105). This layering might be expected to make for a more fluid, questioning attitude toward individual and collective identity, but in this situation it seems to uphold the rigid certainty exhibited by the believers.

Like the Iranian Behzad, Naipaul's best interpreter in Pakistan, Ahmed, is spontaneous and physically attractive—an attribute always noted by Naipaul where he has to negotiate strangeness. He cherishes the physical ease that comes with attractiveness mitigating a stranger's separateness, but here their similarities end. Ahmed, a high-ranking official, has recently found Islam and likes to have a "witness" to his new identity as believer, "someone from the other side" of secular culture that he left behind (p. 106). This is at first helpful to Naipaul, who finds Islam in Pakistan more bewildering than in Iran. Like any good utopian traveler since More's Hythloday, Naipaul listens without comment to Ahmed's praises of the radically different and (therefore) better solution of entrenched social problems: Islam is the most evolved religion, combining Moses' passion for the law and Jesus' compassion for the needy. He is clearly impressed by Ahmed's passion to make sense of his life, "leaning" on this sudden friendship to learn more about Islamic institutions and experiments. Ahmed's "rationality" is important to Naipaul (p. 107), because it seems to shift the question of cultural meaning from the opaque collective to the distinct historical individual. The core of Islam for Ahmed is charity as a personal and not a collective virtue, focused on the individual with a tenderness that moves Naipaul, who is also attracted to Ahmed's quiet and gentle son, a young physician working with the poor.

In contrast, a renowned Pakistani intellectual and expert on the Islamization of institutions refers to his own "God-intoxicated" authority (p. 108), insisting on the unity of the political and the spiritual. Naipaul will learn that this view, if not the intense mysticism, is quite common among Pakistani professionals, newspaper editors and businessmen who see the early Islamic state, the creation of the Prophet, as the ideal for Pakistani Islam.[26] Though troubled by this view, Naipaul finds himself personally attracted to an Indian Muslim, a prominent Karachi lawyer and a member of the influential Islamic Ideology Council who devotes much of his time to Pakistani public issues. Naipaul notes with pleasure the man's solid tallness and "slow, dry humor, the eye for human quirkiness," speculating that in this case "passion for his faith" has not interfered with com-mon sense, because Islam has been for the Indian Muslim the civilization and culture "fundamental" to his self-perception (p. 111). Importantly, this particu-lar man's faith has enabled him to be sufficiently settled to take responsibility for himself and for others, to be a competent adult, a good father—qualities essential to cultural well-being because they support the ability to acknowledge the plural, multivocal, unpredictable presence of others. The father-gods of fun-damentalist believers, regardless of their denomination, have been notoriously suspicious of plurality in their insistence on the monological solidarity of faith. Naipaul's fondness for that fatherly lawyer who speaks for Islam passionately and rationally reflects his own early experiences of unsettledness and the role reversal in the relationship with his troubled if loving father. Adulthood is an individual and a cultural quality; people are helped, or hindered, to become adults by their cultural environments.[27]

For the lawyer, the equality of people is in obedience to the law, with the mosque as the great equalizer; the Islamic enterprise means the creation of a theocratic state whose institutions could function in the modern world. The problem lies with the "modernists" among Islamizers, newcomers to Islam who prefer mysticism over political information. Like the mullahs whom the mili-tary government enlisted to help with Islamization, they see everything in terms of the true believer as the good leader, not in terms of good institutions. Given the gap between the ideal of the pure faith and the reality of Pakistan's political insecurity, the pure faith provides only negations: no alcohol, no (female) im-modesty, no political parties, no secular courts of law. Existing institutions are declared un-Islamic and the political vacuum calls for army rule (pp. 111–12). In Pakistan, the political vacuum is created not by chaos, as it is in Africa and the Caribbean, but by the tightly arranged, elaborate sets of rules that account for the purity and wholeness, the fearful innocence of the faith.[28]

This innocence is predicated on an eclectic and distorting view of the past, the kind of opaque "datelessness" Naipaul had encountered when researching his family history in Trinidad.[29] Encouraged by Ahmed to see Islamic charity in action at a Sufi center, Naipaul observes the feeding of the poor in a religious community and is struck by the extraordinary beauty of a young helper. But he seems unfocused, floating, a "wayfarer" without any sense of how to find his way—like many others, a particle of Pakistan's migrant populations (p. 141). The ability to project, plan, structure, and control that goes with settledness is precious to Naipaul, who knows from experience that to be unsettled most often does not mean freedom but rather the bondage of disorder. A traveler con-fronted with the unpredictable, he appreciates civilized places precisely because they can accommodate contingencies, at least to a degree, and the Sufi center is not one of them. An overseer, seemingly uneasy about his contact with the young man, impresses on him the importance of the *murshid*, the local saint, as the medium for meeting Allah (p. 142): all charity at the Sufi center hap-pens through the *murshid*. But abruptly the man breaks off his chanting "as if enervated by the mid-afternoon heat, the dust, the desert, the life, the boredom"

(p. 144). They are the concrete experiences underlying the religious fervor which fuels the center, a phenomenon both obvious and not fully accessible to the observer. The people who come to the center to be fed and to have bad spirits exorcized may find it a whole world, but to the outsider it seems the enactment of a script in which they are all caught without any clues how to escape it. Naipaul is apprehensive for them, unable to become intimate momentarily with their radical strangeness but keeping his distance to see them more clearly.

Understanding them is a different matter. Ahmed's sudden withdrawal is a great disappointment because it leaves Naipaul with the unsolved puzzle of how "the religion of revelation and rules" could mix so easily with the "religion of asceticism and unconfined meditation" (p. 147). Like Behzar, Ahmed has tried to make sense of his world for Naipaul, but at a certain point his belief makes him separate, remote. Where Naipaul follows reasoned evidence wherever it takes him, Ahmed and other believers work with assumptions arranged in elaborate structures that cannot be perturbed by evidence for fear of collapsing them. Naipaul does not explore that fear beyond its effects, their own acts and words. The documentarist's intention is to record the believers as they present themselves, describing what they allow him to see. But it is also true that what he has been allowed to see is visible because he has looked at it in his own way. The inevitable hermeneutic circle is here instructively mitigated by the combined rational detachment and acknowledged anxiousness of the documentarist who feels swept away by a strangeness that may never yield to familiarity.

In his reactions to their retreating from him, Naipaul is frightened by the believers' simplicity because he finds in it the terrible finality of a profound and basic tension between East and West on which all these Islamic fundamentalisms thrive. He is disturbed not so much by their general rejection of Western rationality as by their lack of interest in secular political and cultural institutions that would enable the individual to feel at home in the world for a time. Naipaul has never censored his reactions of dismay when confronted with unpleasant or dangerous living conditions: attributes like "desolate" and "derelict" assigned to the (Caribbean) island of *Guerrillas* or the Africa of *A Bend in the River* echo the descriptions by earlier travelers of the "wretched" life of certain peoples they encountered, for example, the inhabitants of Terra del Fuego in Georg Forster's *A Voyage around the World.* Anticipating multiculturalist positions two centuries later, Herder admonished the readers of Forster's account (largely also his readers) to embrace the Fuegans' way of life in the spirit of "natural" brotherhood and thereby affirm it as one of many different possibilities of being human. But as Forster argued against him, such embracing is not "natural" but ideological ("principled"), despite its good intentions. Natural is the European explorers' dismayed pity with the people living in such poor conditions: in *any* human perspective, the people observed by Forster and his companions *were* distressed; they *did* suffer badly from cold, hunger, and illness. It would not have been "brotherly" to refrain from responding to their physical misery as they witnessed it. But Herder, the "intellectual traveling in his armchair" and arguing from principle rather than evidence, had no physical and emotional experience of extreme cultural difference and therefore speculated too easily about its meanings. To the observer who shared with the observed a time and place, the Fuegans' vulnerable nakedness in that situation was not natural but culturally inept. As Forster and his companions discovered, another group living close to them under similar climatic conditions had managed much better to protect and feed themselves.[30] Like Forster's, Naipaul's judgments do not signify Western prejudicial preference on principle for complexity over simplicity, but rather an intelligible assessment of different ways and degrees of cultural functioning.

In Malaysia and Indonesia, Naipaul's Muslim interlocutors appear more conflicted about the relation between past and present, because here Islam has ideologically camouflaged rather than openly exploited the tension between archaic stasis and modern mobility. The central character of "Conversations in Malaysia: The Primitive Faith" is like Behzad and Ahmed in that he both mediates and withholds, reveals and hides, and is both attractive and ultimately inaccessible to Naipaul. But unlike them, the intelligent, self-possessed young Shafi, an official of the Malaysian Muslim youth movement in Kuala Lumpur, yearns for the lost paradise of the village he left behind for the educational opportunities of the city. Where his desire to regain "a sense of the fitness and wholeness of things" in multiracial Malaysia would be more easily fulfilled by Islam, his professional self is a creation of the city which set free his intelligence by allowing him to change. Naipaul is interested in the cultural dimension of the (for Shafi) difficult psychological dynamics between his traditional rural and progressive urban "identities": the problematic relation between the collective and the individual exacerbated by profound changes in the village brought about by increasing globalization (p. 220).

Shafi's memories of his village are focused on the simple, pure religious life, in stark contrast to the neighboring Chinese village, which he remembers as dirty and overrun by pigs. People in his village are "good persons" precisely because they remain "self-sufficient," namely uninterested in technology. In Shafi's scenario, village life will endure, given some "good basic amenities"— reliable and frequent bus service and a good school (pp. 225–26). Oddly, he does not realize that this alone would change the continuity of village life already undermined by his leaving the village with the help of the Scout movement, a British institution. In his interview with Naipaul, Shafi has difficulties talking in his own words about the conflict revealed in their conversation between his love for the pure life in the village and his recognition of the "backwardness" of Malaysia. Resorting to the ready-made phrases of Islam, he can gloss over the inconsistencies of his nostalgia. One of the most common human experiences, it can be accommodated if the individual takes responsibility for himself, but Shafi thinks his expulsion from paradise a unique experience for which not he but the world outside is responsible and which only Islam can heal (pp. 227–28).

On some level, intelligent, competent Shafi has not been able to become an adult.

This interview reveals a potential flaw in Naipaul's perception of people whose behavior he thinks unexpectedly inexplicable. Traveling to the village for which Shafi grieves to better understand his conflict, Naipaul finds himself in a small, rickety colonial town. Shafi's contacts insist that they are content: they live well on their secure government pay, do not like competition, and trust Allah to provide for their large families. It is the life that Shafi remembers with yearning, but his own transformation has changed his idea of meaningful community. Their Islam means passive contentment, stagnation; he wants his Islam to be radically upsetting, the "energizer and purifier of Malays, the destroyer of false ways and false longings" (p. 264). Deeply upset by Naipaul's uncovering of his delusion, the discrepancy between reality and memory, Shafi refuses any further contact with him. In their interviews, Naipaul noted with sympathy his difficulties when urged to explain *his* Islam, but Naipaul does not connect this observation with Shafi's surprising withdrawal. Failing to explain the conflicts of his position in his own words, Shafi would finally become inaccessible to Naipaul. But by pressuring him to explain what he could not explain in words he did not have, Naipaul has also become inaccessible to Shafi, who, on some level, has himself been concerned about his failure. Naipaul's going to the village to see for himself did not ease the tension between them, since it made Shafi's estrangement from his real past more explicit; his attempts at making sense of Shafi are not, or only very tentatively, aware of Shafi's attempts at making sense of the stranger who asks him unexpected, uncomfortable questions. Naipaul may suggest that Shafi's—or other informants'—behavior is in some ways a reaction to his questions, but he does not explore the connection. He arrives, engages with his informants, and explains to his reader how these relationships influence his conducting the interviews. He leaves, seemingly unconcerned about his impact on the people he talked to. Yet, like his reticence where private psychological problems are concerned, this apparent lack of empathy or identification affirms the goal of documentary representation to maintain as much as possible the distinctness of its subject in that subject's terms. This goal is arguably best served by a flexible distance between observer and observed. Naipaul's explicit expressions of regret about his informants' withdrawal are as important to the narration of his encounters with believers as are his explicit expressions of appreciation when he connects with them. In both cases he emphasizes their cultural distinctness as he saw it at a certain time in a certain place from a certain position. His report is not concerned with the ways in which he might have influenced their attitude toward Islam, other than suggesting that they withdrew from him because his presence, his questions, were incompatible with their belief.

In fictional discourse, the author asserts his authority by being in charge of his protagonists; in documentary discourse he does so by documenting that he is responsible to people as he finds them. In Indonesia Naipaul finally finds the village Shati grieves for, that is, the village worth grieving for: "an enchanted, complete world where everything—food, houses, tools, rituals, reverences—had evolved over the centuries and had reached a kind of perfection. Everything locked together, as the rice-fields just outside, some no more than half an acre, fitted together" (p. 320). That particular village is the home of the young poet Linus. His father, the village headman, had converted to the Catholic faith of his wife, and it is she who is for Naipaul "the representative of a high civilization." Dressed with great care in her blouse, sash, and sarong, her manners were exquisite, her face "serene and open": "she held her head up with a slight backward tilt; her bones were fine, her eyes bright, though depressed in their sockets, and her lips were perfectly shaped over her perfect teeth. Her speech—without constraint or embarrassment—always appeared to be about to turn to laughter" (p. 322). Naipaul's delight in what he sees easily persuades the reader of its value, and it echoes Forster's delight with the people of O-Taheitee in that beautiful natural setting enhanced by their responsive culture. But if it is absolutely clear to Naipaul, as it was to Forster, that he could not even wish to stay in this perfect place, Linus, proud of his earthly paradise, has already left it. As the person he has become he depends on the city, with its newspapers to write for, its poetry readings, its incipient business of culture—as the young writer Naipaul had depended on London.

Linus's writing poetry, the realization of his talent, cannot be a part of his mother's achieved civilization, which neither requires nor tolerates additions. That beauty is perfect in ways which would have paralyzed him if he had not left it behind, alive in remembrance. As old as human consciousness, remembrance has been potentially life-enhancing but also deadening. For Linus the remembered perfection of his origin, his mother in the place and time of his childhood, is indeed paradise. Exempt from change and corruption, it is a fiction whose purity, no matter how pleasing and nourishing, cannot be imposed on the impure, changing presence without doing damage to it. As a visitor not intending to stay, his memory does not betray him, and Naipaul benefits from its truthfulness which has its source in its acknowledged limitations. Linus is helped here by two aspects of his "privileged" situation. The first one, familiar to Naipaul who shares it, concerns his particular talent: as a writer, a poet, "he had a sense of who he was; he could be a man apart" (p. 326). He *could* be: there is no claim made for the young man's artistic talent, as Naipaul makes none for his own. The claim, instead, is made for the potential of the position of the "man apart," a position congenial to that of the writer. In making something that is his, that comes out of his own way of looking, he can develop a sense of himself in the world. Without the desire for a preauthorized identity, he will not easily be seduced by ideological prejudgments. This, clearly, is important to Naipaul's self-perception as a man apart, a traveler and looker. The other, related aspect concerns the *particular* kind of perfection left behind and reconstituted in remembrance. As Naipaul points out, both Christianity, the religion of the colonizing power, and Islam, the formal faith of the people sustaining their pride under Dutch rule, have been complementary to the old faiths of the village: "People lived with everything at once: the mosque, the church, Krishna, the rice goddess, a remnant of Hindu caste, the Buddhist idea of nirvana, the Muslim idea of paradise" (p. 326). No one could say exactly what or who they *were;* they *did* things together.

The composite, delicately balanced perfection of Linus's village is of course highly precarious. Like all village civilizations, it is threatened by globalization of technical innovations and modern perception of time. Everywhere technology has brought profound changes to the old cultural structures and rhythms—a threat seized upon with great passion by late-twentieth-century revolutionary Islam. Preaching the wickedness of the machine, it proclaims to deal with contemporary political issues by going back to its religio-political roots. These roots, the pure Islam of the Prophet, are a fiction, but they cannot be acknowledged as such. Not only does this new-old revolutionary Islam not have any political solutions for a complex contemporary world; worse, the faith it offers is one of violence and domination, because it insists on total leadership by the Prophet, who is no longer there. The paradox of absence and power at the core of the old-new political Islam accounts for its "rage," its "anarchy" (p. 331). Whether he realized it or not, Naipaul's observations among Islamic fundamentalists uncover patterns of reactions very similar to European reactions between the two world wars that were essential to the rise of leaders like Hitler or Stalin. The shock caused by their regimes, especially the Hitler regime, because it grew out of a homogeneously complex, highly developed civilization, is partly responsible for the end of colonial rule and the beginning of the migrations of the late twentieth century. It is a shock that has, like the brutal but infinitely more "innocent" terror of the French Revolution, brought about a radical questioning of Western Enlightenment culture that sustained achievements like Forster's and without which Naipaul's more ambiguously and painfully illuminating insights would not have been possible.

5   Stories of Other Lives: Documentaries

Beyond Belief: Islamic Excursions among the Converted Peoples

Iran

In 1995, Naipaul went back to fundamentalist Islam, recording the results of traveling for five months in four non-Arab Muslim countries.[1] The book was preceded by an essay about Iran in the *New Yorker* (26 May 1997) that explored the connections between the processual, incomplete nature of knowledge and the goal of documentary accuracy. Revisiting Tehran after sixteen years, Naipaul charts transformations of experience and perception, and the stories he records also document, along with the social and political changes of the place and its people, changes in the observer. Their thoughts about their situation emerge more distinctly but also more ambiguously and inconclusively—like his own realization, after days of looking at the view from his hotel window, that one of the hills he sees is actually the infamous Evin prison, where the revolution killed its children. Once he knows what he sees, it is no longer hidden; but what does its distinctness now say about its hidden meanings then?

The essay on the second visit to Tehran explores the variables of spatial and temporal distance that define and change information, dealing with aspects of representation that Naipaul had developed in the meantime in *Enigma of Arrival* and *A Way in the World*. The result is a documentary essay about the documentary method that would help him achieve a better understanding of fundamentalist Islam in the nineties, namely the intensified politicization of religious belief through an increasingly institutionalized entwinement of religious and political energies. This development is partly a reaction to globalization, the spread of seemingly unstoppable technocracy that calls up profoundly ambivalent desires for all things Western and, at the same time, their resentful rejection. But why this peculiarly single-minded, religio-political militancy? In the "Prologue" to *Beyond Belief,* Naipaul proposes to answer this question by tracing the "theme" of Islam's "imperial demands" on the believers, beyond the privacy of conscience and religious belief. The believers in these non-Arab countries are converts, and the point of Islam's imperialism has been to make converts. However, that "theme" is not meant to dominate the book, which is explicitly "about people," a book of "stories" rather than "opinion" or "conclusions" (pp. xi–xii). Moreover, these are stories meant to carry accurate information, and Naipaul's observations on that trip in 1995 have largely been verified by the events of 1998 in Indonesia and Malaysia, recent developments in Iran, where religious rule is now under attack but still powerful, and Pakistan, where it has been growing, and in Afghanistan, the home of fundamentalist terrorism into the twenty-first century.

A shadowy presence, looking and listening, the writer "steadily retreats" in the "cultural explorations" of his later travel books.[2] In *Beyond Belief* he has "become again what I was in the beginning: a manager of narrative"—the young writer creating his characters out of their voices recorded in his memory and in his father's materials. The meaning of stories, to differing degrees "true" or invented, is "to give news about a changing society, to describe mental states" (p. xii). Since these are stories of individuals struggling with the promises and responsibilities of their belief, they will contain contradictions, lacunae, and obscurities. It is his retreating behind these stories told by the people who lived them, giving them center stage, that accounts for their haunting presence. We learn what they think and feel about Islam and can draw our own conclusions about the social and psychological effects of political re-Islamization. We can also draw connections to other politically potent belief systems, notably fascism and communism, from the statements of people living under the rule of faith gathered in Naipaul's book. If, in his retelling, he could not but shape them in some ways, he did so as "a manager of narrative" whose first responsibility is to the recording of others' stories and whose interventions are meant to enhance their explanatory power.

A poignant and delicate example of balancing distance and closeness toward another person's story is Naipaul's account of his second visit with the Javanese poet Linus, who was young and on the brink of fame in 1979. The long elegiac poem he was working on then, a tribute to the rich culture of old Java, would indeed be a great success. It seemed that he had captured something precious about to disappear (to Naipaul it had then seemed charmed in its timeless perfection), and almost two decades later that poem is still his best-known work and largely untranslatable.[3] The particularity of that rich and complete rice culture would disappear without leaving any traces but taboos and clan names, since there had never been any felt need for recordings: "Once the old world was lost, its ways of feeling could not be reconstructed" (p. 76). It is the inevitability of that loss and the impossibility of mitigating it in verbal representation that makes Linus's story resonate so strongly with Naipaul's concerns about the finality of the writer's failure to speak intelligibly about his world, his responsibility for the finality of its disappearance.

Naipaul came back to retrieve the perfect "pastoral morning" of twenty years ago that had remained with him so clearly: the purposefully ordered vegetation around the houses, the shrines of the rice goddess, the traditional Javanese elegance of Linus's mother, "refusing to take the business of his poetry seriously, since in her perfect world all poetry had already been written, and new poetry was an absurdity." But Linus wrote his new poem celebrating the old perfection precisely because he feared that it would not endure. Signs of the new "Muslim aggressiveness" can be seen everywhere (pp. 77–78), and the Catholic Linus is in serious trouble with young Muslim fundamentalists because he allegedly "mocks Muslims" (p. 83). The village and the house to which he more and more retreats have become shabby and his beautiful mother "shrunken and dimmed by age." When his parents converted to Catholicism in 1938, they simply added their new religion to their familiar Javanist practices, a local mix of Hinduism, Buddhism, and animism. Unlike Islam, Catholicism has not demanded a break with the past but allowed for more gentle transitions. Linus is upset by the ruptures of the surfaces and rhythms of daily life: the controlling loudspeakers on the enlarged village mosque, the strange, ungainly shapes of covered and veiled women in the shimmering tropical heat. These new restrictions and exclusions also mean a diminishing interest in Javanese customs and ritual, for Linus not only an aesthetic but also a political loss. At the funeral of Linus's father a Christian led the prayers, but non-Christian mourners, including the Muslim *coum* who washes and buries the village dead according to Javanese custom, were asked to offer prayers for the dead man in their own way. For Linus this was the way of "tolerance and equilibrium" in the village which is now in danger of being lost (p. 84).

The unwelcome changes have hollowed out Linus's once perfectly balanced, richly layered world. Underneath the luxuriant vegetation of his village—like Trinidad's, a composite of plants from the Old and the New World—were the ruins of Hindu, Buddhist, and Hindu-Buddhist temples. They had been buried over thousands of years in the fertile soil produced by the eruptions of the volcano Merapi that also preserved the traces of peoples even more ancient. But if Naipaul empathizes with Linus's experience of loss, he is also alarmed by his intense Catholic-Javanist spiritualism, not least for its undeniable emotional logic. Linus and his "mystical group" receive encouraging messages from the Indian-Javanese divinity Siddhartha (p. 89), claiming the same status as Jesus and Mohammed, who represent the two revealed, converting religions of Indonesia. They can draw on Siddhartha in their attempts at keeping alive, at least in religious and poetic communication, the old Javanese world that is changing beyond recognition as they look on impotently. Linus's large collection of antique krises, some of them from the sixth and seventh centuries, suggests repressed rage. Their real value for him is their power to give off "vibrations of energy" tapped by the old kris makers' ability to obtain the blessing of the god of animals' magic. Admiring them, Naipaul thinks the krises "fearful things, their blades jagged and sharp, different leaves or layers of metal showing." They remind him of Linus's mentally disturbed sister and her three-day rages, "and then they set the teeth on edge" (p. 90).

The terrible, helpless rages of the shadowy young woman excluded from Naipaul's memory of that idyllic Javanese morning two decades ago are now evoked to suggest the depth of Linus's seemingly quiet despair. Shared with his mother and many other villagers, this despair acknowledges the decline of the rice culture that sends all the educable young men away from the villages, into the cities. Work in the rice fields has become "a torment" because the cycle has been speeded up too much: change has accelerated. Emblematic of the dubious blessings of globalization, the new fast growing, tasteless, less nutritious rice developed in a Western laboratory has contributed to the loss of the old colorful village life: the music made with the old instruments, and the night-long shadow theater with its familiar characters and stories, Linus's great love. Too exhausted in the evening now, the farmers only want to look at the images flickering on the TV screen, like Linus's mother absorbed in her favorite Latin-American soap opera, "leaping the hemisphere, leaping cultures" (p. 89). Linus the poet is a prisoner in his language as well as in his village, because it is only here that he can find sensory and spiritual nourishment. This conundrum is more painful because it is more powerfully concrete now than when he was young; it is also the reason for Naipaul's deep and delicate sympathy for him—not unlike Linus's sadness for his irredeemably damaged sister. The importance of Linus's story may be relatively minor in its political and religious Indonesian context. But for Naipaul it speaks powerfully to the problems inherent in technocratic globalization for groups that have managed to endure for a very long time in their pleasing and nourishing balance of natural and cultural environment, stasis and change, sameness and difference.

Beyond Belief starts with the story of the Indonesian "man of the moment," the university teacher of engineering and preacher of Islam, Imaduddin—a story Naipaul also published in *New York Review of Books* at the height of the Indonesian financial crisis.[4] It seemed to him a particularly clear example for the connection between the cultural and political archaism of Islamic fundamentalism and the seductive force of the latest Western technology used to buttress the power of religious community. Fired because of his religiosity in the late seventies, Imaduddin has become the new Indonesian incarnate, complete with a Mercedes, an expensive house, and a successful TV program in Jakarta. It is not by accident that he is now also the close friend of the Indonesian minister for research and technology, B. J. Habibie, a pious Muslim whose all-absorbing "scientific" interest is the development of Indonesian aeronautics. At the twelfth Islam Unity Conference, he declared 10 August 1995, the day on which the first plane built entirely in Indonesia flew for about an hour at a respectable altitude, as National Technological Reawakening Day.

Both men are members of the Association of Muslim Intellectuals, the religious-political power base of a new elite. Imaduddin is charged with paying regular visits to the many Indonesian students dispersed over the Western world at institutions of higher learning to encourage them in their loyalty to the unity of science and the purity of Islam personified in Habibie, whose office is lavishly financing their education. Imaduddin is now concentrating entirely on the profession of preacher and missionary to increase the number of good, that is, pious men whose scientific education will bear fruit because it is supported by the purity of their belief.

Imaduddin talked to Naipaul a few years before the Indonesian financial crisis, supporting the government of Suharto, the master of Javanese clan politics and the good Muslim with little interest in material things.[5] This perspective conveniently disregarded the overwhelming evidence of Suharto's feudalist politics that had used the "new economy" of high technology to enormously enrich his extended family but done nothing to educate the Indonesian people in their dealings with a rapidly expanding Internet and highly volatile stock market. Naipaul's earlier interview had focused precisely on the detrimental combination of feudalism, theocracy, and Western technology as he found it in the various new Islam fundamentalisms, and it had implicitly predicted the Indonesian crisis.

Like all of Naipaul's writing, *Beyond Belief* deals with the heritage of empire in the second half of the twentieth century, the temporal simultaneity and increasing spatial vicinity of vastly different cultures. With Forster, who traveled two centuries before him, Naipaul shares the fascination with what can be seen (heard, smelled, touched) and how it could be looked at so that it would make sense: a documentary imagination whose source is the reality principle of others' perceptions, questions, and critical comments. When Forster went with Cook's party to have another look at groups they had already visited, they wanted to see what they had missed before. It was a process of accumulating information about essentially static societies, and it was meant to check their previous findings. Whether these societies were or were not static depends on observational perspective and is not the question here. The existence of what to the Europeans seemed timeless, unchanging cultural environments became an important issue in the eighteenth-century debates for and against the possibility and desirability of further evolution: the notorious question of a progress of mankind in which the early and frequently mentioned possibly negative consequences of change through contact certainly played a part.[6] Over the next two centuries, the conflicts of contact would become much more clearly articulated and intense but also much more complicated.

When Naipaul went back to the four Islamic societies, he found the results of a great deal of social and political change but also of an enduring, increasingly ideologized sameness. The troubling combination was expected, but he found himself surprised by its specific variations: the different ways in which changes brought about by technological globalization were absorbed in an expanding sameness of the same. On his first visit to Indonesia in 1979, he was advised to talk with the chairman of the Islamic village boarding school movement of Indonesia, Mr. Wahid, because his religious educational organization was seen as the vanguard of the modern Muslim movement. Sixteen years later, Wahid is openly critical of Habibie's cutting-edge mix of technocratic politics and religious fundamentalism and also of Suharto's newfound, energetically displayed piousness. But Naipaul remembers the depressing sight of young boys gathered in camps to learn village crafts and skills they could easily pick up at home and spending most of the day memorizing, in large groups, simple religious texts that they "read" in "private study" in the evening, unable to make out the letters in the dark (pp. 22–23). One memory image in particular from that first visit has remained with him: a young teacher chanting a lesson in Arabic law to his class from the small verandah of his small house. The house and tiny monthly stipend were provided by Wahib's organization, the food by the villagers. For Naipaul he is part of the long tradition of the "wise man and spiritual lightning-conductor," living off other people's labor (p. 23). His literally mind-numbing spiritual teaching is more harmful now than it might have been in the simpler past because global modernization has created growing needs and desires which will have to be filled somehow—most simply by an ideology of religious identity. Presented to Naipaul by Mr. Wahib, the teacher stood humbly before them "in the great gloom, very small and pious and hunched, with very thick lenses to his glasses," praised for his "marvelous" knowledge of the Koran. He seemed undisturbed by Naipaul's disappointment when told that he had memorized only half, "piously accepting and converting into religious merit whatever rebuke we might have offered him. And I feel that he was ready to round his shoulders a little more and a little more until he might have looked like a man whose head grew beneath his shoulders" (p. 24)—a fairy-tale figure, like the Taliban twenty years before they had the fascinated, appalled attention of the West.

Remembering Naipaul's sardonic remarks about the backwardness of Ugandan culture and politics during his stint as guest lecturer in Kampala, Theroux described nicely how "Vidia had appeared like a dust devil, had sternly questioned every received opinion and demanded answers, and then, like a dust devil, he had whirled away—shivered into the distance, leaving a small scoured trail in the earth." There was his much resented "nagging" the local Indians about their "exit strategy" should things get worse—he rightly assumed they would. There were his frequent violations of the convention not to express one's low opinion of the local students and his awarding only one prize: "Third Prize, to Winston Wabamba, and no one found it funny."[7] Neither did Naipaul, apprehensive about the consequences of what, rightly or wrongly, he thought willful stupidity. His cruelly comical description of Mr. Wahib's treasured supermemorizer was a reaction to the literal dimness of the young man, whose piety seemed to have swallowed all of his own and his students' intelligence and curiosity. If Naipaul's judgments seem harsh, even arrogant, they do take the judged seriously because he cannot but imagine himself in their place: the terrible waste of spending long years learning the Koran by heart in Arabic. Having Wahib correct him that the young teacher had memorized half the Koran is a brilliant touch because it makes concrete the grotesque burden of that kind of route learning. Memorizing all of it, on the other hand, suggests the "marvelous" closure of a task fulfilled that somehow erases the memory of its endless, stultifying boredom.

Naipaul does not identify with other people; his aim is to understand, not to be understanding of, the cultural conditions of other lives, and that requires putting himself in their place temporarily. They may appear disturbingly, on occasion grotesquely alien, but as he saw them they are real, and increasingly, with globalization, their strangeness will have real consequences for other people in other places. His rejection of particular cultural practices, especially relating to education, is less concerned, in this second book on Islam, with individual lives—though he can be sharply aware of the painful impact on them of severe limitations in this respect—than with larger cultural-political trends. Wahib, once a thorn in the side of the then less pious Association of Muslim Intellectuals, has not become any less religious, just more suspicious of technology in its new symbiosis with religion. The now much greater role of technology in Indonesian culture has not changed his educational program; route learning of religious texts still takes precedence over studying languages, mathematics, and science, not to mention computers. This is a situation common to developing countries where Islamic fundamentalism is growing and the reason for Naipaul's portrait of the young Indonesian teacher who had nothing to teach. In a report for the *New York Times* in the summer of 2000, Jeffrey Goldberg describes in detail the conditions in a religious school in the northwest of Pakistan, the Haqqania madrasah, which has the highest record of placing its absolvents in the Taliban leadership.[8] The age range of the students is eight to thirty-five, and the youngest boys spend between four and eight hours every day memorizing the Koran. Like Naipaul, Goldberg observes the children being read the passages in their original Arabic and repeating them. Not only do they have to memorize the text in a language not their own but in a language they do not understand at all: a meaningless sequence of sound patterns.[9] The Haqqania students come mostly from the ethnic group of Pathan, the majority in that area of Pakistan and in much of neighboring Afghanistan. They are enrolled in an eight-year course of Islamic studies and go on to the "mufti course" in preparation for becoming clerics who can issue religious rulings, fatwas, on a wide range of questions from family law to jihad and death sentences. There are no courses in subjects like world history, or foreign languages, or mathematics, no computers, no science labs.

One of the bigger madrasahs in Pakistan, the Haqqania has more than twenty-eight hundred students recruited mostly from very poor families and completely supported by the madrasah that is funded by wealthy Pakistanis and Islamists from countries in the Persian Gulf. There are about a million students in Pakistan's madrasahs, many of them small and located in villages; all of them centered in militant Islam. Some of them are associated with the mujahedeen groups waging jihad against India in Kashmir, and Goldberg refers to the Haqqania madrasah as a de facto "jihad factory." Its chancellor, Samiul Haq, habitually sent students to Afghanistan to help the Taliban in their civil war with the Northern Alliance. He refused to tell Goldberg how many of the students were killed; however, when asked about their parents' feelings should they be killed, all the students said they would be very proud. This reaction seems to surprise Goldberg, who mentions it several times. But since for the Taliban all enemies are eo ipso a threat to the purity of the faith, any conflict is a jihad and all the men and boys killed in battle are martyrs going straight to paradise. There can be no higher glory if one is on the side of the Taliban, and the great majority of the students and their parents seemed to be.[10]

Mullah Haq has been involved in radical Islamic politics, wanting Pakistan to be ruled by religious law, *Sharia*. Instructively, the school's first and only honorary degree went to the Taliban leader, Mullah Omar.[11] Haq, as he tells Goldberg, has also been a friend and supporter of Osama bin Laden, sharing his radically antimodernist, anti-American views, even to the point of endorsing fatwas to kill Americans (p. 3). The influence of men like Haq on large numbers of young, dramatically undereducated Pakistanis—Goldberg has stunning examples of the students' highly exploitable "innocence" (pp. 7–8)—has contributed to a growing sympathy among Pakistani Muslims for the Taliban, and this radicalization, also referred to as "Talibanization," has been very troubling. In Goldberg's view, Pakistan was showing "early signs of coming apart at the seams" (p. 3)—it seemed so to Naipaul in 1995.[12] In the aftermath of September 11th, Haq's referring matter-of-factly to his friendship with Mullah Omar and Osama bin Laden seems in the distant past, prehistory.

What Pakistan did not have in 1995 was "the bomb." Goldberg was invited to a birthday party, complete with a huge vanilla sheet cake inscribed with lemon frosting: "Second Anniversary Celebrations of the Day of God's Greatness." It was the day on which Pakistan exploded its first nuclear bomb, 28 May 1998, and on which, according to the science minister, Allah restored "greatness" to Pakistan. Among the many dignitaries attending the bomb's birthday party was Pakistan's "chief executive," General Pervez Musharraf, who in October 1999 had smoothly deposed the elected prime minister, Nawaz Sharif, and put him on trial for "corruption." What by Western standards is considered corruption has been common practice in Pakistan since the inception of the Muslim state and so, logically, is the accusation of corruption against a political enemy. It is possible that Musharraf was at some point interested in making stability an issue, but not himself an Islamic fundamentalist, he has, like the deposed Sharif, been forced to deal with fundamentalist politics. A modern businessman depending on fax, email, and the Internet, Sharif had decided in August 1998, a situation of economic crisis, to give constitutional status to *Sharia*. He did not have the support of orthodox Muslims, to whom this decision was blatantly self-serving politics, and he did not succeed. But the importance of the bomb for Pakistan's political-religious identity survived his loss of power. Musharraf, whom the West wanted to think of—and since September 11th has needed to think of—as a reasonable man, reassured Goldberg that the bomb would not fall into the wrong hands. Responding to Goldberg's concern about the religious associations of the birthday celebration, the bomb as Allah's gift, he said that deferring to "Allah's will" did not mean "we aren't using our brains, that we are trigger-happy fundamentalists." But talking about jihad, Musharraf sounded to Goldberg like a fundamentalist, relying on the support of the pro-Taliban Pathans and the jihad against India in Kashmir.[13]

In the Afghan city of Kandahar, the Taliban heartland where many Haqqania madrasah students were going, Goldberg's official "guide" in the summer of 2000 was the seventeen-year-old Mullah Muhammad, who had memorized the whole Koran by the age of nine and was now "teaching" nine-year-old boys to do the same at the Jihadi madrasah. When Goldberg complained about his boorishness and "strange ideas" to the more moderate Taliban foreign minister Wakil Ahmed Muttawakil—Muhammad had insisted that the Koran forbids non-Muslims entrance to a madrasah and was amazed that the Koran was translated into other languages so that "infidels" like Goldberg could read it—he was told firmly that "this was the fault of the Clinton administration": young people hated the Americans because of their missile attacks and their desire to kill Osama bin Laden, "a great hero of the Muslims." However, Muttawakil did acknowledge that "average" Afghanis might feel differently out of a sense of gratitude for America's help to the mujahedeen during the struggle against the Soviets—actually a surprising (momentary?) flexibility on his part, if not appreciated by his American interviewer (p. 13).

The Taliban foreign minister and the exemplary "student" and "teacher" of the Koran, the teenager Muhammad, are not "average" Muslims but radical fundamentalists, and to the Western observer they appear paranoid. Is their paranoia simply an "American creation"? Goldberg's ironical question put to Muttawakil receives the expected answer: "we haven't done anything to the Americans, why are they out to destroy us?" But if the Taliban paranoia is too simple, so is the Western temptation to simply forget the Afghan experience of American cold war politics. The Muhammad of Goldberg's story is a very unpleasant young man. Bigoted and obtuse, he is the product of his group's history: born in Kandahar, he lived for a while near Quetta, a city that had to absorb millions of refugees during the Afghan wars; he only attended madrasahs, has never studied anything but the Koran, cannot see any reason why he should, has not had any contact with women other than his sisters, does not listen to music, has never seen a movie, has already fought with the mujahedeen against the Northern Alliance and might do so again; if he is not martyred, he will go back to teaching. In Goldberg's view, his limitations, among them prominently his dislike of and disinterest in America, make him too contemptible to have feelings of desire, anxiety, frustration. It seems impossible for Goldberg to imagine what contact with a person like himself might mean for Muhammad: knowing the Koran by heart defines his place in the world, and he cannot let it be challenged by an infidel's claim to have read the holy text in English and to have the authority to correct him, the believer. When pressed that there *must* be something he likes about America and he answers "candy," this is for Goldberg not a poignant reminder that his surly guide, even though he has the power to irritate the Western visitor, is also by that visitor's standards a severely undereducated, slow-witted teenager, deprived of all sensual and intellectual stimuli, not to speak of pleasures. Suspending his responsibility to these standards, Goldberg does not ask, much less consider, what the madrasah experience has meant to this dirt-poor boy and hundreds of thousands like him. It gave them a sense of belonging, structure, and purpose, in some ways not unlike the appeal of joining the army (or a gang) to young, poor minority men and women trying to escape from the chaos of American inner cities. But in Afghanistan and Pakistan these young people are also peculiarly limited, pared down intellectually and emotionally, by the Manichean scenario of radical Islam that divides the world into "us," the Muslim *dar-al-Islam* (realm of peace), against the rest of the world, the non-Muslim *dar-al-harb* (realm of war). In the 1980s, Islamic fundamentalists found the purest expression of the *dar-al-harb* in the Soviet Union; in 2000 it was in America, and on September 11th, still in the future for Goldberg and the readers of his article, the hatred for the "not us" would explode the most visible symbols of U.S. economic and military might in New York and Washington. Goldberg thinks that non-Muslim and moderate Muslim political leaders are faced with the "vexing" question how "America, which supported—created, some would say—the jihad movement against the Soviets, came to become the No. 1 enemy of hardcore Islamists." Arguably, the militant simplifications of their Manichean scenario have become such a serious problem also because the West has never shown much interest in what American cold war politics have meant in concrete detail for the people of Afghanistan and parts of Pakistan; nor in what the unconditional, unquestioning American support over many decades for Israel has meant to the Arabs in the region. America did not create the Afghan jihad but did unleash it for reasons of political self-interest, and without giving much thought to the resulting disastrous destruction of natural and cultural resources that has been one of the major reasons for the growing attraction of Islamic radicalism in the region.[14]

Goldberg's interviews are informative, and they largely confirm Naipaul's analyses of militant Islam five years earlier. But in contrast to him, Naipaul has tried to understand how people had been shaped—pared down, diminished—by the cultural and political power of belief systems. More important, he has been interested in the greatly varied processes of such shaping, and the stories he records retain the individuality of the people who told them, because he rightly feared that they could easily be swept away by larger political developments. If Naipaul does not presume to identify with their pain and confusion, he does try to imagine the extent of their losses. Since his early fiction and travel writing, he has been interested above all in understanding what it feels like to be that particular person in that particular place and time. What does it feel like to be the teenaged Mullah Muhammad or, for that matter, the Taliban foreign minister Muttawakil? What is their state of mind, their sense of themselves? What does their rage against America, the West, the whole non-Muslim world mean to them? Since this rage defines their identity, the questions may seem circular. But there could be some gaps in that circularity, since one rage is never entirely like another—a truism not taken sufficiently seriously by Goldberg, as in his interview with Muttawakil: "The foreign minister is a man completely lacking in charm, and he has a beard that has crawled up to within an inch of his eyes. He is touted as one of the sophisticates of the Taliban, a new face of moderation. He is not an easy small-talker, and so to thaw him out, I asked him how many children he has. 'I have four boys and one girl,' he said, and then offered, with no prompting: 'The girl is my most beloved of all.' Even the Taliban engages in spin" (p. 13). Perhaps; perhaps not quite. But why did Goldberg not ask him how the Taliban attitude toward schooling for girls went together with his particular love for his daughter? The Taliban father who may indeed truly love his daughter might have revealed an unpredictably illuminating version of the predictable contradiction.

Of the people interviewed by Goldberg nothing remains but their deplorably backward bigotry that (somehow) reflects also on their great destructive potential: blowing up the world they will still be seen as backward, shabby, contemptible, at best a feeble imitation of the West—the Western view of them complementary to their megalomania. Goldberg quotes two opposing perspectives on Islamist militancy: in the Islamic fundamentalist view, U.S. imperialism and globalization is to blame for everything; in Samuel P. Huntington's hypothesis of "Islam's bloody borders," militancy is inherent to Islam. Wherever Islam comes into contact with other civilizations, Jewish, Christian, Hindu, there seems to be war. Goldberg sides with the latter but forgets to add that Huntington's much debated *The Clash of Civilizations and the Remaking of World Order* (1998) warns explicitly of the dangers of Western intervention into the affairs of non-Western countries, the Afghan debacle being a particularly good example. Haq sees Islam as the only viable position against the world's infidels, and he believes, as do many Pakistani moderates, in a Jewish-Hindu conspiracy that directs American policy toward Muslims—a position that Goldberg rejects as both ridiculous and morally offensive. But the influence of Aipac, the highly successful pro-Israel lobby, on American attitudes toward Islam cannot be that easily dismissed, even if the complaints of the Pakistani general interviewed by Goldberg may have been motivated by anti-Jewish sentiments (p. 14). For Naipaul, a Hindu by birth and strong advocate of (Western) rational political institutions, the anti-Hinduism or, for that matter, anti-Semitism of radical Islam is not so much immoral as another troubling aspect of the irrationalism often found where religion and politics mix—a symbiosis whose history needs to be explored rather than simply rejected.

Naipaul's perspective in *Beyond Belief* is focused more on the larger historical-cultural meanings of re-Islamization reflected in the individual stories than on the personal ironies and conflicts of faith as he explored them in *Among the Believers*. The politics of Islamic fundamentalism have become more powerful and more troubling over the last two decades, and his way of looking has changed with the excursions into the puzzles of memory and history in *The Enigma of Arrival* and *A Way in the World*. The stories he is told now seem to have more ambiguities and lacunae, more hidden parts underneath their coherent surface, some of them forgotten. Memories appear more unstable because they are of traumatic experiences, and, listening, Naipaul has to guess what the whole story might have been like so that he can look for help to fill in the gaps and straighten out inconsistencies. His going back to individual informants to ask more questions about their stories mirrors his revisiting fundamentalist Islam. The frame for these stories is the political history of the intervening years, which for many of his informants means the aftermath of great cultural upheaval, in some cases revolution and war. Often their willingness to help him understand their experiences adds to his difficulties, which, as "manager" of their stories, he not only acknowledges but works into his narrative in order to maintain the distinctness of their past states of mind. Inevitably, such imagining of the past is tainted by the needs of the present: their need now to talk about their past thoughts and acts in certain ways; his need to be responsible, in the mid-nineties, to both their stories and the history of which they are a part and to which, telling their stories, they contribute.

This is particularly true for the stories Naipaul recorded in Iran and in Pakistan. He had last seen the founder and former editor of the *Tehran Times,* Mr. Parvez, on a bitterly cold day in February 1980 in a "desolate" office and very nervous about the seizing of the U.S. embassy by revolutionary students searching for "revealing" evidence. Almost two decades later, Mr. Parvez will say that on the whole he has not done so badly under the mullahs: some of them were reasonable and "the authorities" treated him with respect, though they did take away his paper in 1981. The Shah's "formal censorship" turned into "self-censorship" after the revolution, but in the late nineties political criticism could be surprisingly open if it respected the "basic system," that is, the "institution of leadership and obedience"—the theocratic principles of that state.

Mr. Parvez had "never been 'Islamic as such'" but had hoped for a Western-style democracy like India's. In the yes-or-no referendum of 1980 he voted for the Islamic republic, as did 85 percent of the population, without knowing what this republic might be like. He supported Khomeini because of his concern for the Third World and his promises to increase employment (instead it dropped dramatically after the revolution). In Mr. Parvez's view, Khomeini was sincere but could not implement his plans because of the war with Iraq (p. 153). And the loss of his paper was connected with the American hostage crisis, which seemed more important to him than the revolution. Parvez is an important informant because he was very much involved in the events both personally and professionally and at the same time self-consciously "objective," struggling to maintain a relatively reliable observational perspective. Not surprising given the difficulties and confusions of the situation, some of his explanations were too simplistic, distorting, or self-contradictory. Naipaul understands that he "had gone through a great deal; he would have done many things to survive. It would have been unfair to go too far into the uncertainties I had noticed in his narrative" (p. 154). When he first met him, in August 1979, the *Tehran Times* seemed very successful, Parvez and his fellow directors planning expansion. A shy and gentle man, Parvez looked Indian rather than Iranian to Naipaul, and when asked he said he was an Iranian of Indian origin. This was for Naipaul "a neat way of putting something complicated," and he assumed Parvez was an Indian Shia who had come to Iran as the "Shia heartland" (p. 143).

Naipaul liked Mr. Parvez from the beginning and his account is sympathetic. Trying to imagine what it must have been like for Parvez, he neither identifies with the man nor shrinks away from what he might have had to do. Revisiting him after so many tumultuous years and then, during that second visit, going back to him with more questions establishes the interplay of continuation and change, sameness and variation in the flux of time that has always intrigued Naipaul. Since changes accelerate with rapidly growing technocracy, the promises and threats of the future multiply, transforming the shapes of belief and thus the shaping of memories. Parvez does not appear to have changed much, yet he is different—a difference that is left elusive, part of a changed environment. For this reason, too, Naipaul is very attentive to the physical context in which people tell him their stories. When Mr. Parvez is taking him to an empty office to have their lunch and talk without being disturbed, the spacious, well-lit attic room is pleasant and reassuring. Growing up in crowded spaces and severe asthma have made Naipaul particularly sensitive to the ways in which perception is shaped by the conditions of space—bright or dim, clean or dirty, orderly or disorderly—that make it easier or more difficult to breathe, to see, to think. But in the middle of the room are newspaper sheets spread on the floor to suggest a prayer rug pointing toward Mecca and a cake of earth of the kind that Shias touch with their foreheads when praying. Naipaul's detailed description of the arrangement suggests intrusion into the civilized space reserved for their lunch (p. 147). But he is also surprised by his host's open reaction of "weariness and distance" noticing it: living under the rule of the Shah and surviving more than fifteen years of the revolution must have undermined his Shia "certainties, if they had existed" (p. 147).

There was another journalist to whom Naipaul talked on his first visit, an energetic Indian Shia from Lucknow who was eating lunch at their first meeting when he should have been fasting for Ramadan. Mr. Jaffrey had come to Iran from India via Pakistan, found the Shah's worldly regime tyrannical, and welcomed revolutionary religious power. However, as he told Naipaul then, the revolution had immediately deteriorated, a judgment that Mr. Parvez did not share at the time. In contrast to him, Mr. Jaffrey believed firmly in the political principle of separation between state and religion, complaining that the ayatollahs had not handed over authority to the politicians and that Iran was now ruled by religious "fanatics." Naipaul had liked his lively, cantankerous journalism and been intrigued by his dream of a society of believers like the small earliest Islam community which, led by the Prophet, was spontaneously both spiritual and secular. In the modern world this dream, with its desire for security and exclusivity, could be a "dangerous fantasy" of a rigidly homogeneous, ethnically cleansed society (p. 145)—in some ways like the creation of Pakistan or Israel, founded on such desire for safety in shared religious identity and its oneness with political rule. Khomeini's absolute political and spiritual rule did not square with the journalist's Indian-British education and experience of democratic law and institutions. Yet, both pious and suffering from the tyranny of the religious state, Mr. Jaffrey became himself one of the "fanatics," rejecting the impure and judging the quality of others' faith (p. 145). Mr. Parvez tells the story of his friend, hunted by revolutionary students because of some minor connection with the demonized U.S. embassy, leaving for Pakistan in his big old Chevrolet, a dangerous, uncertain journey at the time, and starting work in Islamabad, where he died ten years later. His dream of a just, pure society of believers had ended badly, whereas Mr. Parvez, not a dreamer and judger of other people's faith, had been in a better position to survive. He still misses his friend and thinks that he should have stayed and worked it out with the authorities, remembering in "a kind of final tribute" how Mr. Jaffrey had loved playing bridge and how under the Shah many Iranians shared his passion (p. 149). Playing cards was now banned as "un-Islamic"—the utopian imposition of prohibitions that would turn small, harmless pleasures into serious sinful transgressions.

Mr. Jaffrey's faith is particularly difficult to understand because he was in many ways more worldly and rational than his less pious, surviving friend. For Naipaul, this enduring alienness brings into sharp focus the issue of individual piety as a larger cultural problem. Through his interpreter Mehrdad, like Behzad sixteen years earlier an intelligent and reliable guide, Naipaul listens to the bitter complaints of a severely wounded Basiji about the postwar rejection of the once revered volunteers whose battalions, always the first to attack, sustained the greatest losses. Now these small groups of survivors are collectively hated because some of them police violations of Islamic rules to blackmail war profiteers. Willingly and in great detail, he describes the routines to prepare the young men for battle: two hours of religious chanting and rhythmical beating of chests that filled them with "thoughts of death and martyrdom and going to paradise and having freedom," and after that usually less than two hours for writing letters and wills, washing themselves, and checking their gear and their underpants, since, expecting to be martyred in the holy war against secular Iraq, they wanted to be nice and clean for their meeting with God (p. 161).

Naipaul is perplexed by the absence of wounds and death in this narrative, which, for all the man's rage about the lack of respect for the veterans, stays close to the surface routines of the war. Only when asked directly, and then reluctantly, does he talk about the dead: from his battalion of fourteen hundred only four hundred came back. Mehrdad tries to explain to Naipaul the veteran's literal sense of having been robbed by those who did not suffer but benefited from this traumatic war, even though, or perhaps because, he had once literally believed in the blessings of martyrdom. Together with his observation of Mehrdad's quiet despair over the traumatic change of his once comfortably middle-class family under Islamic rule, the veteran's story and Mehrdad's comments suggest pain that the people who suffer it think cannot be expressed.

At first an additional barrier to understanding, this inability proves useful for Naipaul on several levels because it calls up a particular kind of sympathy. Mehrdad is very much concerned about his sister, who will not be able to find a husband because so few men have survived, and she, as an unmarried woman, has no freedom of movement under Islamic rule. Naipaul understands very well his emotional distress in response to his sister's profound frustration, her overwhelming sensation of being caught, immobilized. And Mehrdad, precisely because he doubts that Naipaul will really be able to understand people's "whole" stories, will help him to re-ask and re-phrase questions and puzzle over the answers till he thinks that Naipaul got it right. It was Mehrdad's insistence that Naipaul rent a hotel room looking out to the northern hills which set into motion the process of his orientation in a literal and figurative sense. At first what he sees from his window appears to be normal suburban growth on these hills, but closer inspection leads to the realization that one of them is Evin prison, which was the scene of the many executions ordered by Ayatollah Khalkhalli, the hanging judge of the revolution. The change in his perception of that hill changes also his understanding of what he sees, the meanings of the marks left on the land, their transformation in time. There is no magical moment of illumination, but gradual recognition of different conditions of observation, notably changes of light. The great wall of the prison has been there all the time but for a while he did not see it, because it appears only in the sharply molding light of the eastern sun. At other times, sharing the color of the hill, it becomes part of it, merges with it. But once he sees the wall for what it is because he has known about the prison, he cannot but see the "monstrous concrete hangar of a building" and then, little by little, details of the plan of the prison that were camouflaged by his misperception, for instance the high blue gates. In August 1979, when Naipaul first went to Tehran, Khalkhalli had said in an interview with *Tehran Times* (then still owned and edited by Mr. Parvez) that he had "'probably' sentenced three or four hundred people to death. On some nights, he said, the trucks had taken thirty of forty bodies out of the prison. They would have left through the blue gates" (pp. 186–88).

The most important change during the intervening years in Naipaul's documentary perspective has been his focus on the political exploitability of faith, which has also meant a more sympathetic, if skeptical, curiosity about the modalities of spirituality. Inserted between a chapter about his learning how to look at the hills to make out the once deadly prison and a chapter about the former hanging judge is the story of another war veteran, a chapter that both links the two events and at the same time questions the connection. A volunteer at the age of fourteen, Abbas was disappointed by his postwar theological studies in the holy city of Quom and was now trying to come to terms with the war experience by making films and conducting interviews with other veterans. In one of the worst battles of that bitter war he had seen his friends killed in great numbers but knew that the corpses brought back were not his friends: they had gone somewhere else and one day he would follow them. The intensely spiritual experience of omnipresent death was also intensely physical, because his task was to collect for reuse the cartridge belts, harness straps, and shoes (a particularly important item) of the dead men from "the place of ascension," the morgue. Washing their equipment was a "spiritual exercise" because it connected him with the dead, who had gone to a place "which they didn't quite know." This statement may also have meant that the men, despite their uncertainty about where they were going, had gone there "straight and with determination" (p. 191).

When Naipaul calls Abbas's explanation "ambiguous," does he mean that Abbas was not entirely clear on this core experience of faith? or that he did not make himself clear to the interviewer? On one level, the two questions are of course not separable; yet they need to be asked separately to get to the issue of the documentarist's combined acknowledgment of incomplete understanding and desire to get it right. Fitting the story it tells, this chapter deals explicitly with the process of documentation. At first Abbas did not really want to speak about his experiences in the martyrs' battalion, finding his way into his memories only when the light faded and the candles were lit because one of the many power outages, in this case a lucky coincidence. Too engrossed in the story to take notes, Naipaul together with Mehrdad "reconstructed what we had heard" later that evening—including the ambiguity of Abbas's words (p. 190). Did he understand Abbas "correctly," namely, (more or less) according to his intentions? An experienced interviewer and skilled writer, Naipaul of course knows that he "reconstructs" not what Abbas said but what he, the interviewer, understood him to be saying. Despite the documentarist's determination to be truthful to what he is told, there are layers of possible misunderstanding between his being given and his receiving the information he is seeking. In this instance they relate to the shaping (constructing) properties of memory—even though they are checked by Mehrdad's collaboration—and of the writing process itself. Even if Abbas, having read back to him the reconstructed conversation, agreed with his story as it has been shaped by Naipaul with Mehrdad's assistance, this by itself would not mean that the story records truthfully what Abbas told that stranger about himself in the dark: he could have been persuaded, seduced by that particular shape given to his story in reconstruction. More, he could have been prepared to be seduced: speaking with great intensity about his spiritual experiences, he himself was giving them new, different shapes, excited by speaking about them, prompted, stirred, guided by the stranger's curiosity and attention. As the story of his faith takes shape and becomes more coherent, so his faith becomes more coherent; both Naipaul and Abbas, in their stories, would have reacted to that growing coherence. What most intrigues Naipaul here—and he explicitly writes of his and Mehrdad's fascination with the wholeness of Abbas's faith and its representation—is the degree of congruence between his reconstruction of Abbas's experience and Abbas's narration.

There is a story Abbas tells them about a miraculous cure for blindness caused by his head wound when he visited, against the advice of his doctors, the shrine of Shah Cheragh, making a vow to Allah to go back to the front if given back his eyes. The doctors did not believe such a cure could have happened and warned him against making it public because people would indeed believe him, and seek to participate in the miracle, rip off his clothes for relics and perhaps, as had happened during the revolution, tear him apart. Naipaul's narration distinguishes between different levels of faith, different kinds of believers. He, not Abbas, recounts the "religious miracle" that the doctors did not believe "could happen," but in a way that preserves, in the wording and shape, the rhythm of Abbas's sentences. He does the same with Abbas's reluctance to go into what happened too deeply. Did he reject the doctors' skepticism? Did he accept, even welcome it? Does he need to protect his faith? Does the faith protect him? Does the faith strengthen or diminish the separation between private and public experience? These are complicated questions that go to the heart of Naipaul's inquiry, and therefore Abbas's experience and his attitude toward talking about it are of great importance. Repeating and reshaping Abbas's words—"reconstructing" them from the memory of that remarkable evening at the publisher's office—Naipaul emphasizes, by articulating it, this importance. The remarks of the publisher's assistant in support of the doctors' warning are presented as a direct quote. Whether or not he really uttered these exact sentences, whether or not Naipaul remembered his utterances verbatim: what the documentarist has him say here is presumably true to the meaning of the assistant's observations on the blind, destructive energies of certain groups of believers.

Incomplete understanding between differently acculturated individuals and groups has been the theme of Naipaul's traveling and writing from the beginning, and it has shaped the narrative strategies of his fictions and documentaries. However, the older writer has focused increasingly on the documentarist's groping processes of understanding, his incomplete authority. He really cannot be sure that he has understood, especially where it concerns another person's attempts at understanding himself in his world. It was of course impossible to "share"—the shibboleth of Western multiculturalism—Abbas's experience. Visiting the shrine of Shah Cheragh at dusk some days later, Naipaul finds an atmosphere like that at a fairground around and inside the shrine and points out that "to see what Abbas had seen, to enter the common pool of feeling here, you had to bring some feeling of your own. You had to bring the faith, the theology, the passion and need" (p. 193). Obviously, he does not, does not wish to, cannot, but he restates the nonbeliever's limited imagination because he is about to go back, once more, to Abbas's attempts at explaining "the effect of his experience on his faith" (p. 194). This time Abbas speaks in his own voice, if through Mehrdad's translation, and Naipaul lets it "stand as it was spoken" because there does not seem to be a better, that is, clearer way of talking about his experiencing the spiritual in the extreme material destruction of the battlefield (p. 194).

After the war, Abbas wanted to hold on to his "treasure" of spirituality, because he could draw on it for guidance in everyday life. Circumspect, cautious Mehrmad expresses great admiration for Abbas's conduct as a soldier and as a civilian; he is to Mehrmad "a real hero" (p. 197), and he translates carefully Abbas's often groping answers to Naipaul's insistent questions. Exhausted at the end of the interview, Abbas thought that he had said more than he should, had talked "like a drunken man." Mehrdad immediately corrects his translation: "A drunken man doesn't know what he says, and I feel I have been like that" (p. 197), and there is indeed a shift in emphasis from talking to knowing. Pushed to explain something that, in his experience, he could and need not explain, Abbas did not know exactly what he was saying because he did not know exactly how to say it. Yet on a certain level he had made sense to Naipaul, even if he could not make fully accessible the details of his experience. Perhaps from his Hindu background, Naipaul did have some access to Abbas's "treasure" of spirituality as derived from extreme physical experience—understood, explained in relation to normality.

Naipaul's focus has changed, subtly but unmistakably, since his historical explorations in *A Way in the World*. In a sense the temporal distance, the insurmountable strangeness of historical actors like Columbus and Raleigh, who at the same time contributed to the reassuringly familiar surprises of the modern world, made him more curious about the different realizations of faith in the conduct of believers. Abbas's passion for spirituality seemed admirably directed by a sense of responsibility to what he might be able to do in the world. He needed to go beyond the common desire for self-definition in obedience to religious rituals and rules, but he did not claim that this would make him the better man: "The Koran says that we do things according to our capacity. So I would do whatever I can, and they would do whatever they can" (p. 194). After his return from Quom, where he finished the five-year course in three years but did not find much spirituality, he swiftly and competently got his high school diploma and a place at the university: the young woman he wanted to marry was a student at Tehran University and her family would not permit marriage unless he had the same level of education, but his had stopped at the age of fourteen, when he went to war. Quom had, if anything, set him back.

Abbas impressed Naipaul because he had insisted on finding his own way. But though his spirituality, different from the reigning religion, was his own, his search was shared by other Iranians who as young men had participated in the revolution and the war.[15] Both experiences are taken seriously by Naipaul as they have been by few Western observers. The extraordinarily brutal war with Iraq might as well have taken place on another planet; and the sociopsychological difficulties of this generation of Iranians seemed irrelevant, because their revolt against what they saw as the Shah's peculiarly corrupting blend of traditional tribalism and modern technocracy seemed so simplistically irrational. Looking to the French Revolution as the arch-model for activist political progressivism and conveniently forgetting the bloodiness of its fundamentalist perversion of reason, Western intellectuals have tended to judge revolutions from the "right" as, at best, unserious and, at worst, evil.[16]

Naipaul's account of his second visit to Ayatollah Khalkhalli, the hanging judge of the revolution, is a haunting reminder of the from hindsight mostly futile but at the time terrible destructiveness of ideological passion. On his first visit, during the revolution, he had been accompanied by his interpreter Behzad, a communist revolutionary who believed that what Stalin had done in Russia needed to be done in Iran: "a lot of killing" (p. 201). For him as for Khalkhalli, all revolution had to be paid for with blood, and Naipaul remembers how the short, bald judge, "a clerical gnome, messily attired," was bragging and joking about the executions for the benefit of his adoring court (p. 201). Now he is almost forgotten and his house, on the edge of the city in 1979, is hidden deep within it because of rapid urban growth. Looking at the many photos of Khalkhalli and Khomeini in the reception room, Naipaul is intrigued by one that shows Khomeini laughing at Khalkhalli's jokes. The photos were meant to document the past glory of Khalkhalli, his closeness to the center of power. But in the future they might also show men of the revolution, now robbed of the glamour of holiness, for what they were: murderers for political gain. When asked about the future of the revolution, the frail old man answers in generalities, and Naipaul, unable to focus the meandering interview, does not think of asking him about the photographs to get to something specific; the thought occurred to him only later when he went back to his notes. Khalkhalli, a historic figure who co-determined the course of the revolution, seems to have no historical memory—the fate of many radical leaders. The changes that he helped to bring about have consumed it.

Murderous and ludicrous, the hanging judge embodied the revolution that Naipaul saw reflected in the "closed, foolish, exalted face" of the guard who had frisked him at his first visit with the ayatollah. The high drama of the Islamic revolution, feeding on the reality of torture and death, has turned into a system of invasive and deforming rules that make no sense but control Iranian society. Hidden under chador and headdress, young women are harassed by the constant control and questioning of young male guards whenever they venture into public spaces. In February of 1980, Naipaul saw women students in guerrilla garb camped outside the U.S. embassy in the cold, excited by the "theater of revolution." There is a vivid memory image of a young woman carrying a mug of "steaming tea for one of the men: her face bright with the idea of serving the revolution and the warriors of the revolution" (p. 225). They belonged to the group Muslim Students Following the Line of Ayatollah Khomeini (feared by Mr. Parvez for their eager "revelations"), and their posters proclaimed shared goals with the Nicaraguan revolution, a "universal movement forward." Many of them would be dead by now, as would be many of the young communists; none of them would have dreamt that the revolution would end the way it had: "with an old-fashioned tormenting of women, and with the helicopters in the sky looking for satellite dishes" (p. 225).

Iranian obedience to an intricate system of rules jealously controlled by power-hungry religious leaders in 1995 is explained by Mehrdad: "They are the rule-makers. If you deny the rules you are denying the rule-makers. If you put the rule-maker away you are against the Leader. If you oppose the Leader you are against the Holy Prophet. If you are against the Holy Prophet you are against the Holy Book, and the Holy Book comes from God. Someone against God must be killed. But who does the killing? Only the rule-maker. Not God" (p. 224). Yet it is God on whom they base their authority to kill—does Mehrdad understand the implications of that connection? Does he care? He shows Naipaul one of the many collections of rules published by Khomeini, all of them in paperback and seemingly everywhere. This one takes care of three thousand problems with rules that are either nonsensical or irrelevant or both, and yet they have power. Mehrdad does not fast, does not go to a mosque, does not, in fact, obey any of the rules, though he knows most of them. But women, he points out, cannot disobey them so easily. Their literal diminishment—down to details like half the amount of the blood money asked for a man as listed in Khomeini's collection—is ominous for the whole society, and Mehrdad, ironically matter-of-fact on most issues, is deeply disturbed by his sister's unhappiness and uncertain future.

The building up of complex systems of rules and their enforcement, to Naipaul the most striking, puzzling phenomenon on his second visit to Iran, has been a common feature of re-Islamization. The new Islamic religio-political fundamentalisms tend to construct fictitiously complete and unambiguous pasts, since they are the result not of historical time but of suprahistorical creation. These theocratic utopian communities are governed by performative speech-acts: like God, radical Islamic leaders create the world by speaking it. Their words are enacted, their rules are enforced, and their speech is preauthorized because, like the Holy Book, it comes from God and brooks no contradiction. Membership in utopia, where it is not inherited, always requires conversion: the converters who establish the rules and the converted who obey them. Ideally, both believe in the perfect presence of pure belief, which, set against the ravages of time and human nature, is itself a rejection of the historical past. (That rejection would include the Muslim Students Following the Line of Ayatollah Khomeini, innocently and dangerously excited "warriors" of the revolution in its early stages, since their revolutionary belief in a "universal movement forward" would be perceived to be a threat to the perfection of the rules and their enforcement.) Re-Islamization concerned with reestablishing Islamic law requires perfect obedience to the rules, and that means a conversion to the purity of the faith thought compromised by moderate Muslims.

Naipaul's conversion hypothesis is not interested in the utopian psychological-political dynamics of belief sketched here, but in a larger historical explanation of the troubling "imperial," "hegemonial" aspects of political Islam as he observed them in non-Arab Muslim societies. For him the importance of conversion to militant fundamentalist Islam is located in its origins as an Arab religion: believers are more ideologically absolutist and controlling if their religion is not indigenous but has been imposed in the past by superior military force and political domination. It is true, a history of forced conversion may have left traces in certain aspects of Islam, for instance the insistence on the purity of the faith, which would be important for the control of new believers, converts. But the new traditionalist emphasis on remaking the self by going back to the "the roots," reestablishing the old religious laws to stem political and social modernization, is also the concern of many Arab Muslims; and many "converted" Muslims do not support the new efforts to collapse the separation between religious and political governance. Has it been Islam's historical "imperial" intention to convert because converts make the most fervent believers and therefore the most obedient subjects, or to conquer because the subjugated make the most docile believers? The strategic interdependency of these two drives has certainly been important to the success of historical Islam as well as of the new fundamentalisms, and it may offer some explanation of the new Islamic fundamentalist militancy. But here the Pakistani Samiul Haq's anti-American, anti-modernist Islamic fundamentalism does not differ much from his friend Osama bin Laden's Saudi version.[17]

However, the most serious argument against Naipaul's particular approach to the phenomenon of conversion is that it contradicts his documented interest in the varieties of religious belief, which he hopes will help him in his explorations of its underlying sameness. He lists the utopianist features of conversion—the rejection or reinterpretation of history, the rebirth of utopian man leaving the old self behind—but the connection to the actual histories of conversions remains speculative and unconvincing: "The convert has to turn away from everything that is his. The disturbance for societies is immense, and even after a thousand years can remain unresolved; the turning away has to be done again and again. People develop fantasies about who and what they are; and in the Islam of converted countries there is an element of neurosis and nihilism. These countries can be easily set on the boil" (p. xi). So can Arab countries; so, for that matter, can all countries that have experienced major social and political ruptures, a good example being Weimar Germany. All these societies are vulnerable to revolution and utopianist reconstruction, with the ensuing rejection of a "bad" recent (prerevolutionary) historical past and rebirth into a "good" mythical present that, depending on the circumstances, can be the reconstructed distant mythical past.[18] Naipaul claims that he saw the "theme of conversion" already on his first Islamic excursion, but not as clearly as on the second journey (pp. xi–xii), and there certainly is a continuity in what he observed then and now. But the value of the interviews he conducted on his second visit to Iran lies in his powerful evocation, through the individual stories, of the repressive institutionalization of religious politics. Since his visit in 1995 there have been changes toward moderation, but political maneuvering in the interest of gradual liberalization has still been precarious. As the events in the spring and summer of 2000 show, the political gains of the moderate leadership are by no means secure, and in 2002 the religious leadership still holds the real power, and the moderate political leader speaks of preserving the "purity" of the revolution.

In 1995, Naipaul notes, nobody even spoke of revolution: the idea, the term itself, had been spoilt by the religious state with its complete, hidden machinery of control. Someone referred to the government as "occult" (p. 226), and it was the quality of that remoteness coupled with the religious rulers' omnipotence that caused anxiety and uncertainty about the future among the ruled, Mehrdad among them: "Everybody is frightened. I am frightened. My father and mother are frightened" (p. 226). That fear is accompanied by fantastic explanations of political developments that relieve ordinary citizens of their responsibility for the revolution and its aftermath, the more extreme, sinister aspects of the rule of faith. Naipaul quotes Mehrdad's comment: "It's something habitual. Our enemies are always responsible. Blaming others, not ourselves" (p. 227). Yet he and his friends do blame themselves, and their greatest concern are the social consequences of political rule by the demands of belief, resulting in their inability to ask critical, rational questions. There also is a generational shift that seems to elude and exclude them. The younger men who did not have to go to war show less fear of the "occult" regime and more cynicism, expressed in playing the forbidden popular music (produced by Iranians in Los Angeles) or even in openly taunting the Guards. And there are the children of the newly rich, people involved in business, in Mehrdad's view, "not productive people." In the fashionable shopping mall, observing their self-confident daughters in their stylishly short chadors, moving lightly on their high heels, long slender legs in tightly fitting jeans, Mehrdad also points out their good skin "that came with good air and good food and an idea of the future: the skin his own sister didn't have" (p. 227). Does he know what to think of, what to do with this different kind of disobedience?

Naipaul perceives and presents the difficulties of postrevolutionary Iran in physical terms: the "wounds" of the restricted, regulation-ridden lives led by most of the people who appear caught in their enforced immobility: the heavy body of Mehrdad's sister who does not want to leave her room; their shabby, uninviting living spaces that make their hospitality all the more poignant; the omnipresent Guards flitting by on motorcycles in search of the "forbidden" temptations of the West that would provide temporary escape—videos, CDs, drugs. Shackled, the present cannot draw on the past for sustenance of the imagination.

6   Stories of Other Lives: Documentaries

Beyond Belief: Islamic Excursions among the Converted Peoples

Pakistan

On his second visit to Iran, Naipaul saw for the first time historic Isfahan, now again open to tourists. He was familiar with the magnificent seventeenth-century imperial Moghul paintings that presented the emperor Jehangir (1605–27) with images of his great rival Shah Abbas (1587–1629). For Jehangir, the India of his empire and the Shah's Persia were by far the most important powers on the globe, their wealth and might reflected in the splendor of their cities. He was not happy to see what to Naipaul, many centuries later, still appeared the "breathtaking confidence and inventiveness" of Isfahan's architecture.[1] In both cases cultural flowering was of short duration, but the ravages of time were somewhat mitigated by the British colonial administration in India that helped to protect its great historic monuments from oblivion and decay—the fate of much of historic Iranian architecture. Colonial rule, a complex, differentiated experience, has had its positive aspects in certain situations in certain areas of India at certain periods. Despite the irritations and frictions caused by it, the presence of Western educational and political institutions contributed to the development of Indian reformist, democratic politics. Without it, Iran's attempts at political modernization have met with many more obstacles, partly due to the steadily growing influence of conservative Islam through the migrations since the 1940s of the Iranian rural poor to the cities, where they soon outnumbered the more secular urban population. Retaining their Muslim identity, their sons gained influence as businessmen and civil servants in rapidly and eclectically modernizing Iran, but unlike the small Western educated old urban elites that supported the Shah, these sons also tended to assimilate Marxism into their Islam. When they became revolutionary leaders, their links with the villages and small towns provided the revolutionary masses, and the Shah's despotic resistance to the development of political institutions helped the growth of Islamic organizations that criticized his regime for its un-Islamic social and political policies.

Naipaul's host in Isfahan, a European-educated, retired diplomat, was deeply divided over the issue of the revolution and the war and like many former supporters of the Shah was disaffected but still nationalist. His haunting stories about the war showed what it had done to the children who willingly sacrificed themselves, yet he also "knew in his bones" that this terrible, inconclusive war "had to be fought" to stave off the Iraqis (p. 236). Khomeini's reviving of the old Arab-Iranian confrontation could be seen as a necessary creation of Iranian nationalism. Calling himself "Victor of Ghadessiah," Saddam Hussein exploited the memory of the disastrous Persian defeat at the hands of the Arabs in A.D. 637, the beginning of the Muslim invasion—a memory the Shah had sought to neutralize by claiming for Iran the greatness of the pre-Islamic Persian past to establish a Western (progressive) cultural continuity.

Like his civilized host, Naipaul thinks the collective memory of Persian defeat destructive to contemporary Iran because it obscures a positive historical memory of the successes of Shah Abbas's Persia (p. 234). Under his rule order was established in Persia, and its dominions reached from the Tigris to the Indus. He distinguished himself not only by his military power and high-cultural achievements, but also by his progressive administrative reforms and support of commerce through the building of highways and bridges and his openness to foreigners, especially Christians. In the terms of his time, he was an extraordinarily successful and in many ways enlightened ruler. The issue here is not to prove or disprove a causal connection between the memory of the mythical Persian defeat in battle and the historical decline of Abbas's stabilized, "modernized" Persia. Myths have often been more powerful than historical memories, and their connection in this case might illuminate the centrality of battle in Islamic fundamentalism, its energizing thought-image and bloody reality.

In order to remake himself in the absolutist terms of the pure faith that promises the metahuman future of paradise, the convert has to turn away completely from the person he has become over time in contacts with others. The man-children, going to battle intoxicated by this promise, wearing the key to paradise around their necks, are a deeply unsettling proof of the power of pure faith, converts to its radicalism. Since the believer's reinvention by means of erasing all traces of his all-too-human self has to be inhumanly complete, it has to be repeated again and again (p. xi), in battle after battle, literal or figurative. Cultures of conversion rule out the development of a modern, fluid self, open to changes in time and to the importance of accident and contingency in human affairs. It is precisely their rigid fear of the openness of the future that makes these cultures so unstable and prone to violence. The power of the believers' stories in Naipaul's narration lies in the literalness of their narrative perspective where it concerns the uncertainties and insecurities of peoples in transition. The anxiety of not knowing how to proceed, not feeling safe moving into the future is characteristic of cultural migrations. When Naipaul draws attention to the "neurotic" or "nihilistic" aspects of such anxiety, he fears the destabilizing effect of individual and collective unhappiness, depression, and fear. Collective remembrance of the enforced conversion to Islam, the arch-battle in the distant past, energizes a contemporary regressive myth of the certainty and simplicity of faith needed to act into the opaque present. Such literal going back into the past under the unreflected conditions of the present tends to deny the many potential meanings of the past and thereby its openness to the future. The future—the believers' present—could not have been different from what it turned out to be because it is not, in the manner of futures, to a high degree unpredictable, but a deliberately selective, utopianist reconstruction of the old that has passed. This is what Naipaul shows in the stories he retells. An important aspect of the new Islamic traditionalism, especially in its radical, militant form, is the believers' rejection of their own recent past—the regime of the Shah, U.S. presence in Afghanistan, Israel's presence in Palestine—and it is the basis for their leaders' "pure" claims to power.

Re-Islamization took root in the profound uneasiness shared by large populations about the new technocracy and its cultural consequences: changes in the work world, the family, the status of women, and sexuality. The loss of the familiar in many aspects of their lives made attractive the idea of simply looking at the modern world as a bad recent past. But this radically simplifying perspective has, if anything, intensified the tension of holding on to the certainties and control of belief while sharing in the promises of modern science and technology. It is not so much the fact of combining the very new and the very old but rather the nature of its symbiosis: the substitution of modern political structures and institutions with paternalistic clan loyalty, putting the interest of bloodlines over historical developments, group solidarity over legal and political institutions, determinism over the reality of accident, and the possibility of rational decisions on the basis of information.

Naipaul's exploration of radical Islam in Iran and Pakistan has yielded a rich documentation of its strangeness in modernity that has clarified the threat of its power. His motivation for bringing together these different sets of complex and often contradictory stories has little to do with an assumed "Hindu rage" against Muslims.[2] His critique is not directed at traditional Islam but at the political goals of re-Islamization, which tend to aggravate rather than mitigate the very real cultural difficulties of global modernization. At issue is the problem of contact, increasingly difficult since the eighteenth century, between groups with different concepts of cultural complexity and competence. In Naipaul's view, re-Islamized Pakistan as well as Iran have in important ways gone back behind the achievements of Moghul culture.[3] Whether Islam was forced on Indian populations by violent means is a matter of debate between historians—they will also differ in their interpretations of the impact of British rule—but there was not one decisive battle and archetypical defeat as there was in Iran.[4] The great majority of contemporary Indian and Pakistani Muslims are descended from indigenous converts to Islam, some of whom may have been impressed by the newcomers' military power. Moreover, Islam was attractive to low-cast Hindus because it promised equality among believers through education, notably literacy, often at Sufi centers in the countryside. The attitudes of Moghul rulers toward non-Muslims was on the whole benign, refraining from pressure to convert and relying heavily on non-Muslim officials—as they would in the earlier stages of British presence in India rely on British administrators who adapted themselves to Moghlai culture and to Persian as the language of administration. Some Moghuls, importantly Akbar and his successors (1542–1605), also took an active interest in Hindu philosophy and traditions. Many of his sons and grandsons, including the emperor Jehangir admired by Naipaul, had Hindu wives. It is true, Islam and Hinduism have contrasted sharply where the "purity" of belief is concerned. Where monotheist Islam has been rigid and exclusive in controlling and enforcing among Muslims the teachings of the Koran, Hinduism has been flexible and inclusive in its teachings, syncretist where it concerns religious philosophy if not religious (social) practices. Both Akbar and his great-grandson Aurangzeb tried to outlaw certain Hindu practices such as *sati* (the burning of a widow on her husband's funeral pyre), the prohibition of remarrying for widows, and child marriages. At the same time, Akbar abolished the taxes on Hindu pilgrims and banned the slaughter of cows. Clearly, there were some important cross-influences during the time of the Moghuls, Muslim practices reflecting Hindu preoccupation with physical purity and pollution and with observation of life-cycle rituals.

Persian was replaced by English as official language in 1830, and when the East India Company, pressured by the British government, got involved in educating the indigenous population, English was the language of instruction. Until 1813, the company had resisted the British government's demands that it open its territory to missionaries, fearing that they would disturb lucrative trade arrangements by interfering with native religious practices. The missionaries' real influence would actually be in the area of Western-style education, which was successful among Indians, many of whom were already multilingual. However, supported by Indian reformers, the missionaries' activism against *sati* and related "backward" social practices created resentment of the interference with religious traditions, leading to the First War of Independence (1857). In the bloody battle for Delhi (1858), the archetypical battle of defeat for India, the British were helped by the latest technology, the new telegraph service, and just opened Suez Canal. India was now a colony of Great Britain, with institutions of higher learning in Delhi, Calcutta, and Bombay. Anti-Muslim sentiment because of the last Moghul's leading role in the uprising motivated initial favoring of Hindus, and resentment of the exiling of the Moghul to Burma contributed to Muslim resistance to British education, perhaps supporting tendencies in Islam to emphasize religious teaching. But British mapping of the caste and religious composition of India also created a heightened awareness of the advantages and disadvantages of religious difference that led to self-conscious membership in the "majority" or "minority." Was that the result of a deliberate British attempt to rule by division or just the in part unpredictable outcome of British administrative tidiness, unsuitable for the huge and hugely diverse subcontinent? The meanings of India's complex colonial history depend to a large part on the historian's perspective, and here the attempts at religious and social reform made by Western-educated Indians are a good case in point. Their efforts were focused on the position of women, because missionaries and colonial officials tended to use the "status of women" to rank the cultural values of south Asia below those of Europe, and the result was an increasing acceptance of education for girls. When Naipaul emphasized Hindu rejuvenation in Bengal where "the New Learning of Europe" was welcomed, he may have had in mind the "rational" Hinduism of Brahmo Samaj, a religious and social reform movement that abolished religious images and castes and supported education of women and their participation in ritual, but soon lost popularity because of its seemingly too radical and abstract critique of indigenous culture.

The political reform movement, started by educated Indians desiring participation in government, led to the founding of the Indian National Congress in 1885 by a small elite group of Indians and an Englishman. The membership remained small and the language of meetings and resolutions was English, as was the case in the Muslim League, founded in 1907 to further Muslim interests. When direct elections to municipal, district, and provincial administrations were granted in 1909, separate Muslim electorates were provided by the British, who were then accused, as in the case of the census, of trying to "divide and rule" and to ultimately prepare the ground for partition. The popularity of Ghandi's person and his agenda among ordinary Indians changed the Indian National Congress movement into a nationalist mass party, declaring in 1928 to outlaw untouchability, get the vote for women, and make Hindustani the national language. Its refusal to set aside separate electorates for Muslims and the language issue caused the departure from the party of Mohamed Ali Jinnah, who had been an important political supporter of Hindu-Muslim unity. He eventually became the leader of the Muslim League, which, following Gandhi's strategies, he reorganized into a mass-based party. Not himself a religious person, he campaigned for a Muslim homeland in an area where Muslims were the majority, a "land of the pure," a *Pakistan,* where they could live without fear of Hindu majority rule.

Naipaul sees "Muslim insecurity" as reason both for the creation of Pakistan and its enduring problems with theocracy (p. 247), but the difficulties faced by the new political entity were staggering. The extreme violence of partition, the enduring serious tensions over the issues of language, and the settlement of refugees coming from India demonstrated that sharing the same religion did not guarantee the integration of different populations. Jinnah's sudden death in 1948 left the new state without a clear concept of the proposed parliamentary democracy or of its Islamic aspects, and there followed several periods of martial law. Under General Zia, who had ended Bhutto's "Islamic socialism," Islamic politics and law gained in influence, and they continued to do so (as did the influence of the military) when Bhutto's daughter came to power after Zia's sudden death in 1988—ironically, he had just proclaimed elections for a return to civilian rule. Naipaul analyzes the consequences of these developments in *Among the Believers* and, with increased foreboding, in *Beyond Belief.* Before partition, the Indian prime minister Nehru's greatest concern had been the control of the Muslim state by feudal, despotic landowners—and it proved to be justified. Founded as the utopian "Homeland" for Indian Muslims, in important ways not unlike the Jewish state, Pakistan was politically compromised from its inception by theocratic energies that more often than not have impeded the development of functioning political institutions over the last half-century.[5]

Certainly connected but also too easily excused with the foreign politics of the U.S., this failure has been largely responsible for Pakistan's re-Islamization, with its increasing insistence on the purity of belief.[6] The consequences of the new-old theocratic laws with their archaic, literal concepts of punishment and retribution—mutilation in the case of offenses against material property, execution in the case of offenses against sexual property (adultery)—have been especially, if not exclusively, grave for Muslim women. But the provincial nationalist, religio-cultural traditionalisms have become globally dangerous because they share, at least selectively, in global technological "progressivism." Fairy-tale woodsmen wrapped into their hip-length beards, the Taliban used sophisticated weapons and the Internet. The terrorist attack on the Twin Towers as the symbol of Western economic and technological hubris was a terrifyingly literal example of the explosive new-old symbiosis: refunctioning the modern jet to become itself the instrument of destruction by the premodern, nonsymbolic act of human sacrifice. For Naipaul, the political instability of cultures of belief is all the more troubling because they profit "parasitically" from Western scientific and technological culture. This does not mean that technologically developing countries cannot make legitimate use of Western scientific and technological achievements, or that such achievements eo ipso constitute the greater value of a culture. It means that there is a dangerous contradiction at the center of the new fundamentalisms: their profound lack of interest in the secular cultural and political preconditions of Western scientific and technological progress while making use of its achievements in battles against modernity. That the West itself has given them the weapons to do so for a host of reasons from muddled to highly suspect is another question.

The cultural centrality of the faith has weakened the ability to create modern political institutions, and that in turn has caused Pakistan's elites to connect the decline of the state not with the possibly problematic nature of the faith, but rather the natural human inability to keep the faith pure. Again and again, on both visits, Pakistani intellectuals despairing of their "Homeland" asserted that Islam saves Muslims: the Islamic state has to evolve out of the pure faith, untainted by human intentions and acts. To a lesser or greater degree, all the new traditionalisms share this preoccupation with the purity of the faith leveling the diversity of believers. Ironically, the rapid globalization of Western technocratic culture has in many cases led to a rejection or reversal of the most important Western political achievements, the creation of relatively fair and reliable political institutions. The global village is then not a place of global understanding but of global prejudices and bigotry, enforced with the most sophisticated weapons. It has been unfashionable among Western intellectuals to even acknowledge, much less have a hard look at, the difficulties of cultural difference, but it has to be done if one hopes to deal rationally with the conflicts of contact. The failure to do so was the perhaps most important reason why Zionist groups who had since the twenties pleaded for reconciliation between Jews and Arabs, even, as late as 1948, for a binational state in Palestine, did not prevail. It proved impossible to share the cultural contributions of Jewish settlers, turning desert into fertile land and later creating political institutions to secure the principle of equality as equal opportunity for heterogeneous populations. These institutions were reserved first for the Zionist settlements and then for the Jewish state—as befits a utopia, only for its Jewish subjects and only with ideological (theocratic) control.[7] In the view of the Arab peoples of the region, of Islamic developing countries, Israel has stood for the self-centered, self-interested, aggressive politics of water and weapons, and for superior Western technology, whose arrogant omnipresence was made more intolerable by Israel's special relationship with the U.S. This global Western magic could only be countered by something fundamentally different: the new Islamic traditionalisms fueled by the tribal battles of the cold war that have been fought with superpower technology in the most remote, underdeveloped areas of the planet. Naipaul sees retribalization—Muslims can only live with Muslims—as an enduring problem for Pakistan, stemming from the time before its inception: in 1930 the poet Mohammed Iqbal made the first serious case for a separate Muslim polity in a speech before the Muslim League, arguing that in Islam the "religious ideal" meant "legal concepts" with "civic significance," the construction and control of social order.[8] A national concept of India displacing "the Islamic principle of solidarity" was unthinkable to a Muslim.[9] He poetically invoked rather than rationally defined the Muslim polity that was to come with the new state: Muslim faith would somehow inevitably create it. Iqbal's evocation of Islamic identity served well the pre-Partition politics of protest, but after the victory of the faith it became clear that this political will could not be expressed in modern political institutions. The reinstitution of Koranic punishments in 1979 was a great success as far as public floggings were concerned; there was public outcry when they were suspended in 1986. But like the amputations resisted by physicians and the severe laws about drinking, gambling, and fornication that are mostly bypassed, they have remained on the books and given the state a different and (for Naipaul) frightening identity: "They outlined the kind of tyranny that, in a crisis, people might talk themselves into" (p. 250). There is much anecdotal evidence that Pakistanis are apprehensive about sexual intercourse outside of marriage because a vengeful neighbor might give them away. Their Western partners think it ridiculous, exciting, slightly forbidding—a not entirely unpleasant mix. But Naipaul, always sensitive to the possibility of the darker side of a situation, is appalled by Pakistan's political regression.

An unsentimental, sympathetic observer, Naipaul has been very sensitive to the experience of aggression: ravaged land and cities, damaged individuals and groups. Listening, taking notes, he has shaped coherent narratives that support the speakers' authority over their stories, shielding their distinctness and, in many cases, their unbridgeable difference. In a shelter for battered women in Lahore, Naipaul met a young woman whose husband had "butchered her nose." With her lower face covered by gauze, she stood out in the group of women in the shelter, all very quiet, the "passive half-dead faces of women taken by suffering beyond shame and perhaps even feeling." A few days later he saw her with her face uncovered and the wound looked less terrible than he had feared, the tip of the nose not cut off but looking as if it was pinched with a hot instrument (p. 253). Small, thin, and dark, she seemed the proverbial victim of others' superstition and unthinking cruelty. Her illiterate parents prevented her from attending the village school and made her marry an occasional laborer. Having married her "only for God," without a dowry, he has been treating her and their children badly. She has had no support from her family and, most painful to her, had to take her children out of school. The woman lawyer connected with the shelter presents her to Naipaul as "a victim of feudal society," but she herself blames her individual family: she mentions the village school she and her children could have gone to and describes the landlord her uncaring parents and brutal husband work for as "a respectful man, and very nice" (p. 254).

This woman is truly without any resources, without a personal or group history. Her family is either absent or punishing; there is nothing to remember but other people's anger and rejection, a shapeless experience of physical and psychological aggression. Her husband is simply the person who beats her; she is the person who is beaten. But finally running away seems to have changed her; she has lost her fear and become, in the lawyer's words, "callous": hardened, indifferent, unfeeling. She says, "I am not supposed to feel pleasure or happiness," and, a shock to Naipaul, she suddenly begins to laugh—at him, his strange questions, his different clothes, his speaking another language: "The laughter had been building up inside her, and when it came she couldn't control it, remembering only, for manner's sake, to turn aside and cover her mouth and butchered nose with her palm" (p. 255). The laughter is not bitter but irredeemably distancing; the visitor's obviously well-intentioned interest in her desperate situation is a part of his utter strangeness, his comical irrelevance.

As it is told, the incident is curiously affecting because the woman is both distinctly present and remote. She may yet be able to get some education; most probably her children will, but that is in the still uncertain future. What counts is that she can be seen clearly as she is now: in all the cultural strangeness of her familiar predicament of spousal abuse. Her story is entirely hers but also symptomatic of the failure of the new state of Pakistan to develop functioning social and political institutions. The responsibility for this failure lies largely with the political power of religious Islam that has dominated Pakistan's short history. In Naipaul's view, that power has drawn support from India's lack of a political tradition and history due in some part to British colonization, but also to the military and political experiences that preceded it. The decay of Lahore's Moghul monuments, ironical in view of Pakistan's self-perception as successor to Moghul power, can be attributed to the country's serious social problems with education and poverty. But there is also what Naipaul sees as "the Muslim convert's attitude to the land where he lives. To the convert his land is of no religious or historical importance; its relics are of no account; only the sands of Arabia are sacred" (p. 256). The reference to "conversion" here emphasizes the utopianism of fundamentalist Islam: the straining toward a perfection of the system of rules that guards an absolute purity of the faith and thereby undermines the attempts at building a modern polity.[10]

Where the Moghul monuments are decaying, the solid, beautifully land-scaped British administrative buildings still house many of the institutions indispensable to the new state, "as if the British out of their experience elsewhere on the subcontinent, knew from the beginning what they had to set down in central Lahore: the civil service academy, the state guest house, the college for the sons of local chieftains, the governor's house, the British club, the public gardens, the courts, the post office, the museum" (p. 256). It is the larger colonial order that could be both nurturing and diminishing. The courts set up by the British and their procedural laws of 1898 and 1908 are still in use for want of better arrangements. Naipaul is introduced to them by the young Lahore lawyer Rana, a Rajput proud of his Hindu warrior caste but of diminished status since his father sold their land. In the practice of (British-given) law, a complex system of rules, he hoped to find "something like purity, something separate from the disorder and unfairness of the country, something in which a man was judged as a man" (p. 257). Instead he finds the practice of law capricious and corrupted by money—a microcosm of the inefficiency and corruption of the country.

On a Friday, the Sabbath, Rana takes Naipaul for a visit to his ancestral village. Rana's uncles still own all the land, and many of the old ways of living off the land, the rhythms of the seasons, are still intact. But the old beauty of this rural life has its darker side: on a "dreadful stretch of stony, half-made road" Naipaul sees a "narrow-backed boy of about ten pushing hard at a little hand-cart behind the horse cart of his father. The boy was having trouble. He leaned to one side of the cart and then to the other, making the handcart tack from side to side on the stony road." The commonness of insurmountable obstacles is made poignant by the barely outlined figure of the boy and his inept, self-defeating struggle with the cart. When Naipaul asks Rana, "what will happen to that boy?" he is told, "His future is lost" (p. 268). The nameless, slight figure of the young boy seen only from the back at this moment of struggle is an affecting allegory for a whole generation's loss of a future. Does Rana empathize with its plight? Does he take it for granted?

In his ancestral village Rana behaves like the son of the clan chief, proud of his family, praising the well-prepared meal. Pointing out a school building on land donated by one of his uncles, he explains the lack of a teacher. Male teachers did not like to live in the village since they were treated as outsiders, and female teachers were afraid of being kidnapped by the landlords, even though with his "good and kind" uncles they would have had nothing to fear. On closer inspection, the school building is "less than a shell," without either a roof or walls at the back (p. 271), yet another all too hopeful projection of future betterment in the face of obvious failure in the present. The driver of the car taking them to the village talks about his garment business and his "dream of exporting" to England or the U.S., his Urdu spattered with magic English words such as "latest designs," "total design," and "models" (p. 269). The implausibility of the man's hopes and expectations goes beyond a harmless illusion to make a hard, limited life more bearable. It has become a serious self-deception that Naipaul fears can only limit his choices even more.

Naipaul reacts similarly to the erratic rhythm of his day in the village: the many small instances of ineptitude and purposelessness, the plans not carried out, the unreliability of expectations. Rana, on the other hand, is enjoying himself: in loose white pants and a long gold-brown coat he looks and feels princely in the village, where the peasants are serving him willingly.[11] His Rajput pride is sustained by their reverence and he feels whole and cherished, whereas in the city, dressed in his lawyerly black suit and tie, he feels divided and humiliated. His impatience with Pakistan's political incompetence and corruption is connected to this sense of self-division, a diminished self-esteem. His mood is part of a "great underground rage" in Pakistani society and makes him susceptible to fundamentalist politics (p. 274). Yet where he seems to agree with the message extolling the virtues of the simple life carried by the blaring loudspeakers from the village mosque, he also seems to regret that young boy's impossible battle with his crude cart on a road that would never be finished. His world is in transition, holding on to the old ways and straining to get a share of the new technological magic. The difficulties of this situation are obvious, but the memory of his own struggles, which seems to become sharper as he gets older, makes Naipaul a more perceptive but also in certain ways less tolerant observer. There is less time now for illusions that weaken the possibility of purposeful action—Rana's, the tailor's, the boy's; self-deception is an increasingly powerful cultural phenomenon, and the reader is urged to consider its self-destructive energies. Still, Naipaul's promise, particularly in this documentary text, to retreat behind the stories as much as possible as "manager of narrative" is largely upheld. It is true, he brings to this task value judgments that have been shaped by his own experience of transition, its problems and promises, anxieties and desires. But this experience is at the core of all the stories he elicits, and he retells them as an expert who appreciates its complexity and variety.

The most haunting Pakistani story takes place in Baluchistan and explores the ex-revolutionary Shahbaz's faithful, selfless, and thoughtless interventions on behalf of insurgent tribes and the disastrous consequences of his pious political activism. In the chapter "Guerrilla," Naipaul deliberately sets up a narrative that moves back and forth between Shahbaz's past experiences and his talking about them now. He wants to project into the unfolding story, which is in the future relative to the ill-considered acts, their possible, probable consequences, in order to prevent as much as possible the arrogant simplifications of the narrator's hindsight. Listening to Shahbaz's memory story of a series of spectacularly and tragically wrong decisions, the temptations of the hindsight perspective are indeed considerable. But employing narrative strategies common to fiction, the documentarist circumvented them by consistently questioning the progress of the story in the process of narration (pp. 279–80).

When British-educated Shahbaz went back to Pakistan in the seventies, he

was appalled by the entrenched feudal customs practiced even by young Pakistanis whom he had known as fellow students in England. In recounting these
memories matter-of-factly, Naipaul also shows them to be part of a selective
memory story that is organized around the "pain and suffering" of Pakistan in
the sixties. Having become interested in local Left politics in Lahore, Shahbaz's
"true political life" began when he went back to England in 1968, "very emotional" in his stance against the rotten system of Western exploitative capitalism.
Like many Pakistani students he took English literature at one of the newer universities, a light course, "Marxist" in the manner of Fanon and Che Guevara. In
Naipaul's disapproving view, they learned nothing that would help them understand the problems of feudal Pakistan (p. 276). Guided by quotes from his newly
found saints, Shahbaz "found" himself committed to fight for revolution as a
guerrilla in Baluchistan and Afghanistan for ten years. Celibacy was one of the
many hard realities, since adultery among the nomads was its own guerrilla war,
where sexual success was linked to success in fighting and failure was deadly: "A
man thinking of adultery had to go to a woman's tent, awaken her without
awakening her husband, lead her out past relations and past the family flocks,
make love to her, and then take her back, all without being discovered" (pp. 277–
78). Appreciating the complexities, Shabaz settled for observation; the challenge
of making revolution proved to be more than enough.

Naipaul is clearly intrigued by Shahbaz's emotionally intense, active and
passive involvement with revolution as it was shaped by the people and the
land: one wrong decision, like a wrong step, following the other. It happened
inevitably and, not only from hindsight, predictably, since his innocence was so
great, and it was to endure. Several decades later, Shahbaz is still not pained, or
shocked, or just surprised by what happened, because he has never really left
those ten magic years of commitment to "total revolution," when he made all
those terrible mistakes (p. 279). The impact of the story depends largely on the
reader's access to both Naipaul's profound sense of dismay and Shahbaz's profound lack of it.

Shahbaz's commitment to Baluchistan as the "focus" of a revolution in Pakistan would not have been possible without certain leader figures, the first of
them an intense South African Indian. Later, when the man tried to kill him, his
piercing eyes no longer signified the total revolutionary dedication and therefore
charisma that drew Shahbaz to him but rather a classic case of paranoia
(p. 279). Yet he had been instrumental in Shahbaz's joining a training camp in
Baluchistan that would completely change his life. At the end of an arduous
journey, he found himself on a huge, empty desert plateau bordered by distant,
towering, bare mountains, exposed to extreme shifts in temperature, his cloth-
ing and equipment dramatically inadequate to this harsh, hostile new world in
which his habits of mind and body were a distinctly negative asset. Immediately
upon arrival, the fully armed tribesmen handed him weapons and put him on
sentry duty, seemingly unaware of his complete exhaustion and, more important, ignorance: "It was like meeting Martians. I had not mentally prepared myself for the shock of this meeting" (p. 280). Time would take care of its initial

shock, the extreme strangeness of the Baluchis, turning it into a degree of familiarity. But this first contact may hold clues to Shahbaz's enduring inability to understand that the revolution carried by him and his friends like a most precious gift was not what these nomadic tribes needed.

Shahbaz and his comrades took three years to "integrate" by learning the nomads' language and adapting themselves to their routines, moving in the summer, staying in caves in the winter, sharing their monotonous limited diet and their bad water, set apart only by the weakness of their survival skills and the strength of their political belief. Neither workers nor peasants, the Baluchi nomads were different from any group Shahbaz had met before. Not knowing how to look at them, he followed Mao's instruction to consider peasants a blank page that would become whatever was written on it. At the time, Shahbaz might have had some doubts about assuming such responsibility, even some kind of awareness of the revolutionary's arrogance in "rewriting" these people of whose cultural and natural environment he knew so little. But looking back, he repeatedly speaks of this situation as "incredibly creative": "You really felt you were on the cusp of change in the life of a nation" (p. 281)—the call for intervention. This sensation of omnipotence, the illusion of creating a new world *ex nihilo,* has been common to young Marxist revolutionaries, mirroring the illusion of young Muslim terrorists that they are bringing about the destruction of a whole world of infidels.

By temperament, Shahbaz is given to illusions and hero worship. In Baluchistan he came to greatly admire his immediate commander, a shepherd who had fought in the 1963 Baluchi uprising against the Pakistan military government. Summarizing Shahbaz's reactions to the man's humility, moderation, calmness, his way of speaking, Naipaul points out the illiterate's "unclouded instinct for the character and mood of people" that helped him to know instinctively how to talk to people in every situation. Shahbaz and his comrades wanted him to become "the Mao or Ho Chi Minh of the Baluchi, and perhaps also the Pakistani revolution" (p. 281). This archetypical case history of radical political faith never loses sight of the extreme physical and mental conditions under which the small, utterly isolated group of young revolutionaries looked for a great "natural leader" in the man on whom they depended absolutely for their survival. He had to be worthy of their dependence and his political education, and, in Shahbaz's eyes, he took to it "like a duck to water," proving beyond all doubt the universal claims of Marxist revolution (pp. 281–82). If Shahbaz had not been so eager for the admired leader to pass the test, he might have paid more attention to the psychology of the situation: the older, illiterate leader of an indigenous insurgency accepting the authority of the young, grotesquely innocent messengers of the revolution. But Shahbaz was simply unable to imagine the other person independent of his own political agenda. When he says now, "We didn't see ourselves as leaders. We saw ourselves as creating leaders for the people," he is not humble but worse than arrogant (p. 282). His and his comrades' belief in the revolution still seems to him all that was needed to authorize their "creation" of revolutionary leaders and running interference in situations which they were completely incompetent to judge. True believers, they assumed that the real world, no matter how different and difficult, would magically yield to their desires.[12]

When tribal uprisings began all over Baluchistan, they were put down brutally by the well-trained Pakistani army. Shahbaz did not participate in the fighting but ran a camp to provide political education and some medical training for the clansmen and to settle conflicts, mostly concerning farming and flocks. Up to a point he seemed to have been aware of the vulnerability of the nomads, wanderers who traveled light and could be easily destroyed. But his story does not provide details, and Naipaul, trying to imagine the disaster of whole clans disappearing as if pushed off, "brushed away" from that huge, barren, utterly inhospitable plateau, goes back to him for more information. What he gets is from hindsight: "People had lost their livelihoods and their families. The economy of a nomadic family is so fragile. It depends on flocks. All you have to do is to destroy the animals. Which they did. They shot them, rounded them up in big sweeps, thousands and thousands of them. And once you do that, people have nothing to live on" (pp. 283–84).

The revolution collapsed quickly, and the clan chief decided to take twenty-five thousand "abandoned and derelict nomads," many of them women and children, on a trek to Afghanistan. Bombed at and without food, all the routes controlled by the army, the people whose political consciousness Shahbaz had tried to raise died like flies all around him. It was "terrible," he told Naipaul, but he never doubted the revolution was right. Despite the memory of his extraordinarily difficult and mostly wrong decisions concerning the fate of the noncombatants, the terrible human tragedy all around him, he still sees the revolution as the most important, most "creative," "exciting" part of *his* development (p. 285). His memory of details is quite clear: how the army intercepted the camel trains carrying wheat, taking the food and killing the people, how local Baluchi trackers were used to follow the guerrillas' movements and whole nomad settlements were killed where they had hidden. It did upset him but he was comforted by the Baluchi guerrillas' fortitude in adversity: "Because nomadic life is hard, they have a great capacity for absorbing calamities. I learnt that stoicism and patience from them" (p. 285).

After Bhutto's fall, amnesty was declared. Deeply divided over the issue of revolution, "the movement forward" (p. 289), the Baluchi were now consumed by anxiety over the destruction of their livelihood. There were cruel ironies, unforeseeable for the politically inexperienced. Under Russian occupation, Afghanistan was relatively safe for Baluchi refugees, but Afghan refugees went to Baluchistan with their own big flocks, repeopling and deforesting the land, taking the best pastures and treating the remaining Baluchi tribes like a minority on their own territory. The Islamic fundamentalism of the Pathan invaders was alien to Baluchi culture and a source of great tension. When Shahbaz joined the clan chief in Afghanistan he was no longer interested in Shahbaz and unwilling to protect him. Deaf in one ear, without teeth, infected with hepatitis and malaria, Shahbaz still insists that he has "no regrets": Baluchistan "was and always will be the most creative, stimulating part of my life. Where I was most energized, and where I learnt so much. I was disappointed by the end result, but that doesn't make me bitter" (p. 286). He rejects Naipaul's suggestions of misused privilege and irresponsibility, since his becoming an adult coincided with guerrilla wars all over the Third World (p. 287). But the willingness itself to accommodate senselessly destructive acts is symptomatic of Shahbaz's enduringly immature idea of education: "It was the strangely colonial idea of his generation in Pakistan born though they were after independence. Education wasn't something you developed in yourself, to meet your own needs. It was something you traveled to, without fear or prejudice now, and when you got to where you were going you simply surrendered to the flow" (p. 287). This is not so much an indictment of colonial rule as of the postcolonial's inability to assume responsibility for himself, the reason for his vulnerability to belief systems, be it in the shape of Marxist activism or Islamic fundamentalism.

Naipaul has never denied the difficulties of the postcolonial experience, and he has been engaged with them more intensely as time went on. The phenomenon of simply going "with the flow" has been very common in the postcolonial situation, where individuals and groups have had easy recourse to the excuse of the damages done by the colonial past, somebody else's "bad history." There are great differences between the various colonial pasts originating in different kinds of conquests and conversions. But Naipaul does have a point when he sees a troubling postcolonial tendency to be disinterested in the larger world, an existential political provincialism. In his own attempts at making contact with people from very different cultures he is attentive to the difficulties of understanding what sets them apart and to what degree he will have to respect their enduring strangeness. On one level, Shahbaz's thoughtless, uninformed, disastrous interventions in Buchanistan are incomprehensible to Naipaul; on another, he understands their inevitability given the nature and the strength of Shahbaz's belief. Misled by his Marxist goal of global political salvation, he has never understood the reasons for the tragedy he and his friends helped to create: the inability of their universalist belief to deal with the reality of the particular, of difference.

Shahbaz did gain a sense of the nomadic tribes' strange ways of survival, their great cultural remoteness that made living among them such a "creative" adventure. Yet he never grasped the fundamental fragility of that survival in their harshly beautiful, extreme environment because it did not fit the grandiose scheme and scenario of the revolution. Naipaul focuses precisely on that fragility: the nomads, their cultural means of survival compromised by the revolutionaries' "well-intentioned" stupidity, are quite literally "brushed away," offered up to unpredictable, uncontrollable natural forces on that bitter high plateau. Naipaul is also appalled by the cost of that disastrous experiment to Shahbaz himself, but its details are recounted in a deliberately detached fashion: if Shahbaz's painful failure is individual and to some degree affecting, it is more important as a frightening, deeply irritating cultural-political phenomenon that does not allow for easy "compassion." The core of this failure is the self-deceiving arrogance of thoughtlessness and weakness, and there is nothing that could be more irritating to Naipaul. Many aspects of tribal Baluchi culture, the legal system and the common ownership of pasture among others, seemed admirable to Shahbaz. Now the traditional law is gone and so is access to the courts, but there are two to three hundred self-destructive blood feuds among the leading families. When Naipaul points this out to him, Shahbaz insists that he had brought the Baluchis nothing but "the truth" (p. 289). Believing in the overriding importance of the revolution, he is absolved by his pure faith from any responsibility for the damage done to the Baluchis and to himself.

He can claim this absolution because the pure faith abstracts. Going over his notes of Shahbaz's story, Naipaul notices that its silences and lacunae are due to the absence of concrete details: of changes brought about by time passing, of landscape, water, and food, and of the tribespeople to whom he brings revolution. Evidently, Shahbaz wanted "to strip people down to their Marxist essentials," much like a pious Muslim wanted "the converted people to be the faith alone, without distorting history and traditions" (p. 288). Instructively, at the conclusion of his story Shahbaz observes that though the source for his political belief had originally been the Western 1968 revolutionary "movement," his motivation was "local," wanting "to do something for my country, especially after the loss of Bangladesh. Today the people who have the answer are the fundamentalists" (p. 289).[13] Shahbaz is now closer to the Pathans than to the Baluchis, among whom he lived those long ten years; "the answer" is the power of belief systems to undermine the capacity for learning from experience. This power is central to fundamentalist Islam, and *Beyond Belief*, a book of documentary argumentation by way of shaping stories into case histories, is meant to show the consequences. More problematically, Naipaul is also trying here to locate the origins: fundamentalism as the political religion of "converted people" desiring an unconditional, unquestioning, unchanging faith has its source in a devastating and enduring experience of conquest, be it military or cultural, be it in the immediate present or the remote past. Conversion under these conditions does to people what Naipaul fears most: it diminishes the individual and the group by demanding the most profound self-deception about the complex and changing reality of social and political power.

Among the Believers was more obviously timely, published right after the Iranian revolution and addressing the then new issue of re-Islamization. The coming to political power of a religious fundamentalist belief system was itself strange, difficult to understand, and the book was focused on that strangeness. Going back almost two decades later, Naipaul wants to show that and how, with the growing sophistication and globalization of technology, the power of faith has become more dangerous in its basic sameness precisely because the power constellations have changed. These changes demand a different approach to the difficulties of understanding: different methods of seeking out informers, recording, and interpreting the different believers' stories. His creating the impression that they speak to the reader on their own authority—always the goal in his mature documentary texts but particularly so in *Beyond Belief*—combines a variety of narrative strategies: the narrator's questions, direct quoting, free indirect discourse retaining elements of the speaker's voice, the narrator's paraphrases, editing and presenting information in his own voice, and indirect and direct comments.[14] The stories are now more in the foreground and in that more clearly the pieces of cultural puzzles that the author puts together in front of the reader. The emphasis is on reconstructing the speakers' cultural environments from their stories while retaining that story's individuality. On his second visit, pieces of the puzzle sometimes fall into place, sometimes not, depending on the kind of changes they signify. The result is a richly layered documentary that gains from its incompleteness. Ironically for such an experienced writer, the formulaic use of the term "conversion" may have been an ill-considered attempt to resolve lingering uncertainties that he would have deemed useful in other documentaries but not here, where he wants to make "absolutely clear" the dangerous political and social power of religious fundamentalism.

Naipaul went back to these questions in a long, two-part essay on becoming a writer, "Reading and Writing" and "The Writer and India."[15] There is now a clearer sense of the different stages in his development and the centrality to it of the intimacy between reading and writing that is characteristic for all his work, particularly so for his approach to the documentary. The boy Naipaul created his own anthology of selected passages from "great" books of Western literature read to him by his father with great infectious enthusiasm. When he later went to the books themselves, he had difficulties going beyond the familiar, "magical" passages; the language was too hard, the details of the social, historical background too unfamiliar and confusing. Written in a very different cultural environment, these books required an "imaginative key" to unlock their meanings which the young Naipaul did not have, and so he copied for a long time his father's habit of literary grazing.[16] No such key was necessary for the *Ramayana* that lived "among us the way epics lived. It had a strong and fast and rich narrative and, even with the divine machinery, the matter was very human. The characters and their motives could always be discussed; the epic was like a moral education for us all" (1, p. 14).

Yet, because he wanted to become a writer, he needed and eventually managed to find access to texts outside his Trinidad Hindu culture, and precisely that process of increasing differentiation would set him free to learn more about the world from which he came, colonial Trinidad and India. He would later find that the "high idea of writing" inherited from his father and his "anthology" were not unlike Conrad's motivations, for whom "the discovery of every tale was a moral one." But first he had to make himself a writer, which meant to be able "to see writing from the other side. Until then I had read blindly, without judgment, not really knowing how made-up stories were to be assessed" (1, p. 14). It was the process of learning how to write that helped him to overcome his difficulties reading English and European fiction, which, in turn, helped his writing. And it was his early fiction, some of it highly successful, that made him understand the exhaustibility of his familiar past: "My material—my past, separated from me by place was fixed and, like childhood itself, complete; it couldn't be added to. This way of writing consumed it. Within five years I had come to an end. My writing imagination was like a chalk-scrawled blackboard, wiped clean in stages, and at the end blank again, tabula rasa" (1, p. 16).

Limited to the familiarity of his past, his vision had been too flat. Over the years, in stages, he discovered the many different layers of his, of everyone's, past, finally envisioning the "vanished aborigines, on whose land and among whose spirits we all lived." The country town where he was born and where as child he saw the local pageant play of the *Ramayana*, the *Ramlila* his ancestors had brought with them in memory, had an aboriginal name. In the course of researching the history of the area in the archives of the British Museum, he came across a small Indian tribe of that name which had provided river guides for English raiders in the early seventeenth century, was collectively punished by the Spanish governor, and had vanished from the records. This altered his understanding of his own past, since he could now no longer think of the *Ramlila* "as occurring at the very beginning of things. I had imaginatively to make room for people of another kind on the *Ramlila* ground. Fiction by itself would not have taken me to this larger comprehension" (1, p. 18).

It was not from fiction but from the historical documents that he learned how to look "through a multiplicity of impressions to a central human narrative"— an approach that he developed further in the long line of "books of travel (or, more properly, inquiry)" he wrote over the next three decades (1, p. 18). The drive of all serious inquiry to go back to before the obvious beginnings has become clearer to Naipaul as he went on writing. With time passing and aging, the desire to make sense of the course of his life, the connections and transitions between his many books, has become stronger.

In the second part of the essay, "The Writer and India," Naipaul explains his need to go back into deeper layers of India's history to understand the reasons for the "extraordinary distress of India" rather than just accept it as a given or, worse, "find a special spirituality in the special Indian distress" (2, p. 12). It took "much writing, in many moods" to see "beyond the dereliction" of India and "the fantasies of Indian political ideas" about the Indian past, because the difficulties of India before British rule had been "obscured" by the struggle for Indian independence: "Evidence of those calamities lay on every side. But the independence movement was like religion; it didn't see what it didn't want to see"—the common sight of a "general wretchedness" of the Indian people noted by seventeenth-century European travelers who also noted the splendor of Moghul palaces.[17] Going back behind the British presence in India "unraveled" for Naipaul the "romance" of the "wholeness of India" with which he had grown up in Trinidad, the ritual evocations of the homeland as a great unbroken ancient civilization. He found that the people he called his ancestors had been as "helpless before the Muslim invaders as the Mexicans and Peruvians were before the Spaniards." "Half destroyed," without the potential for developing political concepts, not to speak of institutions, they were unable to resist the Muslim invaders who for more than six centuries after A.D. 1000 freely "ravaged" the subcontinent, founding kingdoms and empires that fought bloody wars for power and territory. The Muslim invaders had "desecrated" and "obliterated" the temples of indigenous religions in the north and south (2, p. 12). There are parallels to the ravages of the Thirty Years' War in what would in the late nineteenth century become Germany, because this terrible war and its memories retarded the development of political will and intelligence in a large area in the center of Europe. Naipaul's point is this kind of political retardation, not some re-awakened "Hindu rage" against re-Islamization, is what stirred the old hurt of calamitous defeat. He wants to understand why this great ancient culture had not been able to participate more intelligently, benefit more from the undeniable achievements of social and political modernity.

Partly responsible for tearing away the earlier India's past, the Muslim invasions contributed to making its history "unknown, or unknowable or denied" (2, p. 12). Current re-Islamization with its focus on an enduring, universal purity of belief disregards historical particularities unless they concern the politics of the U.S. and Israel in the Middle East, resulting in a largely uninformed, distorted view of Indian (and other groups') history.[18] Writing about the defeat in 1565 of the last great Hindu kingdom of the South, Mysore, and the destruction of its capital city, Naipaul evokes its slaughtered people, the land so "impoverished," so "nearly without creative human resource" that it is hard to imagine that such a great city had ever existed there. Four centuries later, the "terrible ruins" still speak to him of "loot and hate and blood and Hindu defeat" (2, p. 14). It is not so much the historical actors waging wars of aggression he wants to remember, but the appalling physical and mental ruins they left behind that for centuries shrunk the collective Indian imagination for a better society.

Finding the Center and *The Enigma of Arrival*

A Bend in the River (1979), a novel in the strict sense of the author's relative independence from the contingencies of the factual, is narrated by the fictional East Indian merchant Salim. In certain ways he shares his author's voice and provides a bridge to the documentarist Naipaul in *Among the Believers* (1981). Documentary narratives remain "naturally" incomplete because they articulate real lives lived in real places and in real time, something that cannot be fully known. A fictional character, Salim is Naipaul's construction and as such fully knowable to his author if not to himself. Naipaul controls what remains opaque to Salim, and this opaqueness shapes Salim's story as his author has him tell it. An attentive observer, convincingly parochial in his trying to make sense of his life in that place at that time, he cannot think of bringing about change; his self-perception is based on reaction rather than action. The restrictions of his perspective do not leave much room for self-delusions, but they also do not allow for any kind of coherent reflection on the meanings of his position in postcolonial Africa. Roche too, the fictional character in a political environment controlled by his author, is limited in ways that are meant to bring out the obscurities of the postcolonial experience. Writing about his life as a political activist might have led him to a better understanding of his role in its historical context and thus to more thoughtful future actions. But he was designed to keep his (fictional) self-delusions intact, supported by the (real) world's fascination with the activist persona rather than the meanings of that person's past political activities.

One of the interviews recorded in *Among the Believers* deals explicitly with the issue of narrating from a position of incomplete knowledge with the result that the interviewed person assumes traits of a fictional protagonist. When Naipaul first meets the Indonesian Muslim Sitor Situmorang, he sees a small, middle-aged man with a "Chinese-negrito face," "a writer, humane, reflective."[1] The poet Sitor wants to talk about his difficulties with his autobiography rather than his life, notably his imprisonment after Sukarno's fall. With his tribal origins in the wild north of Sumatra, political troubles in Indonesia, and connections with European cultural institutions, Sitor is an intriguing example of extraordinary cultural change. But his in many ways obscure and confusing life also presents peculiar problems to the documentarist: responsible for the stories he is told, he cannot but see them as part of an emerging pattern, which includes

Sitor's search for a narrative that would accommodate his life as a series of dramatic changes.

Sitor wants to write a coherent account of his progress from tribal simplicity to urban complexity, but he has lost touch with his tribal past. So he goes back to his village with a young Canadian woman anthropologist interested mainly in his past as a man of the tribe. There is a photograph of Sitor's reinitiation into the tribe, required after his release from prison in 1975, a ceremony involving the presentation of his grandfather's skull. It shows Sitor with his back to the camera, holding the skull, and the shaman facing the camera, "fury distorting his face, moving swiftly, hair flying." At that moment Sitor seems still unaware of the dramatic clash between two profoundly different worlds. In the perspective of the outraged shaman, and perhaps the photographer, the ritual has been fatally tainted by a gesture made toward the skull by one of his grandsons: a physician, he just put back expertly one of the jaws dislodged during the transfer of the skull to a platter on which it is to be presented by Sitor (p. 293).

Sitor has experienced many such clashes. "Dazzled" by a tall, energetic, much younger Dutch woman, an enthusiastic professional promoter of Indonesian culture, the small, middle-aged man in bad health is excited by her attention and the connections she creates for him in Holland (p. 294). But the village to which he had recommitted himself with the encouragement of another attractive, tall, young Western woman demands a tribal marriage in his father's house of the great chief, now headed by his brother. This occasion produces another photo of Sitor the visitor: he is looking, as if from a great distance, at an old woman bent over a loom, his illiterate sister who has never left the village and is now an unimaginably remote stranger.

Naipaul's comments on Sitor's difficulties with a coherent autobiographical narrative contain the seeds of his own "Prologue to an Autobiography" in *Finding the Center,* which, in turn, led to the autobiographical explorations of *The Enigma of Arrival* and the historical-autobiographical experiments of *A Way in the World.* Sitor has journeyed immense cultural distances, crowding into one generation the experience of four or five centuries. The stuff of his life proves too rich, too extraordinary to express what he wishes to express: "growth through the prism of me as an individual." Sitor has not been able to construct the artistic, personal, political context in which to achieve a "synthesis" of the facts and events he recorded. It took the "skilled questioning" of the young Canadian anthropologist to reconstruct his tribal past so that he, despite his "oddly wordless childhood," could write in his autobiography: "This was how my ancestors lived for eighteen generations." But was it? How did she acquire her skills? What does she really know? Naipaul just quotes Sitor's self-assessment: "I am complicated. But not confused" (pp. 294–95).

Sitor may be complicated, but he is certainly confused about the meanings of modern complexity. The "synthesis" he desires turns out to be his yearning for the paradisiacal simplicity of "the village," so seductive to the neo-Romantic politics of identity in late modernity. Going back to one's "roots" to find one's "true" self means going back to the place (culture, heritage, ancestry) where one could not have lived. Is it possible that Sitor, less preoccupied with his distinct individuality, would have reconstructed his past himself and be content with what he could now see as its modern incompletions, lacunae, and silences? Was not the custom-made past constructed for him by the young anthropologist too complete, too certain to fit him? Did not her flattering, reassuring interest in his tribal wholeness prevent Sitor from asking himself the real, the hard questions that would have to be asked of the modern individual: did your political acts serve any useful purpose? Is your poetry any good? But then, in whose terms could these questions have been reasonably posed or answered?

Naipaul does not ask these questions because they would have silenced Sitor as he understands him. At this point Sitor's most urgent wish is to go back to European "glamour and security," suggesting to Naipaul the familiar fear of being extinguished in his own less accommodating culture. Without the personal and institutional European interest in his specific postcolonial "complication," Sitor could easily be "snuffed out," become superfluous (p. 296). It was only later, writing the chapter on Sitor from his notes, that Naipaul realized the curious absence from their conversations of the years 1945–65, when Sitor was politically connected with Sukarno, and that he understood his own role in creating this gap. Like Sitor himself, he had been more interested in Sitor's beginnings and his present. But in those first twenty years of Indonesian independence, Sitor had become a famous poet, politically powerful and a "figure of threat" to the opponents of the Sukarno regime who had seriously damaged their lives and whom they could never forgive (p. 296). Sitor had not been able to deal with that part of his past and, profoundly uncertain about the significance of his work, his place in the world, his identity, become too dependent on European reassurances.

This regression, the main reason for his difficulties with his autobiography, is linked to the confusions of accelerated cultural change in general and the experienced futility of political intervention in particular. Despite his very different origins and experiences, his clear sense of the significance of his work, Naipaul found certain aspects of Sitor's story familiar in ways which would have contributed to the account of his own "many-sided" background in its relation to his development as a writer.[2] Attempts at understanding where he came from would complicate his narrational position, making him more acutely aware of the interdependencies of traveling and writing, of looking at many different places and recording many different voices without fully knowing how to look and how to listen.

Two centuries earlier, Forster's account of Cook's second circumnavigation was a "natural" outcome of the experience of voyaging for the purpose of exploration. Brought along by his father as a research assistant, the young man did not know how much responsibility he would eventually have for this account, but once he was writing it he could be sure of its value, namely his contemporaries' interest in critically reflected and coherently presented information about what they saw, increasingly, as their world.[3] He could be sure of their enlightened curiosity about different ways of being human on this planet and on their making contact with different cultures through his travelogues. They wanted to know what could be known, and the young Forster in the *Voyage*, though already aware of the European limitations of his observational perspective, was not troubled by their expectations: eventually, the world would be more fully known and his account would have contributed to this process.

In late modernity, globalization has come to mean more complexly entangled connections as well as separations between cultures with different concepts and degrees of complexity. The growing tensions between "developed" and "developing" countries are clearly reflected in Naipaul's writing as it has evolved over time. In "Prologue to an Autobiography," he writes about his attitude to his material, raising questions of authority and cultural value, remembering how "uneasy and uncertain" he was when more than twenty years ago he began "to travel as a writer." Fiction had at first promised greater imaginative freedom than facts, but increasingly he became more fascinated by "people as I found them," with their cultural, political, historical realities (p. ix). "The Crocodiles of Yamoussoukro" records the older, more experienced writer as traveler, meeting new people, adding to and thereby also changing what he already knows about the world. He would be attracted to people not unlike himself in their attempts at finding the "order," the "center" of their world. His discovery of them in the Ivory Coast, then, is as much a part of the story as his attempt at understanding what to him are the puzzles and contradictions of their West African culture. Most important perhaps for the shape this story will take is his conviction that he would have found "equivalent connections with my past and myself wherever I had gone" (p. ix). Drawing him into a changing world, travel has broken his "colonial shell" and become a substitute for the "deepening knowledge of a society" that had not been possible for the young man growing up in Trinidad.[4] Travel enabled him to make good use of his marginality in that it taught him the need to learn "how to move among strangers for the short time one could afford to be among them." Traveling could be as creative and imaginative as the writing process: the absence of rules, the surprise of new places, the possibility of failure, the obscurities and excitements of arrival; then the moments of insight when a place "began to clear up" and its meanings became more accessible (p. xi).

These changing rhythms of travel as they guided the gathering of information were Forster's experiences too. But for the eighteenth-century intellectual and explorer whose beginnings had not been in writing but in voyaging and exploration, and under dramatically more uncertain conditions, they would have been too self-evident to be worth mentioning. It is obvious but still important to remember that with all its initial difficulties, Naipaul's life as a traveler and writer has been immeasurably more secure, coherent, controlled, physically comfortable, pleasurable, and relatively free of pain than that of any of his eighteenth-century European counterparts—as he would be the first to acknowledge, since he has been increasingly concerned with imagining truthfully the facts of past lives.

Finding the Center is about the traveler's narrative—how he came to it as a young writer and how he would learn to expand it through traveling because it would help him to make sense of his experiences. What Naipaul calls his "traveling method" is a dimension of the narrative. It takes "a sifting of impulses, ideas and references that becomes more multifarious as one grows older" to understand the process of living (p. xi), and narrative comes out of this understanding. Naipaul is puzzled by the daily ritual of feeding the sacred, totemic crocodiles of Yamoussoukro that seems to be enacted for the sake of tourists more than Ivorians who in most cases do not have the means of traveling to the remote site. The ruler of the Ivory Coast since independence in 1960, the African president has built a presidential palace in his ancestral village, replacing the forest with plantations and a golf course. He also had strikingly modern, largely unused buildings erected in the wilderness: a university complex to house and educate perhaps sixty students, perhaps six hundred (p. 148)—echoes of *A Bend in the River*. In his *Rhetoric of Empire*, David Spurr criticizes Naipaul's colonialist "gaze" on the African town in transition: "The city itself is ambitious but empty and incomplete, marked by gaps, vacancy, absence. In the judgement passed within Naipaul's gaze, the African town has made progress, but has yet to achieve the status of a 'real town,' has yet to achieve, that is, the reality of modernity and westernization." Naipaul "gazes at an Africa which, left to itself, can only parody the splendors of the West."[5] Spurr's "gaze" does not fit because Naipaul's attentive regard is not rhetorical but *concerned*. There *is* something wrong with that town; it won't do well left to itself. Its Western modern architecture does not reflect a discriminating openness to another civilization but rather the African leader's limiting desire to match its power without making the effort to understand the terms of that power: highly developed science, technology, and (on the whole) functioning political institutions. Tourists are promised "traces" of the president's native village and discovery of "the ultra-modern prefiguration of Africa of tomorrow" (p. 77). But the village and the palaver tree are hidden from view by a high wall, and the feeding ritual, as unsettling to Naipaul as it is "meant to be," brings the threat of darkness and the vanished forest back to the shiny new Yamoussoukro (p. 78). Pale pink pieces of heart and lungs and a sacrificial black chicken are carried in a bucket by the feeder and thrown to the huge, man-eating beasts, whose "twisted snouts" and closed teeth suggest "a long, jagged, irregularly stitched wound" (p. 145). Tall and thin like his long thin knife, the ominously silent feeder in the traditional skullcap and flowered gown is accompanied by an official whose ranger-like outfit and clucking encouragements "swallow, swallow" may be intended to add a touch of touristic familiarity to the intimidating ceremony.

Now an old man, the African president has used well the rich resources of his country, but Naipaul responds to the anxiety of Africa becoming: can Africans function in their new Westernized country without the foreigners who built it for them? They could acquire the needed technical skills but what about the mentality? Yamoussoukro appears as the conflicted "twin reality" of day and night, the latter "ceaselessly undoing" the achievements of the day. The crocodile ritual is part of the night and contributes to the "undoing" (p. 149). Kwame Anthony Appiah, whose father's and mother's families are respectively royal Ghanese and upper-class British, grew up in both worlds and has been equally at ease in them. To him the crocodile ritual is a formality which his politician father observed as a matter of course: treated a certain way, the crocodile can be expected to eat the offered chicken and thereby acknowledge the new leader of the clan. To Naipaul, coming from a different background, the meanings of the ritual are uncertain and potentially frightening. Africans are fully accessible in Appiah's account precisely because he is both one of them but also not limited to that identity. A member of the elite in the Asante part of Ghana and in England, Appiah bridges both worlds more naturally. On occasion he has to cope with some serious African problems like his "evil" murderous aunt, his father's sister, the wife of the Asante king. She wants to organize her brother's funeral, a politically important event, against his stated wishes that his British wife ("my beloved Peggy") and his Methodist church be in control of the ceremonies, and to get her will she uses witchcraft. Though her aggression may seem particularly unsettling to the outsider because of her "supernatural" means, her family knows them to be strategies in the battle for political domination and acts accordingly. Finally things are resolved to everybody's satisfaction, and Appiah, his mother's only son and therefore much involved in the local political feuds with the aunt and, through her, the king, offers the optimistic prediction that things will work themselves out. In his view, multiple identities are beneficial particularly in conflict situations since they can be drawn on to neutralize differences—as he had done by adopting his clan identity for the duration of the feud over the funeral. But the book was written in the late 1980s, and the experience of many African countries, including his own, has been of bloody conflict, stunningly literal brutality, and deep-rooted corruption through the 1990s and into the twenty-first century.[6]

New to West Africa, Naipaul was particularly intrigued by the Ivory Coast because in the "mess of black Africa" in the mid 1980s it stood out for its remarkable political and economic stability. At independence the country had been less concerned with Africanization than with creating wealth from peasant farming by providing security and services, importantly good roads. The president had even tried to "democratize" to counteract any discontent with the cult of personality, but the conventions of village life seemed to hinder the experiment. Impressed by this African success story, Naipaul also begins to see the difficulties. The success rests with the "non-ideological" leader descending from an established ruling family and conforming to the "African idea of authority," which importantly includes magic (p. 87). Naipaul is troubled by the power of magic, even though he understands that it has a plausible psychological basis in many Africans' unease with the new world of highways and skyscrapers. The (on the whole) sensible government newspaper would report matter-of-factly on cases of exorcism, complete with photos of the worried protagonists, to show that the battle of good magic and religion against bad magic and sorcery is no joke (p. 89).

Naipaul's guide to a village where such a battle took place recently is a handsome, well-dressed young man, but his fine-boned African face is unreadable and the adventure ends badly. Naipaul is both intrigued and dismayed by Djédjé, a cultural traditionalist and fervent believer in the supernatural who reacts with rages to his skepticism regarding exorbitant fees and sorcery. Djédjé's stories reveal that he is too alien to be depended on but is not predictably alien to fit an explanatory pattern that might yield a clue to certain puzzling complexities of the West African experience.

The village chief's official line is that he does not believe in sorcery and exorcism, but he strongly advises the visitors to watch out for some well-known djinns near the sharp bend in the road. He also admits to admiration for the cleverness of the devious Evil Spirit that had made the exorcism case and the village famous. Djédjé, duly impressed, comments: "Without civilization, everyone would be a sorcerer." Given his preoccupation with African authenticity and his belief in fetishes, does "civilization" mean for him the old, true ways of ensuring protection by good magic from the random evil of sorcery? Or did he just repeat back to the chief the official affirmation of modern African "development" (p. 124)? More important, are the two explanations irreconcilable?

On his return from the trip, Naipaul felt "Africa as a great melancholy" in its ill-fitting mix of the modern and the archaic: the Evil Spirit happily haunting the well-engineered bend of the expensive new highway. The incongruities are reflected in Djédjé's disturbing "exaggerated" emotions and sudden changes of personality (p. 133). Insisting against Naipaul's wishes that they see the *féticheur*, Djédjé had made the taxi drive around endlessly, obviously without a clue to his whereabouts. Blaming everything on Naipaul, who makes him "feel bad," sweating, his eyes going red, rocking himself, he stops making sense (p. 132)—a fearful withdrawal. Naipaul's anxiousness in this situation may seem exaggerated; a seasoned traveler is not expected to be so easily upset by a bad guide. But as he has pointed out repeatedly, his travel is motivated by the curiosity of the writer, not of the anthropologist or the journalist. Controlled in part by the writer's colonial background (p. 90), this less detached curiosity is shaped by the writer's imagination. On some level, the most alien places "connect" with what he already knows: strange and puzzling, they also seem strangely familiar and on occasion peculiarly threatening because of it. In most cases, the symbiosis of the traveler and writer has helped him meet people whose "varied experience" would enable him to see their world as they were trying to make sense of it (p. 90). They have differed from him by circumstance and yet have been not unlike him in their desire to inform and orient themselves (p. ix). His descriptions of them show the traveler's pleasure at finding them and getting to know who they are and where they might take him, and the writer's pleasure at trying to figure out who they might be and where he would take them.

Naipaul's most important informant about the Ivory Coast is Arlette, a big, black-brown, generous woman who had come there from Martinique via Paris; "reeducated and remade by Africa" (p. 114), she has become its peculiarly persuasive interpreter. Though she shares with many Ivorians a "mystical faith" in Africa that Naipaul finds difficult to grasp, her Africa is still open, not constrained by racial or tribal loyalties.[7] Still, the connection of this mystical faith with the remarkable success of the Ivory Coast remains puzzling. In Guinea, just across the border, with the same ethnic makeup, the same climate, the same kind of African kingship, people had been killed "like cattle" (p. 147) or simply left to die by starvation, the "black diet of Guinea." What was it that had made a difference here? The "ambition" of the president to create Yamoussoukro according to the "highest standards he knew" was both religious and secular: to serve the divinity that protected his kingship proving his right to rule, and to serve the people of the West African forest proving the justness of his rule (p. 148). The crocodile ritual becomes for Naipaul the key that would unlock this particular African place and time, and it seems fitting that he encounters reluctance to talk about the meaning of the ritual. Even Arlette's Africanist friend will only say: "The crocodiles belong to the president. He feeds them" (p. 167). Naming the three symbols of kingship in Africa, the panther on the savannah, the elephant in the forest, the crocodile in the water, he emphasizes the power and wickedness of the crocodile. But what about their connection with the president? Nobody seems to have an answer.

Naipaul accepts the "mystery" but still wants to know what place it has in the new Africa (p. 168). In the growing dusk—another power outage—of the Africanist's university office Naipaul asks about the African funeral custom that requires the burying of wives and servants with their dead master. He is told that there are now government sanctuaries for those who do not wish to comply, but they must get away before the master is quite dead and not all officials can be relied on to uphold sanctuary rules. Thus the funerals of chiefs and other important men who would be particularly intent on taking their dependents with them have to be public. Protecting the living from the powerful dead makes eminent sense to Naipaul, but the Africanist supports emphatically the desire of the dead for comfort in the spirit world, where they are mere shadows, always hungry and cold (p. 160). The first Christian in his family, he is also "profoundly attached" to African animism: "The world of white men is real. *But, but*. We black Africans have all that they have . . . in the world of the night, the world of darkness" (p. 162). This statement must have seemed particularly telling to Naipaul, who took it down verbatim: it confirmed his sense of a double or twin reality when watching the crocodile ritual.

At night Africans have more power of motion and information than whites could ever invent. Converting themselves into "pure energy," they can be transported instantaneously to faraway places to make mental contact with terrestrians and extraterrestrians—a feat eagerly corroborated by Arlette. At night, all power is reversed: women are stronger than men; beggars more respected than kings; black minds more powerful than white science and technology. To Nai-

paul these seem stories that could have been told on a Caribbean slave planta-
tion centuries ago: "White men, creatures of the day, were phantoms with absurd, illusory goals. Power, earth magic, was African and enduring; triumph was
African. But only Africans knew" (p. 165).[8] After the pain of colonialism, the
cultural "density" of African response to it has become the cause of African
intellectuals (p. 166). Arlette's friend is the founder of the new discipline of
"drummologie," the interpretation of African history and philosophy through
the study of drumming and chants, a much sought-after commodity in African-
American Studies programs at U.S. universities.

The president's response to the colonial experience seems quite different.
Naipaul finally gets a "straightforward" answer to the crocodile question from
a former high official: the crocodile is the totemic animal of the president's
family. *Sous-chiefs of* a great African kingdom, they had their power reduced
under colonial rule, but to the people their authority remained intact, and the
president's estates at Yamoussoukro are partly family land. The minister, a calm,
gracious, dignified man who limps because of a twisted foot, does not speak of
opposing worlds of day and night but the interlocking realms of mundane reality and of the spirit. Emphasizing the power of the supernatural, he explains
that Europeans, inventive and creative but spiritually underdeveloped, appear
like enfants terribles to Africans, who, despite their dependence on European
technology, see themselves as "older," more advanced (pp. 170–71). It was only
after their conversation that Naipaul learned about the minister's political imprisonment and the president's pardon after five years. He had told Naipaul that
his family's totemic animal was the prudent panther, leaping only when he was
sure. Was there a connection between the man's limp and the panther's leap?
The information about the ex-minister's political past "cast an extra, retrospec-
tive dignity on the man. And this dignity made more curious his interest in the
supernatural" (p. 171). But it also added yet another aspect to the president's
"ambition" to be the best ruler of his people: had he been despotically harsh to
imprison his minister for five years, perhaps had him tortured—the world of
the crocodile demanding sacrifices? Or had he benevolently pardoned him after
only five years, not too badly damaged—the world of European Yamoussoukro
waiting to become useful? And where does the religious Africanist fit in, telling
true stories of the powers of darkness in his dark university office? and where
the dignified, eminently sensible ex-minister with his modern house, glass and
steel furniture, silent air conditioner, and premonitory dreams?

Presenting these obvious conflicts, Naipaul's narrative retains the inevitable
obscurities of their meaning, the incompleteness of the stranger's understanding. It does not seek out this incompleteness for its own sake but for the sake
of gradually making sense of a situation. In the Ivory Coast, Naipaul is the
traveler-as-writer who for the duration of the visit believes that he can come
closer to understanding the "two ideas of reality that made Africans so appar-
ently indifferent to their material circumstances" (p. 173). His fictional protagonist (and partial alter ego) Salim came to fear this indifference, because in the
town at the bend of the quintessentially African river it fed the chaos of cultural

dysfunction. However, in the (at that time) successful Ivory Coast, Arlette's explanation of the African emphasis on the "inner" world over the "upper" world, if unsettling to Naipaul, is also intriguing. If she makes him feel that the world is constantly shifting, like sand, this may call up the Hindu doctrine of instability. Yet the cultural realizations of this concept are entirely different: the Hindu concept of illusion is derived from the "contemplation of nothingness," Arlette's thought-image of sand comes from her "understanding and admiration of a beautifully organized society," African tribal life with its ceremonies and rituals (p. 175). For the duration of their conversations about Africa Naipaul is persuaded to look through her eyes, content not to ask whether, and then how and why, her Africanness differs from Djédjé's.

The answer might have been that finding the center requires seeing phenomena rather than searching for them and coming to know what one is looking at. These are acts of understanding clearly beyond Djédjé's rigid loyalties and limited vision. But then again, relating to Arlette in a particular way because of his different expectations and her different temperament and talents, Naipaul may not have questioned *her* loyalties sufficiently. Like the crocodile ritual, for her neither a paradox nor a puzzle but an a priori meaningful part of a significant structure, he has to let her be in order to learn from her something of value about Africa. The African "mystery" which he acknowledges but does not embrace still informs his narrative of their conversations: its gradual, partial uncovering of layers of meaning. The issue for the writer as traveler is the changing incompleteness of knowledge. Where the Africanist may have constructed enchantment and Arlette may have found it, Naipaul, by narrating his attempts at understanding their experiences, revises what he thought of West Africa. He is by no means surer now; he may have come to ask different questions.

Naipaul the writer has benefited from the uncertainties of cultural identity. His ability to make the difficulties of writing an autobiography part of the narratives of *Finding the Center* is one example. This integration is not self-reflective but strategic; better, the strategies are not those of (neo-Romantic) self-reflection. They aim to show how the variety and surprises of what he is looking at may retard and deflect but do not frustrate his writing about himself, that is, himself as a writer. The writer's responsibility is to the powerful obscurities of social and political change and his true stories, fictional and documentary, have been shaped by his complete attentiveness—his being "passionate about accuracy"—to the voices of others.[9] With the ordinary experience of the flux of time and the extraordinary impact of accelerated change in late modernity,[10] this accuracy came to require a complementary "imaginative," "personal truth."[11] Shaken by the untimely deaths of his younger sister Sati (1984) and brother Shiva (1985) and extrapolating from the "Prologue to an Autobiography," Naipaul wrote *The Enigma of Arrival*, an autobiographical "Novel in Five Sections" dedicated to his brother's memory.

It is a strangely affecting text, becalmed in its unsettledness. The colonial separations, the disturbing difference of his origins have been neither resolved nor forgotten, but, looked at differently, they have become part of the puzzle of perspective that is central to the book. In the beginning of the first section, "Jack's Garden," Naipaul describes how he gradually oriented himself in the surroundings of his new place, a rented cottage in Wiltshire where he was to stay for ten years. The slowed-down rhythm of his writing reflects the slow process of understanding what he was looking at once he had "undone" the un-prompted associations of the English countryside.[12] It is literally a description of revisions in perception: first he can see almost nothing in the rain, then he sees buildings and fields, glints of light on wet meadows that he later learns to call "watermeadows," and in the background the low hills he will later know as "downs."[13]

New to the countryside, he felt again the stranger's "raw" sensations before they jell into the instinctively shared reactions of familiarity. What he noticed most sharply were the layers of history: the traces of the former activities of old cultivation, of outdated customs and objects, of ruins—decay and desolation different from that of the Caribbean, and differently unsettling to him. He had always lived with the idea of change and found that ideas of pastness, transi-tions, the shortness of human life helped to deal with it (p. 26). So he gave him-self time to piece together his new environment, first noticing the hedge of Jack's garden, "a little wall of mud-spattered green, abrupt in the openness of the driveway, like a vestige, a memory of another kind of house and garden and street, a token of something more complete, more ideal" (pp. 20–21). Naipaul is not in search of himself, reconstructing earlier anxieties of strangeness, but at-tempting to show a writer in acts of looking and thinking, inevitably challenged to understand what he is looking at, thinking when looking. His approach in this book is not so much a new way of merging fiction with documentation, something he had been doing all along, but rather of identifying "my narrator, my seeing eye, my feeling person": himself as the writer shown in instances of thinking about flux and change. In this way fiction writing and travel writing are equally "aspects of one's looking at the world one has lived in."[14]

Patient readers have been open to the book's curiously combined compact-ness and fluidity. Schiff aptly describes the text as coming at its readers "in re-peating waves, depositing bits of information, and then receding, only to surge forward again, a little farther this time, depositing a little bit more": the revi-sions of its author's perceptions.[15] Yet the key issue is still *what* he sees if he looks in that way and *how* it is significant for his understanding the world he has lived in. Looking at Jack's garden, he at first sees its different components as "emanations" of "literature and antiquity and the landscape" (p. 25). A trans-mutation of strangeness occurs as he distinguishes its layered complexities, and the change in his emotional and cognitive response to his changing perceptions will shape his memory, its peculiar selectiveness and lacunae. This shaping guides the writer's later attempts at recovering his memories—not of Jack's gar-den but of the process of seeing it more clearly, understanding better now what he was looking at then.

"With the eyes of pleasure" he saw first the variety of colors before slowly distinguishing different plants and flowers. Remembering that sequence, the narrator now also sees different kinds of learning: not in the "almost instinctive" manner in which he had come to know different flowers as a child in Trinidad, but deliberately, like "learning a second language." He understands that had he known then what he knows now he could reconstruct the seasons of Jack's garden: the way in which he looked at it then controls what he remembers now. He can remember only "simple things" by themselves, not the meaning of their changing patterns: the bulbs of spring, the planting of annuals, the vivid blooming of high summer. He also remembers "flowers like the gladiolus which, to my delight, flourished in both the climate of England and the tropical climate of Trinidad" (pp. 32–33)—the reassuring connection between the familiar and the strange.

This connection, however, is fragile. And so is the stranger's first impression that in the English countryside he has found "an unchanging World," in some ways like the idyllic Indian village conjured up in his father's reconciling stories. He would soon correct it, seeing that people grew old and died, houses changed hands and deteriorated, gardens overgrew, losing the orderly beauty created purposefully by their owners. He made himself look at these unsettling transformations as the inevitable "constancy of change" to help him cope with the distress he felt at "a death, a fence, a departure" that "undid" or "threatened" the perfection he had found" (p. 51). This distress signifies a particular strangeness: to "see the possibility, the certainty, of ruin, even at the moment of creation" was his inherited temperament, confirmed by the circumstances of his early life but also by his education in England. It had given him, with the English language, a particular kind of writerly ambition and a taut apprehensiveness regarding unfamiliar people in unfamiliar situations, nervous about both their perceived retreating from him and trespassing into his private territory.

Given these inhibitions, he found it "soothing" to live in the small cottage on the grounds of an old, once magnificent estate where boundaries seemed fluid. He remembers how the water meadows, the garden and orchard beside them grown wild after Jack's death had for him a limpid beauty also because they seemed to correspond to his childhood ideas of England: this grand Wiltshire estate, now decaying, had been "the apotheosis" of the colonial plantations of Trinidad where his poor Indian ancestors had worked (p. 52). If these "tribal" memories contributed in some indefinable way to his own apprehensive and skeptical temperament, "colonialist" is too undifferentiated and divisive to describe it. Naipaul is much more interested in the particularities of the "historical chain" that brought together his reclusive landlord, living out his days in the decaying glories of the great crumbling house, and the young writer in his cottage, trying to understand different experiences of change in different places and times. The wild garden loved by both serves as a screen from the changes occurring all around them, but also as their metaphorical catalyst. A pretty thatched cottage, once the pride of an old couple, has a succession of renters who do not or cannot see it as anything but a temporary shelter for people who do temporary jobs. Naipaul finds particularly "unsettling" its frequently open front door (p. 55), suggesting a breach in the inviolateness of privacy and intimacy protected by the house. The young woman who likes to sunbathe on the front lawn and leaves the door open will shortly be killed by her jealous husband, one of the new kind of agricultural workers brought in by the management of the estate to drive their big machines on the land to which they have no ties. The dense, astute narrative of his inarticulate, desperate sexual bondage and her cruel, equally desperate self-centeredness ends with Naipaul's speculating about the verdict of the court that the man had been "taunted" beyond endurance (p. 71).

Cutting in his precise description of their new working class appearance and behavior, their preoccupation with clothes guided by the woman's pride in her crude sexual beauty and the man's anxiousness to please her, Naipaul does not condescend to them. Their passions, hers for recognition of her power, his for her acceptance of him, are significant, and Naipaul is troubled by the promptness with which they are erased after the murder: "without disturbance, without many people knowing," the cottage was "cleansed and cleared of its once precious life, its once precious passions" (p. 71). The raw force of these passions may have stayed with him also because they remain disturbingly, destructively alien, Third World countries of the imagination set down in the English countryside. Uneasy about the woman's demanding sexuality also because of its negative influence on the older couple who take good care of the manor, Naipaul holds her more responsible than her killer. Her transgressions of the tacitly honored boundaries between public and private threaten the spread of chaos. Leaving her front door open, she walked freely on the estate grounds, passing too close in front of his window; and her possessive presence in the well-kept quarters of the older couple repeatedly spoiled his treasured, clearly remembered "feeling of space and protection" in the big, warm, inviting manor kitchen, of "doors opening into corridors and big room standing beside big room" (p. 67). It is a feeling shared by his memory of the unassertive young man coming to his door with some vegetables from the manor garden, "offering them with that classical gesture, and a smile of pure goodwill, the smile of a man receiving at that time a little love from the person he loved, and passing a bit of it back to the people around him" (p. 69).

A mysteriously selective, elusive record of temporal experience, memory is fluid, multilayered, porous; and Naipaul's narration in certain ways simulates its both random and patterned redundancies. There are the repeated recallings of that moment of grace that alleviates the emotional burden of social and natural decay, but also of how he had, in the continuously interrupted continuum of the past, again and again questioned his own perceptions: how he saw the well-dressed, well-groomed, troubled young couple, the picturesque thatched cottage, the valley. How others "with another kind of life, different resources, another idea of what was owed them" might have seen them differently, interested neither in the lost orderly quaintness of the cottage nor the conflicting desires for intimacy and sexual power that led to the murder (p. 63). She taunted him, he lost his head; it was all "in the cards," not a tragedy. Naipaul remembers also the people who simply did not share his vision of the valley as a place of inexorable change for the worse, whose vision was "without the decadence that was in my eye; a vision of childhood that would expand in the adult mind" (p. 77). There was Jack, the laborer who created his beautiful garden; there was a working woman from a neighboring town who shows him the place where a family of deer has survived on a piece of land bounded by busy highways and an army firing range: "No decay in that woman's eye. Downs, walks, deer: the wonder of the natural world as available as it had always been" (p. 77).

Naipaul's particular sensitivity to co-existing, often contradictory perspectives on a world simultaneously shared and not shared with others has its source in his core experience of the enigma of arrival, its terror and its exhilarating promises. Traveling and looking, he met again and again the stranger's challenge to find his way in unfamiliar places. As a writer, he did not have, as did Georg Forster, the benefit of the steady company of other similarly interested and informed travelers who could contradict or confirm each other's perceptions. Island after island, arriving and departing, they had to solve the puzzles confronting them or they would not survive. Their strangeness was particular and temporary; enigmas did not endure or recur, they changed with each landing. They could be troubled or happy in different places with different peoples, but it would not interfere with their coming and going to chart new worlds. Their past and their future were in Europe; their present was experience through motion, no matter how much they regretted on occasion that they could not stay. At least this is what their letters suggest—not less complexity, but less information about their emotions, greater risks, and greater reticence.

In some sense the consequence of what these earlier travelers learned through the contacts they made, Naipaul's strangeness has been enduring, composite, and solitary. Looking back, the Wiltshire valley was for him "the second, happier childhood as it were, the second arrival (but with an adult's perception) at a knowledge of natural things, together with the fulfillment of the child's dream of the safe house in the wood" (pp. 83–84). And there is indeed a curiously instructive naïveté, the world's wonder for the child, in Naipaul's learning about other people in their natural and cultural historicity, about himself in his relations to them. The perhaps most rewarding stage of that learning process is over when he leaves the cottage where he has worked so well because of dampness seeping in from the water meadows.

The enigma of arrival retreats into the past when the stranger is no longer a stranger, at least not in the literal sense of having to learn, instant by instant, what it is that he is looking at, but now in most cases can safely guess. This is not true for the writer, for whom the fearfulness of the unfamiliar intensifies the desire to understand it. Quintessentially modern, this desire comes out of knowing the dangers of not knowing, in this case the self-destructive illusions of globalization. At issue are the individual and cultural particularities of this writer's fear of not knowing enough and of his determination to use this fear well. Naipaul is not an exile in Wiltshire (or anywhere); a few miles away from Jack's garden, on drier ground, he will convert two decayed agricultural cottages built on layers of earlier foundations. Generations of agricultural workers and other people lived on that site before the outsider, who is now Naipaul himself, altered the land and created a "potential ruin." Dreaming of the "safe house in the wood," the adult soberly acknowledges its temporariness, its unquestionable vulnerability to change (p. 84). But change has also proved an important component in the perspectival intricacies of approaching the unfamiliar. Like memory, like building on the site of older settlements, understanding other people is a multilayered, open-ended process resonant with the endlessly complicated rhythms of living. There are endings, death and departure, and, like the beginnings and arrivals spawned by them, they seem to be the locus of more questions than can be answered, mysterious.

"Jack's Garden" narrates experience constituted in perception over time, weaving together temporally and spatially distinct acts of perception. In a similar fashion, the second section, "The Journey," shows the development of the writer as traveler beginning with Naipaul's first departure from Trinidad, "the journey that had seeded all the others" (p. 97) and remained the point of reference for all others. That first journey caused the first gap between the person and the writer, a split to be repeated many times and closed only much later (p. 102). Looking back at his excited and apprehensive younger self intent on recording all the adventures of the journey, he can now see why he then left out what he should have used, for the story's sake, but what was then too difficult to cope with, especially unfamiliar kinds of "racial feeling."[16] The development is gradual, a process lit up by subsequent insights into earlier misunderstandings of the connection between the writer's life and the story—a connection that differs with each of his journeys but keeps alive the promises and panics, the mysteries of arrival.

Writing about them many years later, now famous and secure, Naipaul comes back repeatedly to a Chirico painting, *The Enigma of Arrival*, he had found in a book left in the manor cottage, intrigued by its title and the "desolation and mystery" of the classical Mediterranean scene. What he saw was a wharf, walls, the top of the mast of an antique vessel in the background, and two "muffled" people in an otherwise deserted street in the foreground. The pictorial narrative of absences, the painting's brilliantly lit emptiness, may have been one of the reasons why he wanted to write a story about the "beautiful, clear, dangerous world, far removed from the setting in which I had found myself," the cluttered, rainy, misty English winter. He was also trying to get away for awhile from an especially taxing piece of work, a "book about fear" set in postindependence Africa. The Chirico story would be "floating light above" the African mud and chaos. But once the character drawn from the obscure figures in the painting's foreground escaped its emptiness through a gateway in the background, he would "be swallowed by the life and noise of a crowded city (I imagined something like an Indian bazaar scene)." There are echoes of Naipaul's own panic at the Bombay station, and his protagonist, less and less sure about his initial mission, "would begin to know only that he was lost." The adventure gone wrong, he would panic and try to escape with the help of seemingly kind people, only to realize that he was their intended victim in a bloody religious ceremony. Frenzied with fear, he would come across a door, open it, and find himself safely back on the site of his arrival, as he remembered it. But not quite: the mast has disappeared from the picture; the ship has left without him; "the traveller has lived out his life" (pp. 91–93).

There are resonances of his own experiences which become explicit in the connection he establishes only much later between the stranger's mysterious adventures and those of the characters in the African story about two white people caught in a suddenly erupting tribal war. Looking back, he realized that the story of the painting *The Enigma of Arrival,* which seemed to him a release from the more difficult and dark African story, was actually another version of it: both shared the experience of overwhelming chaos, fear, and futility. More important, he understands then how the wintry desolation of Wiltshire, deepened by his feeling of insecurity about his writing, became the African landscape of "In a Free State": how, as a writer, he projected the "solitude and emptiness and menace" of his Africa onto the land around him and how they stayed with the land. Walking in the vicinity of his cottage, forced to turn back from the deep mud of a footpath, he finds himself in a small Ugandan village on a rainy afternoon four years ago, "mired in animal excrement, tormented by the stares and approaches of Africans, who were puzzled by my intrusion, and I had to turn away, get back into the car, drive on." The landscape of his walks began to "radiate or return Africa to me. So man and writer became one; the circle became complete" (pp. 155–56).

As much as he could be whole and secure, writing the African story—one of his most powerful in its evocations of menace and barrenness—healed him.[17] He did not know then that the Wiltshire landscape "was in fact benign, the first landscape to have that quality for me," so much so that it sustained the fearful Africa of his memory and imagination: "That all the resolutions and frankness I was going to arrive at through my writing were to be paralleled by the physical peace of my setting" (p. 157). "In a Free State" is one of his darkest, most violent stories, not, as he himself observed, "in incidents, but in its emotions" (p. 93). That emotional violence is a product of Naipaul's extraordinary "frankness," his unsettling focus on the large, entangled complex of motivations that defies the simplifications of "racism" and accommodates the obscurity of unsolvable political and moral conflicts. Again and again, in this self-reflective, other-centered biography of his writing, he reminds himself and the reader that such vision is largely dependent on a vantage point of relative security and order—in his well documented experience the exception rather than the rule. From it he could see the white couple on a two-day-long drive from the capital of a recently "free" sub-Saharan African state through forest and bush to a government compound in the south. The man, a well-intentioned administrator, speaks of serving rather than running the young country: his business is to deal with its need for food, hospitals, and schools, not to monitor its government. But this enlightened attitude also shields him from uncomfortable questions about the nature of the government and, consequently, of his service. A fictionalizing rather than informed friend of Africa, he envisions a glorious merging of different colors and cultures. When he tries out this fantasy on an African, telling the man of his desire to be reborn as black and beautiful as he is, the African spits into his face. Disregarding difference, he has no respect for its meanings, and his intention to serve the dignity of the new Africa, the new African, is condescending and largely abstract in the terms of that society's, that individual's violent, chaotic reality.

He finally has to confront that reality when he is brutally beaten at a government controlled checkpoint in an area of postindependence tribal conflict. Assuming that government soldiers would be "civilized," he gets out of the car to ask for permission to pass—a crucial mistake that undermines his authority. He manages to escape and drive on, despite his broken wrist, to the relative safety of his destination. But seeing his battered state, the houseboy is openly derisive, and at night the sounds of torture keep him awake. He does not understand that he has no authority in the new Africa and thus cannot read the menacing signs along the road: army trucks, the dead king's abandoned car, his captured and tortured supporters that indicate the bloody tribal insurrection brutally suppressed by the government. The white progressivist's concepts of African dignity and civilization are not Africa's concern. His deliberate ignorance of the "darkness," the difference of Africa, is complemented by the woman's determination to isolate herself from what is going on around her. Waiting for him in the car, she is unaware of his ordeal, complaining that he should not have been so cooperative. In her opinion, Europeans should either stay away from corrupt and brutal Africans or punish them for their misconduct. Her reaction to individual Africans—most basic and powerful, their "smell"—makes her appear "racist" but also questions the usefulness of this censoring definition. Naipaul's narrative has the conventionally bigoted woman appear more unlikable but not really more wrong than the proto-"politically correct" man. The same is true for the unappetizing former British colonel who runs a hunting lodge in the bush and pronounces on African inability to maintain civilization without European control. Given the observable conduct of Africans at that time, in that place, the whites have a point—as would have blacks visiting there from a different, less troubled country—though it may seem mean-spirited to concede it.[18]

If the story succeeds in permitting moral obscurities without trivializing them, it does so in part by situating explosive cultural conflicts in the absorbing ancient sameness of the African landscape that puts them into perspective. So does the Wiltshire landscape where Naipaul wrote *Guerrillas* and *A Bend in the River,* and finally explains, in *The Enigma of Arrival,* the coming apart and then coming together of the man and the writer, the gradual development of his curiosity about the world and its many histories. Arrival is a process. Looking back, his arrival in England in 1950 seems to Naipaul like that of the "earliest Spanish travelers to the New World, medieval men with high faith" who quickly took for granted the "wonders" of God's world they had ostensibly traveled for. Like the Spaniards, "having arrived after so much effort" and interested only in what he expected to find, he had little to record (p. 132). Going back to Trinidad in 1956 he was tense about his family and still apprehensive about being a writer. But returning in 1960, after the completion of *A House for Mr Biswas* (1961), a book he knew to be an important achievement, and commissioned to write about traveling through "colonies, fragments of still surviving empires" in the Caribbean and the Guianas of South America (*The Middle Passage*, 1962), he was in a mood to celebrate. Yet there was still, even increasing, the gap between the person and the writer. At first "glamoured" by the idea of the cosmopolitan traveler starting from Europe, he found it difficult to write his travelogue, since the glamour was in conflict with the "rawness of my nerves as a colonial traveling among colonials." Even though he shared the European traveler's education and sense of adventure, he did not have a metropolitan audience "to report back to" from the requisite distant and therefore interesting point of observation (p. 140).

Naipaul realized then that if he wanted to go on traveling as a writer, he needed to "acknowledge" more of himself, and he did so in his book about India, *An Area of Darkness* (1964). Traveling to the peasant India recreated by his grandfathers in Trinidad, he was traveling "to an un-English fantasy, and a fantasy unknown to Indians of India." How would he find his way? He needed to take his own reactions seriously. He would be the traveler as writer who permits himself to acknowledge his panicked fear at Bombay Station that he might be swallowed, extinguished by the milling crowd. From the starting point of Trinidad, his curiosity "spread in all directions. Every exploration, every book, added to my knowledge, qualified my earlier idea of myself and the world" (p. 141).[19]

This spatial, as it were horizontal enlargement was to be supplemented by a temporal, vertical one. Commissioned by an American publisher to write a book for a series on cities, he chose Port of Spain because he thought it could be done quickly and easily. But the archival materials drew him in much more deeply than he had envisioned. Reading the documents, he had wanted naively to arrive at a "synthesis of the worlds and cultures" that had made him, Columbus, the search for El Dorado, Sir Walter Raleigh, centuries later the growth of the slave plantations and the revolutions: the American and French Revolutions, in their tow the black Haitian revolution; later again the South American revolution, Francisco Miranda, Bolivar, the disappearance of the Spanish Empire. Finally there was Trinidad, now detached from chaotic Venezuela, a British West Indian colony, an "island of sugar and slaves" sinking into its long colonial "torpor" when both are gone. Naipaul learns that the island's drabness, so depressing to the boy, was man-made and temporary rather than an unchanging aspect of geography: "there had been other visions and indeed other landscapes there" (p. 142). But when he travels to the present Trinidad, its many-layered past built up in his imagination over several years of study, he finds a situation of great racial tension threatening revolution, chaos, and destruction that will again obscure his newly found, more differentiated view of the island's past (p. 145). Like the stranger, the home-comer has to cope with the confusions and apprehensions of arrival: the myth of origin is a story that, if told with any degree of cultural intelligence, will change its meaning in time. At Naipaul's first departure two decades ago, the blacks of Trinidad seemed to want to belong; now, at this arrival, they are asserting their separateness. Their aggressiveness promises another "false revolution," the desire to destroy rather than improve fueled by a "simplified and sentimentalized" past. Still, he tries to see the situation from both sides: the blacks, whose hopes and energies will again be squandered; the Asians, "the people mainly threatened, not black, not white" (pp. 146–47), his people.

The enigma of arrival is the unpredictable coming together of perceptions from different times and places. Looking back from this vantage point, Naipaul observes that with him, "everything started from writing" (p. 154), because it was this activity more than anything else that made him aware of the many different ways of seeing the world. In the third and fourth sections of the book, "Ivy" and "Rooks," he reconstructs his life as a writer in the manor cottage by narrating the lives of the people around him as he learns more about them. "Ivy" begins with the statement "I never spoke to my landlord," pointing to the writer-observer's limited access. He has pieced together bits of information for his incomplete portrait of the recluse, among them his love for ivy. His conversations with most of the other people connected with the manor are limited by their inability or unwillingness to speak about themselves. Living among them, Naipaul shapes their world with questions that he tentatively, speculatively answers himself. It emerges from his remembered perceptions of them in their relations among themselves and to him. In its explicit focus on the temporal, cumulative nature of knowledge—of the writer in his physical surroundings and his interaction with other people—Naipaul's approach here differs from that of his documentary texts constructed of others' stories behind which the narrator can (pretend to) retreat. His distinct presence in the narration serves to clarify how these processes of gathering, comparing, and qualifying information draw on uncertain perceptions and unstable memories, his own and others'. The spatial and temporal complexity of perspective is central to the self-explorations of the writer in The Enigma of Arrival. It is also intimately linked to an understanding of his responsibility for a world shared with others. The more certain he is of the importance of such sharing, the more he admits to its uncertainties—not in the sense of self-referential "postmodernist" circularity, which produces an increasingly abstract sameness, but in the modern sense of an ongoing, uncertain, unpredictable process of understanding what is different. However hesitatingly and indirectly, people would eventually tell him something about themselves "because I was a stranger; because I could understand; and because I was interested," responding to his "wish to visualize the details and routine of their lives, to see the world through their eyes" (p. 220).

Yet this wish, essential to the documentarist's enterprise, is here more openly guided by the insight that "the only way we have of understanding another man's condition is through ourselves, our experiences and emotions" (p. 220). The writer can reconstruct others' lives from the observed details of their self-perception and self-presentation: their body, their clothes, their speech, their stories about themselves and others, their memories. He cannot exclude from this process his own perception of himself as shaped by his temperament, his physique, his environment: his multiple physical (smallness, asthma) and psychological (his "many-sided" background) insecurities, his sense of not belonging or of belonging too much, his knowing and fearing dependency. His own experiences make it easier but also more unsettling to understand a person like the gardener, Pitton, who works "in the wilderness of the manor grounds." Coming and going at his own discretion, with his carefully chosen country clothes and precise routines, his handsomely dressed, beautiful wife, he does not fit the image of a gardener. More intelligent, worldly, and ambitious than the simple agricultural laborer Jack, who relishes the physical demands and beauties of his garden, Pitton is also more obedient and vain and therefore more vulnerable to other people's judgment of him (p. 211). A particular incident reminds Naipaul of his own family's "curious instinct" to boast to people who were richer and could "easily see through our vanity." Memories of lies caused by poverty, "some whiff of huts and damp and the swamplands of my childhood," came to him in Pitton's "improved agricultural cottage" (p. 227): a hurt and shame that has stayed with him and become an important aspect of his talent for observation because it enabled him to imagine the other person's vulnerabilities and insecurities without condescension or sentimentality.

"Rooks," named after the birds' noisy protests over the loss of their habitat when the estate's big beech trees are cut down, is the section most pointedly concerned with perceptions of change and forgetting, decay and desolation. Here too the focus is on the differences and commonalities of perspective derived from the often obscure, complex interplay of individual and collective experience. Like Pitton, Alan, a relation of the landlord and minor literary figure, has made his connection with the manor a both essential and elusive part of his place in the world. Alan has built on it his identity as the writer with a particular "sensibility" (p. 260), reminding Naipaul of his own early idea of "the writer" when he first came to England. At that stage he would have envied Alan the "material" of the landlord, the manor, the setting, the London literary parties because he was seeking to "create," fictionalize rather than truthfully, if painfully, recreate his experiences. Alan is caught in the same bind; some unresolved hurt in his past had "committed him to solitude, uncertainty, an imperfect life" (p. 260).

These are echoes of Naipaul's self-perception. But if Alan is soothed, like Naipaul, by the solitude of the manor and its surroundings, this does not make him a serious writer: unable to imagine the sensibilities of other people, Alan cannot envision difference. He visits the manor ostensibly to study the landlord in his environment, collecting samples of the speech habits and social mannerisms of a more gracious, more civilized life before the Second World War, when such people, such environments were still important. The visitor is given a room with an untouched view and a modernized bathroom in a still functioning big house that makes no demands on him. He can just be present, pretending that this life is still there for him to copy into his diary, which will become "the book." Taking notes, he seems curiously unaware of the landlord's debilitating acedia and the physical "dereliction" it has caused all around him, signs of decay that are uppermost in Naipaul's mind. Alan thinks it "creepy" that he has never spoken to the landlord in all that time, but it would have been difficult to meet him in his house and to "note however involuntarily his idiosyncrasies and affectations; it would have undone the magic" (pp. 261–62). The "magic" lies in the contrasting perceptions of the once gifted and privileged, now reclusive, impaired man in the once magnificent, now crumbling manor on whom all the people associated with the estate have depended for their place in the world. Alan in his role of observer and recorder depends on the landlord for the solace of the manor's solitude that keeps at bay the threatening "vision of his own inadequacy" (p. 262). This vision too is familiar to Naipaul, leaving him more sharply aware of its ravages as he finds them in Alan's face: how the skin of his cheeks had become very white and thin and seemed to "flutter above the flesh (as though there was some vacancy between skin and flesh)," like the "outer petal of a blown rose" but also like the "faded, black plastic sheeting that covered the old cottage-shaped hayrick on the driveway, plastic sheeting so beaten about by wind and rain that it had not only lost luster and snap but appeared also to have developed within its thinness little blisters and air-pockets" (p. 264). He saw the threat of disintegration in the live face, suggesting, as in Rembrandt's self-portraits, mere and yet immensely personal matter worked on indifferently by anonymous physical forces.

Alan would soon commit suicide. For the landlord "it was one person less in his shrinking world; another person not to be mentioned again" (p. 265). This shrinking signifies to Naipaul the undoing, by illness and the passing of time, of the man's educated interests and talents and of the beautiful work of carpenters, masons, and bricklayers that had made his house magnificent. He observes scavenging intruders and senses with apprehension the instinct to "hasten decay, to loot, to reduce to junk . . . the secrets of the building and its modest technologies, for so long ordinary, lost" (p. 292)—like the loss of the old civilization of India he had lamented in *An Area of Darkness*. But he is also a stranger to whom it is natural that others have different visions: "The wet river banks, the downs: everyone saw different things. Old Mr. Phillips, with his memories of chalk and moss; my landlord, loving ivy; the builder of the manor garden; Alan, Jack, me" (p. 268). The difference is affirmed rather than bridged by the gift of a newly polished walking stick left to Naipaul by old Mr. Phillips and delivered by his daughter-in-law, an important if elusive figure in the life of the manor. It awakens Trinidad memories of his father's hobby of making walking sticks and Wiltshire memories of his walks with the old man on the manor grounds, the stick pointing out plants to the stranger. The woman already seems to be distancing herself from the old man and her own manor past, adding "a touch of desolation to the beauty of the gift," and he, "as if in response to her new personality, had never felt so close to her" (pp. 302–304). But this fragile, momentary closeness between two people who have been and will remain strangers is not meant to be a consoling closure to the narrative of that troubled, searching, productive decade in the life of the writer. Rather, it calls up once more the enduring enigma of arrival, the gradual shaping in time of the stranger's perception.

In the last section, "The Ceremony of Farewell," the many strands of the book come together in the story of its origin. The original story evoked by a painting and its title had been "modified" over the years to become the journey of the "writer defined by his writing discoveries, his ways of seeing, rather than by his personal adventures." The "motif" of that story was "death and the way of handling it" (p. 309). In the fall of 1984, in his new house in Wiltshire, Naipaul had just decided that writing of Jack's great love of life was the best way into his new book when he got news of the sudden death of his younger sister, Sati, in Trinidad. At what he thought was exactly the time of her cremation, he looked at her photographs taken over the years, concentrating hard on "that person, that life, that unique character" to honor the person "who had lived." His younger brother, Shiva, had arrived from London in time to watch the still glowing pyre, "the terrible final rites of cremation" (pp. 311–12). To see how the flames consume the shape of the person, how nothing familiar is left after the transformation into ashes, is to experience the finality of separation affirmed by the Hindu rites. Naipaul joined his family for the religious ceremony performed for the sister who had not been religious. Questioning the pundit about the cruelty of his mother's death, refusing to accept the idea of karma, Sati's teenage son had not "yielded to the mystery of the ritual" (p. 313). To the boy's "Will she come back?" and the husband's "Will we be together again?" the pundit said, "But you wouldn't know it is her"—the Hindu concept of reincarnation that left them inconsolable (p. 314).

The dead woman had disliked Hindu ritual but her family wanted the rites. Separated from their difficult past by education, travel, and history, they were self-fashioned and had nowhere to go but into the future; in the absence of the promise of redemption, they felt "the need to honor and remember" (pp. 316–18). For Naipaul, looking on death as the unredeemed, "real grief where melancholy had created a vacancy" meant a new imaginative vision of "life and man as the mystery" which enabled him to start writing his book about Jack's garden, the enigma of arrival.

8   Uncertain Histories
A Way in the World

Western concepts of time and history opened distinct temporal spaces that shaped Naipaul's writing. Peter Hughes's observation that he joined the "great modernists" in retrieving through "style" what has been "lost through history" does not take into consideration Naipaul's keen awareness of the historicity of understanding.[1] Coming from a place that he thought had no history, Naipaul has never lost the sense of the precariousness of knowing our place in time. The young man's sense of his native island as outside of history resulted partly from his early questioning of his background in the loving and troubled relationship with his father, but it was also encouraged by the colonial educational system that had stimulated his intellectual curiosity. In the archives established under British rule he would eventually find materials that went into *The Loss of El Dorado* (1969) and, after more transformations, *A Way in the World* (1994). Colonial rule, then, signified both imperialist restrictions and cosmopolitan encouragements. That dual experience came at a cost, yet it gave Naipaul a peculiarly mobile imagination of his own and others' differences and similarities as they were all changing in time. In a 1981 interview he pointed out that in writing about not belonging in the world of *A House for Mr Biswas,* he had still needed to write about it. More important, while he was writing about it, that world turned: Trinidad became independent. The colonial enterprise had created global historical and spatial connections, and the end of Empire meant their undoing: the young writer was now "floating" between many different worlds. He would never lose the sense of the "mystery" of a common, connecting language in writing and talking, given the often enormous, seemingly unbridgeable cultural distances. He also knew that he could not be that Western author who "always has the right passport and continues to pretend that it does not matter."[2]

Neither could he resort to a redemptive significance of "style," not even in his most densely written book, *The Enigma of Arrival.* True, on some level the text's intricate literary patterning of recurrences "creates meaning," but its function is to make more transparent the temporal layers of experience, the responses to changes in time and of places.[3] His later texts, increasingly interwoven compositions of fictional inventions, narrational strategies, and documentary (historical) materials, are stylistically less elaborate because more focused on understanding strangers in unfamiliar settings reluctant to yield their meanings. In *Among the Believers* and *Beyond Belief* the recorded individual voices come together, as if naturally, in a complex, fluid pattern that makes transparent the explosive cultural conflicts of late modernity in the seductively varied realities of other lives. An experienced traveler and looker, Naipaul has developed what one might call a gestalt perception of people in their cultural context, as a good chess player can sum up rapidly the meanings of a complex constellation. Yet if that experienced, skilled perception is his, its representation is meant to enlarge and clarify for the reader what the documentarist saw and heard: he came across those voices; he did not invent them. His responsibility toward them is different in kind from that of the writer of fiction, and so is the reaction of the reader.[4]

The stories Naipaul tells in *A Way in the World* are intended to be true stories: true to the observed, true to the narrative that shapes itself around the observation. But there is a new emphasis on changes in the perspective of the traveler who looks through the experiences of others, merging them with his own. Writing in the material of history, Naipaul is not in the manner of new historicist discourse a "grazer," subjectively selective. The issue is not an a priori lack of transparency with respect to the "Other" but attempts to differentiate between different kinds of others in relation to different kinds of documentarists or historians. Naipaul has always been intent on "getting it right" and sharply aware of the acculturation of perception.[5] Where *The Enigma of Arrival* traced the development of his own culturally composite, other-reflected way of seeing, *A Way in the World* undoes this composition by exploring differently acculturated ways of seeing for the sake of the differences themselves. Seeking to clarify the obscurities of different perspectives in different spaces and times, he has to stay with them. He cannot, as he tried in *The Enigma of Arrival*, go beyond and, to a degree, connect them. If his narrational position has become more openly personal where his characters are historical, this means the construction of a more temporally composite perspective: his "feeling in this history," in these historical actors.[6] The otherness of history is now explored from the inside, within the individuals shaped by it.

Writing out of historical documents and recording interviews requires different documentary approaches: in *Among the Believers* he "never altered" a word he was told; in *A Way in the World* he wanted to reach "another kind of imaginative truth"—for, among others, the experiences of the Venezuelan revolutionary Francisco Miranda on Trinidad in 1806 ("In the Gulf of Desolation"). His career was "just as fabulous and original" as that of Columbus or Raleigh, but it has not become the stuff of historical legend. Miranda is still curiously accessible from his documents, and his historiographer can keep his narration "personal," as if sharing his authority with a subject that is both factual and fictional. Naipaul was particularly intrigued by Miranda's relation to the slave society of Trinidad: when he returned there after many years spent in the U.S., France, and England, trying to sell the idea of Spanish-American liberation, he literally did not see the Negro slaves; they were not for him "true presences." Miranda's peculiar ability to distance himself became "an imaginative moment" for Naipaul, trying to understand how Miranda could nevertheless hold on to his cause, how he had been transformed and yet, in important ways, stayed the same. It required creating his "own construct" of a combined inside and outside perspective that would enable him to represent historical events and actors in the flux of time.[7] The issue is not "reading against the grain," "re-writing," or re-de-constructing historical documents but to having a mobile perspective emerge from them. Unlike historical fiction, this "mixed" approach disrupts and complicates the meanings of historical experience: getting closer to Miranda, we also move further away from him. It is his historically imagined accessibility that makes him more irrevocably a stranger because it enables the reader to see more clearly the differences wrought by temporal distance.

Nothing separates more than time, and nothing is more common and more poignant than the shock of that separation. *A Way in the World* takes temporal alterity literally, as if illuminated by the spatial and cultural distances Naipaul has covered. In the first chapter, "Prelude: An Inheritance," he describes how on his return to Trinidad for the first time after six years plants and houses seemed bigger or smaller than he remembered, people in the streets darker—unless they were old acquaintances whom he could see "more easily."[8] Going back to a past he knew from a present he knows only partly, he experiences a state of "strange and not strange," the "half-dream" of "knowing and not knowing," the "shifting about of reality" (p. 4). He listens to stories about strange people, like a male decorator of cakes and arranger of flowers: the woman teacher who knew him suggests an "inappropriate feeling for beauty"—something that troubled her but that she had not even tried to understand (p. 10). It made Naipaul wonder how such a man had seen himself in that society and how little he would have known about his family history, though the last two centuries of the island's resettlement were documented fully in Port of Spain's registrar general's office. (Working there for a short time before leaving for England, the young Naipaul had never looked for historical documents concerning his own family; historical awareness, the desire to locate past events in the flux of time for orientation in the present, was not part of his West Indian background but of his British education.) The enigma of arrival in a given place, at a given time had remained intact, suggesting that the great distances covered in order to arrive had not really been overcome. Through his name the strangely gentle, sensitive decorator was linked with a Shia Muslim group in India and perhaps with the dancing groups of Lucknow, the "lewd men who painted their faces and tried to live like women," but this would only be a small part of him: "We cannot understand all the traits we have inherited. Sometimes we can be strangers to ourselves" (p. 11).

It is this perception of strangeness within caused by the temporal layers of consciousness, the presence within the individual of unaccounted-for others, that can help the historian to become more attuned to the strangeness of others without. This insight underlies Naipaul's narrative approach to the protagonists of the histories, factual and fictional, whom he brought together in *A Way in the World*. It refutes, more explicitly perhaps than his other texts, the comforting and trivializing assumptions of multiculturalism which erase the very real difficulties of strangeness, prematurely and to the detriment of historical understanding. It also suggests the problems of fitting the expanding "confused, mixed world" of late modernity into more narrowly literary fictions and inhabiting, as a writer, a world where "the other half or three-quarters" are not seen.[9] Naipaul's texts document that he has seen much of the other half and that its reality remains largely uncharted. Yet, insisting on a larger, socially more informed and more intelligent view of the world after independence, he too is parochial in certain ways.[10] He has never reflected seriously on modern Western culture, which in his own estimation has enabled him to acquire that knowledge and to develop that intelligence. Nor have, with very few exceptions, the important "imperial" writers from whom he distances himself here.[11] Like them, Naipaul has shown little interest in the larger cultural meanings of rapidly developing science and technology since the nineteenth century that are of crucial importance to "our confused, mixed world" at the turn of the millennium and will influence greatly, perhaps dangerously, the development of that "other half," beyond the transparent problems of the new fundamentalisms. Unlike them, he has made a good portion of that other half speak to the West in ways which are disturbingly illuminating.

The composite, tentative, self-questioning narratives of Naipaul's time travel in *A Way in the World* are in certain ways prefigured in his documentary on the American South, *A Turn in the South* (1989), which brought him the "great discovery" of a new "form" when the people he interviewed were describing to him "what they felt."[12] With all his usual intelligence and shrewdness of observation, he shows here an unusual eagerness to be persuaded by what he sees and hears. Certain physical and cultural properties of the South stirred in the observer certain memories and associations, suggesting an elusive yet tangible connectedness. In North Carolina he found James Applewhite, a poet and university teacher from an old tobacco family who made him "see" the complex physical and cultural realities of the tobacco culture. Combining "a poet's sensibility," a "farmer's dedication," and an "academic evenness of manner," he "spoke from the heart, without affectation, with a farmer's matter-of-factness, offering me at once, as soon as he saw that I was receptive, thoughts he would have spent some time arriving at."[13] This informant is too good to be true, reflecting Naipaul's determination here to accept a reconciling plausibility over the possibility of misunderstandings.

Naipaul seems to have been persuaded by a peculiarly American ability to create a familiarity between past and future that to a degree assuages even the darkest memories. But though that ability is a powerful fiction and Naipaul's perspective on it too uncritical, what he learned writing *A Turn in the South* stayed with him. The book's dedication to the memory of his father and its motto point to the intrinsic presence of the past, its combined inevitability and strangeness that both demands and challenges understanding. And there is a connection between an inherent plausibility of the stories he hears and retells here and the intricately choreographed fact-fiction combinations in *A Way in the World,* as well as the documentary strategies of the "manager" of others' narratives in *Beyond Belief.* Naipaul has exchanged coherence and completeness of knowledge accumulating from documents and interviews for a greater transparency of individual stories, be they factional or fictional, present or past. It is a transparency that will not diminish strangeness precisely because it seeks to preserve what their protagonists "felt," thereby subverting the often fictitious hindsight cohesion of historical agency, including his own.

A Way in the World has three chapters subtitled "An Unwritten Story." To the reader they may appear as "very dense, written stories," but they are "at once historical and invented," the "writer's fantasy" working within a "crust of fact."[14] However the author may wish to define his experimentation with representational conventions, there will be questions about his choices. Is an "imaginative reconstruction" essential in the case of recovering a "lost" history with large gaps of uncharted spatial and temporal territories? Is the documentary mode more appropriate for less remote, more fully recorded events? Naipaul insists that both approaches can yield "truths"—but truths about whom? For whom? Authorized by whom? The issue is not the fact but the manner of the writer's fantasy working within historical materials, and it will decide the reader's acceptance of the truthfulness of their representation, her willingness to trust it.

The first of the three "unwritten stories," "New Clothes" (chapter 3), is wedged between two autobiographical chapters and set in the present. Preceding the two historical chapters about Raleigh (chapter 6) and Miranda (chapter 8), it explicitly poses the questions of the narrator—which is crucial to understanding them—by means of inserting him into a literally unwritten, fictional story. The idea for it had come to Naipaul on his first trip to South America more than thirty years ago, and he now reconstructs the story in the process of inventing its most suitable narrator. He remembers traveling in Amerindian no-man's land on the frontiers of Venezuela, going upstream in a small boat through "tall, cool woodland," occasionally stopping at small settlements on the high river bank. Pale, dark-haired, the elusive Amerindians would appear momentarily, "holding themselves with an extraordinary stillness on their tree-shaded bank, and looking down without expression at the boat." The mystery of the people who returned his gaze without seeming to do so had stirred his imagination and stayed with him, but the story, like the people, always retreated. Everything he added to that mysterious moment of seeing and not seeing seemed to "falsify what I had felt as a traveller" (p. 46).

The archival research into the history of the area for a book project that was to become *The Loss of El Dorado* (1969) would confirm this perception, changing his sense of himself as a writer because he learned from the historical documents the difficulties of getting to their "truth." In sixteenth- and seventeenth-century records he read about the foundation of Spanish towns in the Amerindian wilderness, expeditions that mostly ended in "death or despair"; petitions to the king that were read, if at all, years later by an anonymous official and promptly forgotten, or took several more years to be acted on. All these one-sided attempts at communication appeared "curiously informal and fresh," the voices of "quarrelsome, self-righteous, stoical people" on the other side of the world clearly audible (p. 47).[15] The documents had preserved for him the strangeness of the past—its remoteness, its dangers, its overwhelming uncertainties. So did the accounts of the French, Dutch, and English adventurers, "interlopers" in that remote corner of the Spanish Empire, trading African slaves for salt or tobacco or setting up their own empires. Remembering what he had first glimpsed from a low-flying plane in late 1960—wild beaches hugely overgrown, "the vast half-drowned confusion of meandering rivers"—he wonders at the extraordinary daring and tenacity of all these people (p. 47). "New Clothes" narrates the taking shape of the story that had emerged from this experience, beginning with the question "Who is the narrator? What can he be made to be?" (p. 47). If he was made a writer and traveler, the story would have been true to the author's experience but it would not have fully integrated its origin: that mysterious moment of seemingly irreversible separation and strangeness. At issue is its imaginative accessibility; if Naipaul had felt its power then and remembered it for so many years, it still remained inarticulate because it was not fully his. He needed to imagine the threatening stillness of that moment, and for that he needed a narrator who had experienced its pure unpredictability and remembered what *he* had felt.

The narrator, then, would be traveling inland on the river on a political mission, looking for signs to orient himself, a man to whom "everything seen on the river has many meanings." His author imagines a revolutionary of the 1970s trying to enlist the help of Amerindians to overthrow the African government on the coast. Two centuries ago, African slaves were running away from Dutch and British slave plantations on the coast and hunted down for bounty by Amerindians. In the present tense of the story, the descendants of these slaves have taken over the power of the old colonial government and are rapidly modernizing where the Amerindians have stayed the same. The balance of power has shifted with the growing disparity from changes in cultural complexity. The British narrator sees this disparity differently than the Africans or the Amerindians, since he has his own cultural and political agenda, his own experiences, memories, ways of looking at the world. Moving along the river, he is moved by purpose; purpose and motion are central to finding one's way in the world. But if this is the story's motivation, there is also its elusive, mysterious, negative energy. Distant, still, expressionless on the bank of the river, the Amerindians are outside of this narrative. They have found what there was to find for them and perfected it to the point where change can signify only betrayal. It was this surreally distinct juxtaposition, the most potent allegory yet of the fearful uncertainties of contact between radically different cultures, that stayed with Naipaul as the unwritten story. If it is to be written, it has to preserve, like the old historical documents, the uncertainties and incompleteness of understanding strangers. Part of the narrator's mission is to find his way among the Amerindians; as he moves along, the difficulties of his enterprise make it less and less certain that he will ever be in control of his narrative. He remains his author's creature, the protagonist of the harsh futilities of contact with profoundly different people in a largely unreadable situation. For the sake of the story that needs to remain incomplete, "unwritten," the author can move into and out of the narrator's consciousness at will and narrate through him, withholding the illusion of control over his own story that comes with first-person narration.

The narrator's first destination where the river becomes unnavigable, stopping the motion, is a religious settlement with African followers on the coast and Amerindian converts in the interior. Run by whites, this church has some authority in the officially antiwhite African country because its international connections seem advantageous to the African political elite and their families. The settlement is infiltrated by the revolutionaries who fit in well with the believers since they share an ideology of "racial brotherhood," the just cause of the oppressed, and the need for redemption (pp. 51–52). At the same time, the narrator's sensory perceptions of the compound have a peculiarly vivid immediacy that might undermine such ideological certainties. The cabin he shares with four Indians smells of "treebark and sawn wood and dirt and oil and rotting leaves," which combined with the "salty" smell of burning wood outside makes a "very deep smell of stale tobacco" (p. 53). Presently, this smell—the smell of the food he is given, the river water, the forest—invades him, and so does the overwhelming singing noise of the forest at night (p. 54). Working for their "cause," the narrator remains a stranger to the Indians and they to him, but on some level their being together in this cabin and in the forest creates an eerily enveloping physical intimacy. Two Indian boys take him through dense, uncharted forest on a trail that he could never follow by himself to a place of which he knows only the name. He is reassured but also troubled by their knowing so well how to survive in the forest—the shelter they build with branches every night, the food and poisons they know where to find. There seems to be no outside; in the absence of comparison, of motion resulting in changes of space, there is nothing beyond the present moment, backward or forward, just blackness (p. 57).

The narrative moves rapidly, making the more intricately structured descriptions and reflections appear not fully integrated: a text not yet finished, a story in the process of being written, still open to changes, "unwritten."[16] Maybe, in the last "written" version, the narrator will be ready to tell his own story and, by signing his name to it, assume responsibility for its confusions and uncertainties, but there may not be such a version. At the end of the first day in the forest, after their separate meals, the sun swiftly dropping away, he asks his first question: "What does your father do?"—to be reprimanded by his author that this was a "foolish question" (p. 57). Yet the answer is important for his slowly developing insight into the strangeness of his mission: the father of one of the boys was killed by the kanaima, the spirit of death of the forests. Inhabiting the body of a living man, the kanaima looks like all the Indians and, a killer somewhere in the forest, kills them all. In this world without time and comparison, without differentiation, life is spent in fear of the kanaima. The narrator is now "filled with shame and grief" for these remote people and their perfect adaptation to the forest, fearful that they cannot be redeemed by the revolution because for them it could only mean diminishment or destruction (p. 58)—a fictional foreshadowing of the real-world revolutionary Shahbaz, recorded in *Beyond Belief.*

Walking through the forest day after day, sleeping under the shelter provided by his young guides, burdened by their expecting him to save them from the kanaima and his reliance on them for survival, the narrator begins to wonder about his mission. Finally they arrive at the village and the boys, offering their company as protection against the kanaima on the prowl, take him for a swim in the river where it is very deep and cool. The blackness of the water is so deep that it is colorless, nothing, giving him the eerie sensation of being out of his body, a moment of not-being, death. He begins to understand the implications of the boys' desire for protection. If, as the Amerindians believe, the kanaima loses its power when seen by a third person, this at the same time increases its power because it confirms the evidence of its presence seen by several people and then the fear to be, to think alone. For that moment of nothingness in the black water the narrator feels the power of the kanaima, as his author felt the inevitability of separateness looking at the Amerindians on the bank of the river who, looking at him, did not return his gaze. It will come back to him in dream images of the forest and the river, recalling his painful love for the people whom he cannot deliver from their constant fear of a death, both fated and arbitrary, and whose particular perfection he cannot protect. The political activist's conflict about a contact both futile and destructive may enable him to keep his own story incomplete—to alter his mission, yet in some form go on with it—but it may also do the opposite. Watching the narrator at that moment, his author decides that pain now "corrupts" everything he sees, and his doubts have turned into the decision to leave these people to their fate (p. 66).

Part of the narrative would be the narrator's planning his escape from the country and the movement. He knows now that he will not be able to help the people, and their expectations are a burden to him. But can he imagine how he, extraordinary in his strangeness, is seen by them? How, committed in every detail to a memory made much more powerful by the lack of writing, his appearance, his voice, his promises, and his betrayals will remain intensely vivid to them? Can the narrator who best suits this unwritten story be expected to imagine himself in the place of these strange people? Or does he suit this story precisely because, acting among incompletely understood strangers, his imagination will be in certain ways limited? Naipaul has long been intrigued by this question, in his political novels as well as his documentaries. He would come back to it in *Beyond Belief,* retelling the faithful, selfless, and stunningly thoughtless interventions of the former political activist Shahbaz, who as a young man carried revolution to Baluchi tribes. They too were extremely fragile in their remoteness and isolation, living in a precariously perfected balance with a harsh environment at the edge of the world, and promptly destroyed by his "gift" of political faith. Shahbaz, in Naipaul's recording of his story, never quite understood the disaster to which his actions had contributed because he had never tried to imagine what it was like for the tribes, what *they* had felt. He knew that they suffered greatly, that they were accustomed to it, and there he stopped.

The documentarist Naipaul would later find, and try to fill out, the blanks of Shahbaz's story, complicating it with his own kind of incomplete understanding. He would do so more tentatively than the author Naipaul, searching for the most suitable narrator of his invented story.

On the day of his arrival, the narrator is taken by his guides to the brother of the dead father, not the contact person he expected. The boys translate into their rudimentary English the story told the uncle by his wife's father, grandfather, or great-grandfather that people had come from the north to look for gold, the archetypical story about the perils of contact. The villagers set fires in the savannah that killed the intruders and then hid in the forest for a very long time. The uncle relates the past cataclysm to the future revolution, asking the narrator, "Are you sure you know what you are doing?" (p. 68). After returning from England where he had gone with an Englishman, their ancestor waited for the English to come and build the houses they had promised; they came several times by the savannah route but never fulfilled their promise. The boy believes the narrator to be his ancestor's English friend who will save them; his coming confirms the promise, as had the gift sent from England which the uncle shows to the narrator: "fawn-colored, perished, but recognizably a doublet of Tudor times, new clothes of three hundred and fifty years before, relic of an old betrayal" (p. 69).

Different perspectives come together in this concluding paragraph: the Indians' hopes for and fears of contact unchanged over centuries and the author's relating both the sameness and the changes. By authorial fiat, the narrator is confined to his unreflected historicity, his specific betrayal. He understands that the Indian, fearing another betrayal, has no sense of historical time, but he cannot fathom this lack in cultural terms.[17] The tribe's complete indifference to temporal distinctness is seen in the personal terms of his own brush with the kanaima, the non-experience of its black nothingness. For the sake of a better understanding of dramatically different cultural responses to temporality, the author has to admit the reader to the process of constructing the narrator's story. Commenting on his experiences as if they were available outside his narration, he shows how the narrator is literally the protagonist of his own story, fighting the author's battles with the distances of space and time.[18]

The (great-great-)grandfather, a figure from the remote past suspended as if outside time in the tribe's memory, might be the Amerindian who accompanies Raleigh in 1618 on his last trip back to England in chapter 6, "A Parcel of Papers, a Roll of Tobacco, a Tortoise: An Unwritten Story." *A Way in the World* was originally conceived as "a series of narrations" of repeated encounters: "People you knew in Trinidad as a child turn up in London and then you see them as big men in Africa, then you see them as criminals making money somewhere else. One had to find a form for that. I hope it will be very light."[19] The historical chapters defeated that hope because their "unwritten stories" deal with the largely unbridgeable strangeness of people who had to find their way in the world, like Columbus or Raleigh, in remote, very different times or in places that share this remoteness. Standing at the easternmost point of Trinidad named

"Galera" by Columbus, Naipaul realizes that he is looking at a "version" of what Columbus had first seen when he came here on his third voyage. The experience of visual continuity has an aspect of the "miraculous" though the rocks are "created out of those Columbus had seen, and wind-beaten trees like the ones before me, ten or twelve or fifteen cycles before" (p. 72). Seen from the land side, the worn-out remnants of the aboriginal island do not suggest the shape of a galley; but from the ocean side, Columbus's observational position from his own small galley, "that first, fifteenth-century Mediterranean view," might still be the same (p. 74). Naipaul's reversal of perspective here depends on his realization that he has been looking at a *version* of the aboriginal rock formation, a kind of continuity that is possible in natural but not in historical time. He can imaginatively reconstruct Columbus's view; he cannot "really" share it. Columbus's understanding of his world, his attempts at being at home in it, like Raleigh's, are irreversibly different; they belong to their cultural time that defines their sense of space. To speak about them historically means to acknowledge their strangeness in relation to their own world, whose strangeness to the historian is then compounded—hence the thought-image of "unwritten stories."

Naipaul saw Raleigh first as a character in a play or screenplay: he would be going back to England on the *Destiny* in 1618, sixty-four years old, ill for many months and soon to die a violent death. The South American river would be "grey when still, muddy when rippled. It is almost dawn. The sky is silver. The two-tiered set is in semi-gloom." The light "begins to show a thin and very old man in Jacobean undress in the captain's quarters" (p. 163). The screenplay, "an unrealizable impulse," remained unwritten, but the setting's interplay of images evokes the old Raleigh's peculiar dark strangeness composed of physical frailty, emotional remoteness, and ambiguous vulnerability. Imprisoned in the Tower for thirteen years, Raleigh has been released to go back to Guiana to find gold in El Dorado. If he does so without creating disturbances between the English and the Spanish, everything is forgiven; if not, he will be executed. He has not found gold, lost too many men, and now has to prepare himself for giving an account of what happened. As the ship's surgeon reminds him, his accounting in *The Discovery of the Large, Rich, and Beautiful Empire of Guiana* (1595) is fraught with deliberate factual inaccuracies, gaps, inadvertent falsehoods or distortions, and memory lapses. When he writes about the Gulf (Trinidad) side, everything is correctly recorded, every Indian tribe, every little Indian port. But on the Orinoco side, where the gold mines are expected to be, he writes "about a strange land of diamond mountains and meadows and deer and birds," as if he were a different author (pp. 174–75). Many brutal incidents were incorrectly recorded or left out, whereas the Spanish were recording every detail, getting it notarized, sending it to Spain on different ships in duplicates and triplicates. This way little information is lost and, as the surgeon observes dryly, the English can get both sides of the story (p. 178).

Naipaul allows Raleigh's story to be incomplete and gives the surgeon a good deal of historical information to better question him about "that version" of his adventures (p. 180). He could be Naipaul's alter ego, nagging his informant about inconsistencies in his story; but there is also the darker aspect of his urging Raleigh to come up with the more coherent account of his doings in the New World that will mean his death. Though he shows kindness to his patient, he also acts in the interest of the king, representing political changes concerning English-Spanish relations in the New World. Raleigh's book is for him a "deliberate mixture of old-fashioned fantasy and modern truth" (p. 175), difficult to disentangle and thus protecting him from having to admit that there was no El Dorado. Yet though he may be right in his judgment of Raleigh's accounting, he also may not understand his motivations, his acts, his sense of his world distilled from experience. Raleigh tries to defend himself against the surgeon's charges with memory stories of exquisite Spanish cruelty and treacherousness toward both the Indians and the English. But he is old and ill, and his stories, though vivid and well told, do not add up in the surgeon's view. How is it possible to know his or Raleigh's "true" feelings toward each other? Their author imagines the scene of their parting on the road to London where Raleigh will die, smiling at each other, the surgeon handing Raleigh a parcel with food and receiving from him the account he had urged him to write (p. 210). Is this the end of a successful political mission? Has Raleigh further incriminated himself? Does it matter? Has not his execution been unavoidable? Is he not old and ill enough to die? Could he be the narrator who best fits his unwritten story?

A Way in the World is about the difficulties of writing history because the past is the ultimate stranger, more unknown than the most distant, most remote physical phenomenon. Each of the nine chapters deals with this strangeness in its own way, but there is the connecting issue of incomplete historical knowledge established in the many cross-references between chapters. It results from the fluidity of historical time and memory and, if acknowledged, can be useful to historiography; it can also be politically exploited. Raleigh's "miraculously rescuing, and naming, the tortured and half-dead Amerindian chiefs of Cumucurapo who had been dispossessed by the Spaniards" is mentioned at the end of "Passenger: A Figure from the Thirties" (chapter 4) in the context of different historical views of the New World (p. 105). This reference serves to modify the surgeon's general skepticism regarding the reliability of Raleigh's memory in chapter 6: he may not have been, as he claimed, the "first man here ever to punish the Spaniards" for their cruelty, but the names of the tortured chiefs *were* listed in his book and corroborated by the duplicate of a Spanish report that had been retrieved from a captured Spanish ship (pp. 178–79). Both facts were known to the surgeon, whose judgment was most probably colored by his own political agenda.

Raleigh's strangeness—his obsession with finding gold, his peculiar unpredictability and ruthlessness, his "floating"—is less inaccessible to Naipaul, his late-twentieth-century observer and creator, than to the early-seventeenth-century English surgeon, much younger than Raleigh, more modern and rational. To an interviewer Naipaul pointed out the ironies of the concept of "safety" in *A Way in the World.*[20] At the end of Raleigh's unwritten story, the Amerindian who accompanied him on his last voyage and witnessed his death is asked about his fear of the ocean, now that he has crossed it twice and experienced that "the ships always knew where they were going." The fear, he admits, is gone; the Europeans, unlike the Indians, "know how to go where they are going" and "for them the world is a safer place" (p. 211).

On his return to New Granada, the Amerindian describes the English attack on the Spanish at San Thomé to a Spanish priest, a chronicler of the Spanish New World. The attack would be terrible news for Raleigh, but the Amerindian's account of it may be the most successful "unwritten" story. Prodded by the experienced chronicler's questions, he provides many factual details that can be added to the official narrative; but he also remembers events of great emotional intensity like the horrors of battle and Raleigh's execution that will subvert its coherence. The priest wants him to come up with a plausible "factual" explanation for Raleigh's behavior on his last journey (p. 197): why did he take on the Indian as his servant and companion, knowing nothing about him but that he carried a letter informing him of the attack at San Thomé and his son's death? The Indian only remembers Raleigh's gaze resting on him at their first encounter: he "wanted my company but he wanted me to stay a stranger" (p. 198). A witness to the killing of the Spanish governor, he was made to wear the dead man's "bloodstained clothes smelling of death and the forest, river water and dead old leaves" (p. 198)—the smell experienced 350 years later by the narrator of "New Clothes" in the impenetrable forest of Guyana. But on the *Destiny* the Indian was given clean clothes and allowed to find his way "back to the beginning" to heal himself from the "chain of death" caused by the Europeans (p. 211). Naipaul made the world safer for the Indian than for the Europeans, but his own sense of safety is another matter. It is out of his imaginative understanding of their fear, and then of his fear for himself, that he culls their haunting, doomed presence that allows them to retain their strangeness.

At the beginning of "Passenger: A Figure from the Thirties," Naipaul's perception that Columbus's first view of the island might still be retrievable is linked to his early feeling of the island's timelessness and emptiness. Its history "burned away" by the aggressive heat and light (p. 74), Trinidad "needed foreign witnesses" to become a distinct presence. Yet the travel books for tourists diminished the reality of the islanders' unwritten history: presented as timeless aborigines rather than people who had come to the island over time from different places and for different reasons, they seemed responsible for the island's "nullity" (p. 79). Naipaul is the first-person narrator in this "autobiographical" chapter, and, claiming for his story the more certain (if unacknowledged) authority of fiction, he gets it written and thus manages to deal with the "nullity" of the place that is at its center.

The story is about his relationship with a British writer, Foster Morris, whose book *The Shadowed Livery,* an account of the historical 1937 strike of Trinidad oilfield workers for higher wages, he had admired when he was young. Led by the charismatic black Barbadian-born Uriah Butler, the strike had attracted also agricultural laborers and public employees and aroused the interest of political radicals who, like the narrator of "New Clothes," wanted revolution.[21] But as in the slave days, it fizzled out and people quickly returned to normality. It seemed to the narrator then that Morris had seen and taken the people of Trinidad seriously, as nobody had before, "as though they were English people—as though they had that kind of social depth and solidity and rootedness." Yet he had also missed their "sense of the absurd, the idea of comedy" central to Trinidad culture that hid from them their "true position" of "floating" rather than orienting themselves in their world (p. 81). Morris's desire to applaud the strike had made it difficult for him to see Butler clearly: presented in the black and white terms of victimization and redemption, the man who had sparked a new kind of politics simply could not be that "crazed and uneducated African preacher" who had quickly become a joke (p. 82). Yet he was; he also had considerable political charisma and, for a short time, power. These contradictions were at the core of the comedy in Naipaul's early fiction, and Morris would again be an important influence. The story of the changing relationship with this man over time and in different places is a story about strangeness as a process: a gradual understanding of different ways of looking at the same events that would affect Naipaul's understanding of his own strangeness in relation to the island.

In the mid-fifties, working on a part-time job for the BBC and very much uncertain of his future as a writer, Naipaul meets Morris, praises *The Shadowed Livery,* and asks him to read a book manuscript he had just finished. Morris's answer is prompt, devastating, essential: scrap the book and learn more about the craft of writing. It sets him free to write competently about what he knows best and has so far suppressed: his inheritance of Trinidad's comedy, both from his "story-telling" Hindu family and the street life he observed in Port of Spain (p. 89). After the publication of *Miguel Street* (1959), they meet for lunch in a place whose brilliantly evoked gloom fits the awkwardness of their conversation. The narrator is surprised by Morris's calling the strike's leadership "a bunch of racial fanatics" and explaining that the domination by the Left of intellectual circles had prevented him from saying so at the time. There had also been the complications of the political situation: the different layers of racial tensions, the oilfields as a colony within a colony. Naipaul had not thought about these aspects of the strike, nor of the dangerous racist sentiments among the preacher's followers as Morris remembers them (pp. 95–96). At first impressed by Morris's shrewdness, the narrator "plays the newsreel back"[22] and begins to doubt Morris's truthfulness: he probably wanted to defend his Trinidad book and put the narrator in his place with overly elaborate praise for the use of comedy in his new book.[23] Yet these comments also reassured him about the more reflected, muted approach to comedy in the new book he was working on, *A House for Mr Biswas* (1961). Morris's later reaction to the young writer's highly successful book, however, will be strangely hostile; he may even have written an anonymous review that harshly judges the book's characters as "sunk in superstition, without an intellectual life, without nobility or potential." Naipaul finds in it the "abuse of colonial days, the opposite of the attitude (and originality) of *The Shadowed Livery*" (p. 100).

A House for Mr Biswas established Naipaul as a writer to be reckoned with. He had found his way—his place, his voice—in the British (Western) literary and intellectual world and could now venture out to chart the largely unknown territory of that "other half." He found a rapidly changing, increasingly unstable but also more connected world, whose "globalizing" energies created new cultural and political constellations much too large and complex for postcolonialist certainties. Much later, after many books that explored these changes, Naipaul invented the difficult, unattractive man and talented but unsuccessful writer Foster Morris to explore his own difficulties in trying to understand the strangeness of Trinidad from the vantage point of his position as a stranger in England. He gives Morris the history of having published, just after World War I and still at Oxford, a minor cult book and then having difficulties finding his "voice"— the identity as a writer he had hoped to establish in *The Shadowed Livery*. In this factual-fictional story about the development of his writing, the book would prove useful to the young colonial, Naipaul, who would find his "voice" in *A House for Mr Biswas*, but, importantly, this would be a temporary identity, to be amplified and complicated by many others. Morris's search, as Naipaul invented it, reminds the much older Naipaul of the cruise ships from Europe and the United States coming to Port of Spain when he was a child. Then these visits "from the great world," reported in the local paper the following day, were for him like something missed, "a blessing in the night." He remembers that he never thought then that his isolated colonial world was "at a great turn in history," and that one day he would be able to understand "what Foster Morris had come out of, and to follow him in all his uncertainties as a writer out to Trinidad" (pp. 104–105). But he did; and so as narrator of their relationship the author ends this chapter with an assessment of his character Morris's contribution to what was in certain aspects a shared enterprise: "incomplete but not bad," his book was original in the ways it presented "subject people as whole, belonging to themselves," a part of the "great chain of changing outside vision of that part of the world." It is a vision that begins with John Hawkins and Sir Walter Raleigh and "constantly changes" over four centuries. A "fair record of one side of a civilization" (p. 105), it is also inevitably provisional, replete with contradictions, obscurities, gaps, and ambiguities.

Morris was invented to show that he could have been the author of a book written out of his particular, by necessity partial understanding of a situation that seemed to him both familiar—a strike against capitalist exploiters—and strange—the physical and mental frenzy of the strikers whipped up by their seemingly half-crazed leader. But it took Naipaul's invention to write the story of the incompleteness of the book and the limitations of its author's understanding and then set it next to the "unwritten story" of the narrator-protagonist of "New Clothes." Does it help to know that Morris is a fictional and not a historical character when trying to navigate Naipaul's intriguing, unsettling mix of fiction and fact, stories and histories—a mix meant to underscore the simultaneity of different truths, the uncertainties of historical knowledge?[24] Or is it irrelevant? What matters is the reader's sense of the author's familiarity with Morris's Victorian habits and hesitations as well as his modern experiences, sensibilities, contradictions, and transformations; knows him so well in fact that Morris *might be* that writer whose book and writerly advice had influenced the development of his own writing. Up to a point, both authors share a culture that has supported writing about what is different and strange, including attempts to make sense of it in accepting the risk of not understanding it fully. The result is the convincing realism, the documentary dimension of this "pure" fiction, both for the reader who knows and who does not know that Morris's existence depended on Naipaul's imagining him in the literal sense of creating him and thereby controlling the written story about the significance of his influence.

There is a historical book that Naipaul might have transformed for his fictional story: *The Life of Captain Cipriani: An Account of British Government in the West Indies* by the Trinidad Marxist writer and revolutionary C. L. R. James.[25] A West Indian nationalist involved in the struggles of Afro-Caribbean industrial workers, Cipriani became a leader of the Trinidad Labor Party. It was his new politics during the thirties that had interested the young James, his ability to stir the political passions and release the energies of Trinidad's urban poor.[26] In the view of some historians, James's book was important to contemporary attempts at a better political understanding of the widespread labor riots in the late thirties.[27] But whether Naipaul "gave" his book to the fictional Morris or not, the historical James is very much present in "On the Run" (chapter 5), the fictional autobiographical story of his relations with Lebrun, a black West Indian communist revolutionary. Like Morris, Lebrun is the author of a book with Caribbean associations, this time on the subject of Spanish-American revolutionaries before Bolivar: Naipaul would have had in mind James's 1938 *The Black Jacobins: Toussaint L'Ouverture and the San Domingo Revolution*, about the only successful slave revolution, resulting in the 1804 foundation of the new state of Haiti.[28] Telling the dramatic story of the uprising, James argues the importance of the collective mobilization of slaves but also of the skilled and moderating leadership of Toussaint, whose early death in French captivity would be disastrous for the new state. There is a clear subtext proposing similar uprisings in Africa; in a 1975 interview, at the height of the political interest in Black Power, James stated that he had meant his book to demonstrate "how the African revolution would develop."[29] His consuming interest in African independence was connected with his hopes for the West Indies. In a 1963 appendix to *The Black Jacobins* he asserted that West Indians, in order to just think of being free and independent, had to first eradicate the "stigma that anything African was inherently inferior and degraded. The road to West Indian nationalism lay through Africa."[30] James's radical internationalism, intrinsic to both his pan-Africanism and Marxism, distinguished his book from other pan-African writings of the 1930s and 1940s: where they "were addressed to the colonial Powers," it was "a declaration of war for liberation."[31]

Naipaul was particularly interested in the activist dimension of James's political thought, first developed in London where he had arrived in 1932, leaving behind Trinidad's limitations. Many young and gifted Trinidad writers would follow his example over the next decades, though James was more politically focused and activist than most of them. He would always acknowledge that the "origins" of his work were in European literature, philosophy, and history, where he had learned his political analysis of "underdeveloped" countries: "I didn't *have* to be an exploited African."[32] At that gloomy London lunch in 1959, Morris would connect racist sentiments against whites during the Trinidad oilfield strike with a man called Lebrun, a communist talking revolution in fluent Spanish around Central America, the West Indies, and West Africa.[33] He was forgotten for a while but would soon be "discovered" as one of the "Pan-African" prophets of black revolution (pp. 95–96). Lebrun's character is a variation on the fallacies and futilities of ideological political activism for which the historical professional revolutionary James provided good examples, though he had had no contact with the fiery Uriah Butler and his equally aggressive and unstable entourage.[34] Mistrusted by established postcolonial rulers, Lebrun continued in his role of "impresario of revolution" without a popular base of his own, attaching himself to leaders more in touch with the "simple people who had given them power and with a simpler idea of that power" (p. 111).[35] His most loyal followers will be Western intellectual admirers, and in more than one sense he has remained "on the run" because he has never stopped to consider the consequences of his political activism for himself and others.

Yet the fictional Lebrun had also written perceptively on Naipaul's early fiction, emphasizing the subversiveness of their comedy.[36] In contrast to Morris's advice, which he would appreciate only later, Lebrun's interpretation had immediately been "a revelation" (pp. 113–14). The black West Indian came to the young writer's books with an intuitively accurate understanding of the characters' particular vulnerability that could not be matched by the English writer, despite his interest in the Trinidad labor unrest. Lebrun's kind of political literary criticism was also a new experience for Naipaul, whereas Morris's expert critique reflected familiar British high-cultural skills and sensibilities. Still, in retrospect the latter had been more helpful for the development of his writing because it had "in fact" freed him to find his own uses of the comical and his own solutions to the "problems of voice and tone and naturalness" (p. 114); like James, Naipaul locates the "origins," the achievement of his writing, in European high culture.[37]

In his relationship with Lebrun, more so than with Morris, Naipaul himself becomes a fictional character: Lebrun introduces him to the radical chic of affluent, white intellectuals in New York who adore the black ideologue's mellifluous disquisitions about black slavery in the Caribbean, which will inevitably create its own special revolution (p. 126). Lebrun presents his "political resolution" as a "re-interpretation of Marx, with special reference to the struggles of non-European peoples in the twentieth century," especially in the Caribbean. In this scenario the historical relevance of figures like Gandhi and Nehru for Asia will be radically diminished, and the meeting of an Indian delegate with Lenin in 1920 will be one of the "crucial events of the century" (pp. 120–21). As he did with Morris's gloomy lunch, Naipaul describes in loving detail the dinner at which Lebrun's eclectically Marxian theories are eagerly discussed: the expensive wines, the choice food, the seductions of abundance. Generous, hospitable, enviably comfortable in their impeccably tasteful environment— something that Naipaul has always taken note of, admired, enjoyed, and here invented from memory—they have invited him to shed his racial or cultural burdens and "be part of their brotherhood" (p. 127). They know all about these burdens because they have made themselves at home in the world with the help of Lebrun's abstracting political rhetoric: the "struggles" with which he regales them are fictitious because they are Lebrun's invention, not because Lebrun is Naipaul's invention. Would Lebrun's patrons ever be able to acknowledge that his information was wrong, that "the special revolution" he had promised for the Caribbean would never happen (p. 129)? His particular blend of anti-imperialism prevented him from seeing that the politics of the islands had never really changed. The leaders who had come to power at the end of the colonial period stayed in power because their local, racial politics were successful: "each man embodying in his territory the idea of black redemption. In the almost mystical relationship between these very local men and their followers there was no room for Lebrun" (p. 129). Drawing on the historical political activist James, Lebrun's creator had given him an idea of revolution too abstract and undifferentiating to work in Africa or anywhere else: a "revolutionary without a revolution."

Yet he also gave him a "political resolution" that despite its shortcomings "enabled him, not to embrace the period of slavery, but to acknowledge it without pain, and, presenting it in his own way, to make a claim for its universality, and even its precedence" (p. 127). Lebrun finds a way to deal with his past that Naipaul knew from his own experience to be workable, if not easy. With "shame, grief, sympathy, admiration, recognizing something of myself in this struggle," Naipaul understands, by making it a part of his fictional character Lebrun, James's need for a political belief system; but it never was his need. Like the fictional Morris, the fictional Lebrun is useful to clarify the younger Naipaul's developing sense of himself as a writer because it distinguishes him so clearly from them. At the time he had strong feelings of physical and social "incompleteness" but his "yearnings" were for "my own earned security, a wish for my writing gift to last and grow, a dream of working at yet unknown books, accumulations of fruitful days, achievement. These yearnings could be assuaged only in the self I knew" (p. 128)—whatever its limitations and obscurities.

When Naipaul finally read Lebrun's first book in a London library, he was amazed how vividly it spoke to him and how similar the course of Lebrun's life was to that of the Spanish-American revolutionaries he was writing about, es-

pecially Miranda. Instead of liberating Venezuela, Miranda had created or trig-
gered anarchy and was finally destroyed by petty colonial irrationalities and intrigues. Naipaul reconstructs the lostness, strangeness, and diminishment of the
failed revolutionary's last years in the "unwritten story" of his being moored in
the "Gulf of Desolation," no longer able to find his way in the world. Lebrun,
too, at the very end of his life, turns against his revolutionary principles by celebrating an ideal Africa cleansed of tyrannical regimes, murderous tribal wars,
and collapsed economies. James's uncritical view of Ghana's Nkrumah, the
folk hero–turned-dictator who fell from power in 1966, led him to disregard
the extraordinary economic mismanagement and dangerous dynamics of one-
party rule and to concentrate instead on certain personality flaws (vanity, paranoia) of his friend. If he offered any criticism of the leader of the People's
Convention Party, it never pointed directly to Nkrumah's corruption and his
share in allowing the rapidly growing, highly problematic influence in Africa of
multinational concerns and superpowers. The third wave of pan-Africanism
was over when James's study *Nkrumah and the Ghana Revolution* came out in
1977. A review in the *Times Literary Supplement* sharply criticized the book
for undoing the "sentimental imperialist myth of African development only
to replace it with a sentimental Pan-African myth about Nkrumah as Lenin,
Gandhi, and Toussaint L'Ouverture all rolled into one."[38]

Like James's, Lebrun's Africa has finally become a utopian fantasy offering
racial redemption by way of radical exclusion (pp. 135–36). Lebrun's attempts
at dealing with the past so that he might be more at home in the world have not
worked; like Miranda's, his failure has had consequences for other people, but
he is never held accountable for the murderous acts of African rulers encouraged by him—echoes of *Guerrillas* and *A Bend in the River*. Now very old and
famous among postcolonialist critics and journalists who have no sense of his,
of colonial history, he has become, like James in some circles, a suprahistorical
legend that they promote "with self-conscious virtue." Naipaul also points out
that supporting a cause that had long since been won and risking nothing, they
are in no position to assess a man who was born into a world much more difficult and complex than theirs. For him the life of the black West Indian "whose
intellectual growth had at every stage been accompanied by a growing rawness
of sensibility, and whose political resolutions, expressing the wish not to go
mad, had been in the nature of spiritual struggles, occurring in the depth of his
being" (pp. 160–61). Lebrun may have misled many people and willfully simplified many issues; he was not trivial. Creating him, Naipaul could see in him
aspects of his own—and his father's—difficulties, but also differences of generation, temperament, and talent. When he drew on the work of the historical
black political activist James for the character of Lebrun, whom he "used" to
reflect on his own work, he partially obscured historical "truth" for the sake of
partial historical clarification.[39]

Naipaul's insistence on the difficulties of writing history, the stories of historical acts, actors, and events that often have to be told in their incomplete

state, "unwritten," comes out of his understanding of the limitations of historical imagination: the past as the multitude of people who lived, felt, and thought
before us has been largely inaccessible to the observer in the present, especially
if they lived in remote pasts or in remote places. This makes all the more important the achievements of modern historiography indispensable to finding
one's way in a world ever more expanding and changing. The core of historiography is the ethos of factual accuracy because it arises from sharing experiences
and information with others and thereby subjecting it to others' critical inquiry
and provisional judgment. Facts are not found "out there" but indeed "made"
(*factum*) in the mind, and in that sense they are like myths, stories. But there is
the fundamental difference that facts are subjected to a critical process of establishing their validity, and that process has to follow the modern standards of
an informed trust in evidence. The processual nature of trusting evidence calls
for the argument of plausibility rather than truth: at this particular time, in this
particular place, to these particular observers certain facts seem more plausible,
certain kinds of evidence more trustworthy than others. We trust in historical
evidence precisely because it is tentative and temporary. When we try to negotiate our understanding of the past, we refer to the partial, limited, relational
authority of a multivocal critical discourse of historiography. Moreover, since
facts are made in the mind and their trustworthiness depends on the shared
effort of constructing evidence, they can also be unmade. In the documentary
discourse of historical inquiry, facts can be and often are revised, evidence re-
argued, the fluidity of memory and identity acknowledged and explored—
hence Naipaul's "redundancies" and recurrences, his revisiting events in the past
and revising his earlier views of them.

This combination of the acknowledged uncertainty of historical knowledge
and straining for instances of getting closer to a historical "truth," however provisionally, underlies Naipaul's desire to write what in his own terms of historical
understanding has not, could not yet have been written because of the difficulties of recording. It goes against a current intellectual reluctance to engage critically with the cognitive and emotional distances and differences created by the
passage of time. In a sense, temporal discrimination is the only remaining ideologically founded and protected discrimination in Western culture. It seems that
the more we open ourselves to cultural pluralism, the more restricted our historical imagination has become where it concerns the particularities of the past,
beyond the generalizing, abstracting scenarios of colonizer and colonized, victimizer and victim, exploiter and exploited. Yet in order to understand the concrete conflicts underlying these scenarios, we have to understand, by imagining
them, the particularities of their histories.

Naipaul's work has been shaped by this challenge. In a review of *The Enigma
of Arrival*, Bernard Levin described the author as an inquiline, an animal that
lives in the nest or abode of another species; it was a reference to the stranger's
in-between status that Naipaul thought fit very well his position as a writer, in
this as in his other works.[40] It seems especially appropriate for his intriguingly
mixed fictional-factual search for *A Way in the World*. This in-between status,

expressed in an increasingly expansive narrative that overflows the borders of "genre," is emblematic for the modern responsibility to know more about our world, the desire to understand and document as much as possible of its baffling diversity and relentless temporality. Moving between different civilizations in the second half of the twentieth century, Naipaul has been a contemporary to modernity in a curiously and instructively literal sense: someone moved to go on redefining himself as a writer by charting changing worlds, an enterprise that, as he learned, cannot but include the strangest of all of them, the past. Its strangeness, its strangers have changed under his attentive and imaginative regard; they have become, if not more familiar, more transparent: more clearly our responsibility.

Notes

Introduction

1. *A Voyage Round the World,* in *Georg Forsters Werke: Sämtliche Schriften, Tage-buecher, Briefe,* ed. Gerhard Steiner (Berlin: Akademie-Verlag, 1958 ff. *AA*), *AA* vol. 1, p. 13.

2. See Forster's 1778 "Antwort an die Göttingischen Rezensenten," arguing against the "unfair prejudice" that all virtue is European and all savages are morally inferior (*AA* 4, pp. 49–60); his almost Darwinian "Zu einer künftigen Geschichte der Menschheit" (*AA* 8, pp. 185–93); and his sharply critical review of the racist writings of the Göttingen philosophy professor Christoph Meiners (*AA* 11, pp. 236–52).

1. Understanding Strangers

1. V. S. Naipaul, *Finding the Center: Two Narratives* (New York: Knopf, 1984); V. S. Naipaul, *The Enigma of Arrival: A Novel in Five Sections* (New York: Knopf, 1987); V. S. Naipaul, *A Way in the World: A Novel* (New York: Knopf, 1994); V. S. Naipaul, *Beyond Belief: Islamic Excursions among the Converted Peoples* (New York: Random House, 1998).

2. Naipaul, "Prologue to an Autobiography," in *Finding the Center,* vii (author's foreword), p. 41; see also ibid., pp. 38–40: the description of a young girl in the "desolation" of the Caribbean coast as "unneeded, one of the many thousands littered in peasants' yards and cast out into the wilderness of Venezuela."

3. For details see Naipaul, "Prologue," in *Finding the Center,* pp. 12–20. See Jan Hamilton, "Without a Place: V. S. Naipaul in Conversation with Jan Hamilton/1971," in *Conversations with V. S. Naipaul,* ed. Feroza Jussawalla (Jackson: University Press of Mississippi, 1997), pp. 14–21.

4. Cathleen Medwick, "Life, Literature, and Politics: An Interview with V. S. Naipaul/ 1981," in *Conversations,* pp. 57–62, 59.

5. Ibid., p. 58.

6. See here also his harsh prediction "Africa has no future" in an interview about *A Bend in the River* (New York: Knopf, 1979): Elizabeth Hardwick, "Meeting V. S. Naipaul/ 1979," in *Conversations,* pp. 45–49, 49.

7. An instructive example is the conciliatory revisions in V. S. Naipaul, *India: A Million Mutinies Now* (New York: Viking, 1990). Timothy F. Weiss praises Naipaul for seeing "the country and its peoples through other's eyes as well as his own, and with a largeness of spirit absent in earlier accounts" (*On the Margins: The Art of Exile in V. S. Naipaul* [Amherst: University of Massachusetts Press, 1992], p. 129). But the selection of voices is Naipaul's, as it was in the earlier accounts; only his perspective is more optimistic.

8. Naipaul, "Prologue," in *Finding the Center,* pp. 26 and 71.

9. To his delight, one of his aunts whom he remembered as constantly screeching and bickering in the overcrowded family compound became a poised, elegant woman in Canada.

10. There is the counterexample of another cousin who "escaped" to Venezuela too

early to have learned enough from the clan, and, "in the emptiness of his Venezuela," turns to the rituals of religion for the general "consolation of hallowed ways" (p. 44). Visiting him, Naipaul is saddened by the desolation around and within the man but depicts pitilessly the illusionary, depleting nature of such consolation.

11. Edward Said, review of *Among the Believers: An Islamic Journey,* by V. S. Naipaul, *New Statesman,* 1981, quoted in Charles Michener, "The Dark Visions of V. S. Naipaul/ 1981," in *Conversations,* pp. 63–74, 63.

12. Edward Said's *Orientalism* (1978) is profoundly eclectic and ahistorical in its choice of materials, lack of distinction between high and popular culture, and lack of interest in the important question of different audiences (differences of period, class, and economic status). John M. MacKenzie rightly observes that Said failed "to recognize that the arts and dominant political ideologies tend to operate in counterpoint rather than conformity. It is from the arts that a counter-hegemonic discourse invariably emerges. It is often tentative and cannot be expected to leap totally out of its period. (Thus Said's disappointment that neither Conrad nor Forster is capable of a full premonition of decolonisation seems hopelessly anachronistic)" (*Orientalism: History, Theory and the Arts* [Manchester and New York: Manchester University Press, 1995], pp. xviii–xix, 1–19, 14).

13. Andrew Robinson, "Stranger in Fiction/1992," in *Conversations,* pp. 130–34, 133.

14. Andrew Robinson, "Going Back for a Turn in the East/1990," in *Conversations,* pp. 110–13, 111.

15. See the passage in the "Traveler's Prelude" to *An Area of Darkness,* the description of a lone cab driver too unaggressive to secure a fare and his horse late at night, a concise, quietly devastating study of frustration.

16. Paul Theroux, *The Great Railway Bazaar by Train through Asia* (Boston: Houghton Mifflin Company, 1975), p. 120.

17. Theroux quotes Naipaul (from "In the Middle of the Journey," *Illustrated Week of India,* 28 October 1962): "for all my life I have expected some recognition of my difference; and it is only in India that I have recognized how necessary this stimulus is to me. . . . To be a member of a minority community has always seemed to me attractive. To be one of four hundred and thirty-nine million Indians [now close to a billion] is terrifying" (Paul Theroux, *V. S. Naipaul: An Introduction to His Work* [New York: Africana, 1972], p. 117).

18. The physical aspect of strangeness has always been important to Naipaul. In his remarkably open interview with Michener, he reminisces about his lack of "personal beauty and charm" when he came to England as a young man, tense, apprehensive, asthmatic. The only thing he had was intelligence and the will to distinguish himself ("The Dark Visions of V. S. Naipaul," in *Conversations,* pp. 64 and 70).

19. Bharati Mukherjee and Robert Boyers, "A Conversation with V. S. Naipaul/1981," in *Conversations,* pp. 75–92, 92.

20. See, however, his recent strangely hostile remarks about his former friend and mentor in *Sir Vidia's Shadow: A Friendship across Five Continents* (Boston and New York: Houghton Mifflin Company, 1998); see also chapter 2 of this study.

21. Michener, "The Dark Visions of V. S. Naipaul," in *Conversations,* p. 70.

22. Medwick, "Life, Literature, and Politics," in *Conversations,* pp. 59 and 61. She sums up other critics' reservations.

23. Mukherjee and Boyers, "A Conversation with V. S. Naipaul," in *Conversations,* pp. 89–90.

24. Ibid., p. 91; Naipaul quotes himself from *The Middle Passage Impressions of Five*

Societies—British, French and Dutch—in the West Indies and South America (1962; reprint, New York: Vintage, 1981), p. 29.

25. Adrian Rowe-Evans, "V. S. Naipaul: A Transition Interview/1971," in *Conversations*, pp. 24–36, 27.

26. Stephen Schiff, "The Ultimate Exile/1994," in *Conversations*, pp. 135–53, 138.

27. Irving Howe, "A Dark Vision," *New York Times Book Review*, 13 May 1979, p. 1. Quoting from this review, Charles Michener emphasizes Howe's appreciation for Naipaul's honesty, not his reservations ("The Dark Visions of V. S. Naipaul," in *Conversations*, pp. 63–74, 63).

28. Medwick, "Life, Literature, and Politics," in *Conversations*, p. 61; she reports that Naipaul is himself "surprised" by the violence.

29. Andrew Robinson, "An Elusive Master: V. S. Naipaul Is Still Searching/1987," in *Conversations*, pp. 106–109, 108.

30. See Naipaul's remarks in Schiff, "The Ultimate Exile," in *Conversations*, p. 148.

31. Medwick, "Life, Literature, and Politics," in *Conversations*, p. 59.

32. Mukherjee and Boyers, "A Conversation with V. S. Naipaul," in *Conversations*, pp. 81–82.

33. Bernard Levin, "V. S. Naipaul: A Perpetual Voyager/1983," in *Conversations*, pp. 93–98, 98.

34. Naipaul, *Enigma of Arrival*, p. 12.

35. Mukherjee and Boyers, "A Conversation with V. S. Naipaul," in *Conversations*, p. 91.

36. Michener, "The Dark Visions of V. S. Naipaul," in *Conversations*, p. 65.

37. Hardwick, "Meeting V. S. Naipaul," in *Conversations*, p. 48.

38. Naipaul has often described how hard but also how essential it was for him to learn to write well as quickly as possible: interview with Schiff, "The Ultimate Exile," in *Conversations*, p. 153.

39. Michener, "The Dark Visions of V. S. Naipaul," in *Conversations*, p. 66.

40. Naipaul, "Prologue," in *Finding the Center*, p. 32.

41. Michener, "The Dark Visions of V. S. Naipaul," in *Conversations*, p. 66.

42. Note the titles of the interviews mentioned above. See also Naipaul to Robinson, "An Elusive Master," in *Conversations*, p. 109: he declared with uncharacteristic charity that "Americans are really very nice, very humane people. What a humane civilization and culture to have been created from a big melting pot." Asked whether he would like to live in the U.S., he said that it "would be nice to be in a place where nearly everyone you meet is a stranger. As one gets older one does feel more of a stranger here. But this is not a profound or settled attitude of mine."

43. Robert Boyer's assessment, stated in Scott Winokur, "The Unsparing Vision of V. S. Naipaul/1991," in *Conversations*, pp. 114–29, 128.

44. Medwick, "Life, Literature, and Politics," in *Conversations*, p. 60. Naipaul understands now that one "can't go around being too dramatic about being rootless" (ibid.). But he also takes care to have a well-ordered home to come back to. See here Linda Blanford, "Man in a Glass Box/1979," in *Conversations*, pp. 50–56, 55, an interview with Naipaul's long-suffering, all-supportive British wife Pat, a gentle, shadowy, prematurely silver-haired presence confiding that "Vidia hates messes."

45. Schiff, "The Ultimate Exile," in *Conversations*, p. 145: Naipaul has stated repeatedly the central importance to him of that security.

46. Ibid.

47. Medwick, "Life, Literature, and Politics," in *Conversations*, p. 60.

48. V. S. Naipaul, "What's Wrong with Being a Snob?" now in *Critical Perspectives on V. S. Naipaul,* ed. Robert D. Hammer (Washington, D.C.: Three Continents Press, 1977), pp. 34–38, 37.

49. Ibid., p. 37.

50. Michener, "The Dark Visions of V. S. Naipaul," in *Conversations,* p. 64.

51. The reality of the social experience in many postcolonial societies goes largely unrecognized in the global parochialism of much postcolonialist theory, despite some critical voices coming from feminist positions: see Sara Suleri, "Woman Skin Deep: Feminism and the Postcolonial Condition," *Critical Inquiry* 18 (Summer 1992): pp. 756–69, on the consequences for women of the "Hadd" (limit) category for punishment in the re-Islamized Pakistani criminal legal system. Regrettably, her critique of fellow postcolonialists for their lack of interest in the concretely dangerous aspects of the new traditionalisms still blames mainly U.S. intervention, not the "terrors of Islam" (p. 768). An analysis of interdependencies might be more helpful. See Naipaul to Robinson, "Stranger in Fiction," in *Conversations,* p. 131: having caused tribal warfare in Afghanistan by encouraging fundamentalists in their fight against the Soviet Union, the U.S. ought to admit that it "cracked these barbarians up to be freedom fighters" and feel responsible for the consequences.

52. See Mukherjee's critique of Naipaul's general lack of solidarity with and "compassion" for the people of places like Trinidad or Calcutta and his argument against "too many lovers of India loving them for their wretchedness and their misery and their slavery and their wish to keep others trapped" ("A Conversation with V. S. Naipaul," in *Conversations,* pp. 89–90).

53. Winokur, "The Unsparing Vision of V. S. Naipaul," in *Conversations,* p. 123.

54. Ibid., p. 122.

55. Derek Walcott, quoted in Winokur, "The Unsparing Vision of V. S. Naipaul," in *Conversations,* p. 121.

56. Quoted in ibid., p. 121.

57. Quoted in Winokur, ibid.; the last phrase is paraphrased by the interviewer.

58. Naipaul to Medwick, "Life, Literature, and Politics," in *Conversations,* p. 61.

59. Winokur, "The Unsparing Vision of V. S. Naipaul," in *Conversations,* p. 123.

60. He left his publisher when he found himself advertised as a "West Indian writer" (Schiff, "The Ultimate Exile," in *Conversations,* p. 139).

61. Boyers in Winokur, "The Unsparing Vision of V. S. Naipaul," in *Conversations,* p. 123.

62. It is from this experience rather than from a "Westernized" perspective that Naipaul has argued for English as the literary language of India.

63. Mukherjee and Boyers, "A Conversation with V. S. Naipaul," in *Conversations,* pp. 83–84.

64. Winokur, "The Unsparing Vision of V. S. Naipaul," in *Conversations,* pp. 119–20.

65. Schiff, "The Ultimate Exile," in *Conversations,* p. 138.

66. Ibid., p. 137.

67. Hass, quoted in Winokur, "The Unsparing Vision of V. S. Naipaul," in *Conversations,* p. 118.

68. Hass, quoted in ibid., p. 128.

69. For an approving collection of quotes see Rob Nixon, *London Calling V. S. Naipaul, Postcolonial Mandarin* (Oxford: Oxford University Press, 1992), pp. 4–5. Offering some interesting insights into the complexities of Naipaul's position, the study is marred by conceptual confusion and ideological rigidity. For the "authoritative" post-

colonialist position on Naipaul see Fawzia Mustafa, *V. S. Naipaul*, Cambridge Studies in African and Caribbean Literature (London and Cambridge: Cambridge University Press, 1995), pp. 1–29. Emphatic in her praise of Nixon's study (p. 23), Mustafa sorts out Naipaul criticism neatly and inexorably: only correctly postcolonialist readings need apply. Not unexpected but still amazing in its completeness and sameness is the incantation of "authorities" that support Mustafa's judgments, a list of names unfailingly repeated in every academic statement on the subject.

70. Mustafa, *V. S. Naipaul*, pp. 7, 9, 29.

71. Ibid., p. 7.

72. The subtitle in the British edition (London: Heinemann, 1994) is "A Sequence"; Knopf chose "Novel" for marketing reasons.

73. Mustafa, *V. S. Naipaul*, p. 18.

74. V. S. Naipaul, "Trinidad," in *The Middle Passage*, p. 68; Mustafa, *V. S. Naipaul*, p. 4.

75. Mustafa, *V. S. Naipaul*, p. 4.

76. Homi K. Bhabha, "Signs Taken for Wonders: Questions of Ambivalence and Authority under a Tree Outside Delhi, May 1817," in *"Race," Writing, and Difference*, ed. Henry Louis Gates Jr. (Chicago: University of Chicago Press, 1985), pp. 165–68; quoted in Mustafa, *V. S. Naipaul*, p. 4.

77. Mustafa, *V. S. Naipaul*, p. 5.

78. Ibid., pp. 5–6.

79. Ibid., pp. 6–7. Mustafa refers here to a study of "anxieties" typical of all Caribbean writers.

80. Informal polling on several university campuses yielded the information that English majors in the pre–Nobel Prize period never heard of Naipaul but had had the experience of "incomprehensible" lectures by Homi Bhabha and Gayatri Spivak.

81. Mustafa, *V. S. Naipaul*, pp. 6–7.

82. Ibid., p. 17. See here Homi K. Bhabha, "Of Mimicry and Man: The Ambivalence of Colonial Discourse" (1984), in *The Location of Culture* (New York and London: Routledge, 1994), pp. 85–92.

83. Naipaul, *Finding the Center*, p. 20.

84. Naipaul, "Conrad's Darkness," in *Critical Perspectives*, 54–65.

85. Mustafa, *V. S. Naipaul*, p. 28.

86. The Lacanian reading of Naipaul in Judith Levy, *V. S. Naipaul: Displacement and Autobiography* (New York and London: Garland, 1995), is too exclusively preoccupied with myths of origin and non-origin but is useful in its loose and fragmentary connecting them with questions of Naipaul's "postcolonial condition," since it does so without postcolonialist moralizing.

87. References to Said have assumed biblical authority in postcolonialist discourse, where dropping the correct authority at every turn of the argument nicely demonstrates the fundamentalist loyalties of the believer.

88. Mustafa, *V. S. Naipaul*, p. 27. "Bookishness" refers to Bhabha's argument about the "triumph of the colonialist moment," which is "the discovery of the book."

89. Ibid.

90. Ibid., p. 28.

91. See, however, the recent critical assessment of postcolonialist theorizing in Richard M. Eaton, "(Re)imag(in)ing Other^{2}ness: A Postmortem for the Postmodern in India," *Journal of World History* 11, no. 1 (2000): pp. 57–78.

92. Naipaul, "Conrad's Darkness," in *Critical Perspectives*, p. 59.

93. Mustafa, *V. S. Naipaul*, p. 3.

94. Quoted in Naipaul, "Conrad's Darkness," in *Critical Perspectives*, p. 56, from a preface written by Conrad for a collection of his stories.

95. Peter Hughes, *V. S. Naipaul* (London: Routledge, 1988), pp. 42 and 94, emphasizes rightly the great importance of Conrad to Naipaul, but the concept of "truth" with which he works here is too broad and too assertive, precisely because the issue is fiction, a fact that Naipaul is well aware of.

96. See Conrad's argument that precisely the extraordinary experience "laid me under the obligation of a more scrupulous fidelity to the truth of my own sensations. The problem was to make unfamiliar things credible. To do that I had to create for them, to reproduce for them, to envelop them in their proper atmosphere of actuality. This was the hardest task of all and the most important, in view of that conscientious rendering of truth in thought and fact which has been always my aim" (quoted in Naipaul, "Conrad's Darkness," in *Critical Perspectives*, p. 56).

97. Naipaul, "Conrad's Darkness," in *Critical Perspectives*, pp. 64–65.

2. Postcoloniality and Historicity

1. Paul Theroux, *Sir Vidia's Shadow: A Friendship across Five Continents* (Boston and New York: Houghton Mifflin Company, 1998); Derek Walcott, "The Garden Path: V. S. Naipaul," first published in *The New Republic*, 13 April 1987, now in *What the Twilight Says: Essays* (New York: Farrar, Straus and Giroux, 1998), pp. 121–33.

2. See Theroux, *Sir Vidia's Shadow*, chapter 19, "Exchanges."

3. Ibid., pp. 285–89.

4. In Walcott, *Twilight*, pp. 135–45, 141–42.

5. Ibid., all quotes pp. 126–28.

6. See here the even-handed account of Walcott's critical attitude toward Naipaul in Robert D. Hammer, *Derek Walcott* (New York: Twayne Publishers, 1993), pp. 159–60.

7. John Thieme, *Derek Walcott* (Manchester: Manchester University Press, 1999), pp. 152–53.

8. Walcott, "The Antilles: Fragments of Epic Memory" (1992), in *Twilight*, pp. 65–84.

9. Walcott mentions Naipaul's early work approvingly in his one-paragraph roll-call of fellow Caribbean writers in the Nobel address (p. 72): "the streets and yards that Naipaul commemorates, its lanes as short and brilliant as his sentences."

10. "For every poet there is always morning in the world. History a forgotten insomniac night; History and elemental awe are always our early beginning, because the fate of poetry is to fall in love with the world, in spite of History" (Walcott, "The Antilles," in *Twilight*, p. 79).

11. Walcott, "The Garden Path," in *Twilight*, p. 122.

12. Walcott, "The Antilles," in *Twilight*, p. 77.

13. Walcott, "The Garden Path," in *Twilight*, pp. 128–29. Walcott uses this accusation complete with references to Naipaul's admirers several times: Naipaul's "self-disfiguring sneer" at blacks "praised for its probity" (pp. 131–32).

14. Walcott, "The Garden Path," in *Twilight*, p. 129. These are accusations repeated in many variations in the chat rooms of South Asian postcolonialists or students interested in the topic: Naipaul encouraging English, being "contemptuous" of native languages. They misunderstand his concern about audiences.

15. V. S. Naipaul, *Finding the Center: Two Narratives* (New York: Knopf, 1984), p. x.

16. V. S. Naipaul, *The Enigma of Arrival: A Novel in Five Sections* (New York: Knopf, 1987), p. 12.

17. Theroux's recent harsh criticisms of Naipaul in *Sir Vidia's Shadow,* like many postcolonialist condemnations, impose on him an affirmation of ethnic and racial diversity for its own sake. This attitude is itself ethnocentric, since it does not allow Naipaul to set his own standards or to assert his own views as they have grown out of *his* experiences, which in most cases differ dramatically from theirs. Theroux differentiated more intelligently in his useful analysis of Naipaul's early texts: *V. S. Naipaul: An Introduction to His Work* (New York: Africana, 1972).

18. See Richard M. Eaton, "(Re)imag(in)ing Other^{2}ness: A Postmortem for the Postmodern in India," *Journal of World History* 11, no. 1 (2000): pp. 57–78, 57–58.

19. Ranajit Guha, ed., *Subaltern Studies One: Writings on South Asian History and Society* (Delhi: Oxford University Press, 1982), p. 7; Ranajit Guha, ed., *Subaltern Studies: Writings on South Asian History and Society Four* (Delhi: Oxford University Press, 1985).

20. Eaton, "Postmortem," p. 60.

21. In Guha, *Subaltern Studies Four,* p. 342. Those "positivist" historians interested in subalterns would of course have no way of recovering their consciousness, which is Spivak's signature feat: the deconstructing construction of the consciousness of its recovery—or, since we are just dealing with "discourse," recovery of its consciousness.

22. Ibid., p. 345.

23. Manifesto, in Guha, *Subaltern Studies One,* p. 7: "It is the study of this historic failure of the nation to come into its own, a failure due to the inadequacy of the bourgeoisie as well as the working class to lead it into a decisive victory over colonialism . . . which constitutes the central problematic of the historiography of colonial India."

24. Eaton, "Postmortem," p. 61.

25. See Nicholas Dirks, ed., *Colononialism and Culture* (Ann Arbor: University of Michigan Press, 1992), p. 14: "We kept trying to find new ways to rescue subaltern voices among the colonized, only to find that colonialism was about the history by which categories such as colonizer as well as the colonized, elite as well as subaltern, became established and deployed." Dirk concedes at some point in his introduction that colonialism was "neither monolithic nor unchanging through history. Any attempt to make a systematic statement about the colonial project runs the risk of denying the fundamental historicity of colonialism" (p. 7). But neither his nor his fellow postcolonialists' arguments in this volume reflect this caveat. See also the argument in Gauri Viswanathan, *Masks of Conquest: Literary Study and British Rule in India* (New York: Columbia University Press, 1989), that British colonial hegemony in India was mainly based on the teaching of English literature.

26. See Tapan Basu et al., *Khaki Shorts and Saffron Flags: A Critique of the Hindu Right* (New Delhi: Orient Longman, 1993), p. 5: "It may be observed that a notion of an all-powerful colonial discourse tends to cast Indians in the role of simple victims and exempts them from their own initiative or agency."

27. John M. MacKenzie, "Edward Said and the Historians," *Nineteenth Century Contexts* 18 (1994): "Above all, it is difficult for historians to find in all his work a single instance in which cultural artifacts are directly influenced by specific events or themselves have bearing on individual decision-making or developments in the European imperial relationship with particular territories, although such connections abound" (p. 20). See also Richard Price on the impact of postmodernist "theory" on the study of nineteenth-century England in "Historiography, Narrative, and the Nineteenth Century," *Journal of British Studies* 35 (1996): "If meaning is understood as a never-ending series of discursive codes, texts behind texts (raising the quest of infinite regress), and if relationships are essentially chaotic rather than structured, then the notion of change as

a historical process as opposed to a matter of continual, shifting indeterminacy is both moot and unimportant" (p. 238).

28. Kwame Anthony Appiah, *In My Father's House: Africa in the Philosophy of Culture* (New York: Oxford University Press, 1992), p. 149.

29. Eaton, "Postmortem," p. 68, rightly points out the "conservative" nature of these ideas. There are clear resonances in these self-stylizations of Toennies's originally "value free" distinction between "Gemeinschaft" and "Gesellschaft," which became a loaded dichotomy at the end of the nineteenth century, when the difficulties of modernity had become an issue, and intensified during the period between the two world wars: see my *Weimar Intellectuals and the Threat of Modernity* (Bloomington: Indiana University Press, 1988). Coming from authentically postcolonial intellectuals, these ideas found an easy acceptance at progressivist American universities. Anouar Majid, "Can the Postcolonial Critic Speak? Orientalism and the Rushdie Affair," *Cultural Critique* 32 (1995–96), laments about "Cultural imperialism" and the hard fate of Third World intellectuals in the West: "no radical or leftist Western scholar seems to measure accurately the degree of our alienation, to read the exotic presence of the Other in the Academy as a reminder of our vulnerabilities and organic uprootedness" (pp. 26–27). See, in contrast, Thomas Blom Hansen, "Inside the Romanticist Episteme," *Thesis Eleven* 48 (1997): "As the Western Other articulated through the colonial and post-colonial state is posited as alien, nonauthentic and outside the inside, the popular and subordinated becomes, by implication, both authentic and original" (p. 27).

30. See Eaton, "Postmortem," pp. 69–70.

31. See Gyan Prakash, "Postcolonial Criticism and Indian Historiography," *Social Text* 31–32 (1992): p. 17: "History and colonialism arose together in India. As India was introduced to history, it was also stripped of a meaningful past; it became a historyless society brought into the age of History."

32. Dirks, *Colonialism and Culture,* p. 3.

33. Ibid., pp. 3 and 8–9.

34. Ibid., pp. 9 and 7.

35. Eaton, "Postmortem," p. 71.

36. Ibid., pp. 74–78, offers two interesting sixteenth-century "antecedents of what has thus far passed for 'British colonial discourse,'" namely, discussions of connections between knowledge and power that Eaton reads as "a generic discourse of imperialism, quite independent of this or that ethnic identity or imperial tradition" (p. 75).

37. Ibid., p. 73.

38. See here also Dane Kennedy, "Imperial History and Post-colonial Theory," *Journal of Imperial and Commonwealth History* 24 (1996): pp. 355–56. Eaton agrees with Kennedy's critique of the tendency in literary studies of colonial encounters to focus too much on European rather than non-European writers and that, contrary to Said's opinion, Fanon and Yeats could not be fully representative of the experience of colonial rule.

3. Stories of Other Lives: Novels

1. V. S. Naipaul, *Between Father and Son: Family Letters,* ed. Gillon Aitken (New York: Knopf, 2000), p. 58 (27 January 1951); p. 198 (28 September 1952); pp. 262 and 264 (8 October 1953); p. 265 (10 October 1953).

2. Ibid., p. 260 (24 September 1953).

3. Ibid., pp. 280–81 (6 April 1955); p. 283 (8 December 1955); pp. 284–85 (10 February 1956). The last letter in the correspondence is to his mother (pp. 286–87 [20 June

1957]), with a long quote from a very positive review of the *Mystic Masseur,* news about interviews for jobs that he did not like and about his busy writing schedule.

4. On Naipaul's relations with his first wife, Patricia Hale, see Paul Theroux, *Sir Vidia's Shadow: A Friendship across Five Continents* (Boston and New York: Houghton Mifflin Company, 1998), chapter 17, "A Wedding Is a Happy Funeral." Theroux had befriended the shy woman who was completely devoted to Naipaul's work, and some of his observations here make good sense. See Naipaul's descriptions of her to his suspicious family: a fellow student, "not unintelligent, nor altogether unattractive," she "put up with all my moods—my coarseness, and my fits of anguish," "she is good, and simple. Perhaps a bit too idealistic, and this I find on occasion rather irritating," "she shares my literary tastes." There is much talk about his sister's attractiveness and liveliness in the letters and "Pat" remains a shadow. Both families had great reservations about mixed marriages (*Between Father and Son,* p. 195 [6 September 1952]; p. 197 [17 September 1952]).

5. Bharati Mukherjee and Robert Boyers, "A Conversation with V. S. Naipaul/1981," in *Conversations with V. S. Naipaul,* ed. Feroza Jussawalla (Jackson: University Press of Mississippi, 1997), pp. 75–92, 78. See also Theroux, *Sir Vidia's Shadow,* p. 326.

6. See Timothy F. Weiss, *On the Margins: The Art of Exile in V. S. Naipaul* (Amherst: University of Massachusetts Press, 1992), p. 47.

7. Ibid., p. 48.

8. V. S. Naipaul, "Prologue to an Autobiography," in *Finding the Center: Two Narratives* (New York: Knopf, 1984), p. 60.

9. In a letter from Oxford, 5 August 1953 Naipaul had complained to his father about his difficulties with dialogue in a story set in Trinidad: "The people at home are becoming more and more indistinct in my mind, and I wish I were more alive to their affairs and speech" (*Between Father and Son,* p. 242).

10. Scott Winokur, "The Unsparing Vision of V. S. Naipaul/1991," in *Conversations,* pp. 114–29, 116.

11. V. S. Naipaul, *A House for Mr Biswas* (New York: Penguin, 1981), pp. 13–14.

12. See Naipaul on his luck in writing Bogart's story, the most important character in *Miguel Street* (1959; Somerset Maugham Award): not knowing his full story he had been "free to simplify and work fast" ("Prologue," in *Finding the Center,* p. 34).

13. A large part of the correspondence between father and son is about the importance and the difficulties of writing, how to improve it, and where to find good models, receptive editors, decent pay to keep the writer going, and a typewriter of one's own. The suggestion made by a BBC editor to publish at the same time a book of the father's stories and of his own first attempt at a novel has Naipaul writing home excitedly: "So it appears that, with luck, Father and son will have first books out at almost the same time. I hope that one of us does strike the jackpot!" (*Between Father and Son,* p. 121 [20 September 1951]).

14. V. S. Naipaul, *Guerrillas* (New York: Knopf, 1976); *A Bend in the River* (New York: Knopf, 1979; reprint, New York: Vintage International, 1989); references are to the Vintage edition.

15. Weiss, *On the Margins,* p. 177. For a discussion of "In a Free State," see below, chapter 7, "Uncertain Histories."

16. See also his later account of the incident in V. S. Naipaul, *The Return of Eva Peron (with The Killings in Trinidad)* (London: André Deutsch, 1980).

17. "It was written with great excitement": Naipaul to Scott Winokur, "The Unsparing Vision of V. S. Naipaul," in *Conversations,* p. 128.

18. The image of Roche's molars, a somewhat overworked metaphor for cultural cor-

ruption, disease, and mortality, reappears throughout the novel, also at the moment of declaring his intention to leave, his ultimate failure (p. 132).

19. Some critics have seen Jimmy as too much of a caricature: Weiss, *On the Margins*, pp. 182–84. Naipaul is mainly interested in how Jimmy is seen by others, how their desires and fears reflect back on him, the political-psychological meanings of the characters' interplay.

20. It is also a highly constructed narrative with carefully orchestrated recurrent perceptions that foreshadow and interpret events: Jane's recurring and also remembered perception of Roche's "tall, blackened molars" (first pp. 6–7) in different but related contexts of individual and cultural precariousness, the city becoming stranger, more dangerous for people who have come from elsewhere (pp. 44, 48, 121, 132, 184). Another recurring issue is Roche's refugee status on the island pointed out by Jane (pp. 46, 48, 219) and in his radio interview with Meredith Herbert (pp. 199–200). The reader has to be attentive not only to the different views of different characters but also note how they are presented and where and how misunderstanding occurs. Doubling and repetition of scenes is used to emphasize double or multiple perspectives on the same situation which then no longer is the same: pp. 14 and 153; 10–11 and 243–44; 7 and 44; 85, 238; 112 and 164.

21. This fond portrait using speech patterns recalls Naipaul's early fiction.

22. See the most recent version of the once politically involved intellectual whose activist "persona" changes with changing times and politics: Lebrun in *A Way in the World*, chapter 5, "On the Run."

23. Roche uses this explanation repeatedly: pp. 23–24, 219.

24. Peter Hughes, *V. S. Naipaul* (London: Routledge, 1988), p. 77, points out rightly Naipaul's critique of "brutal and parasitic superstition based on a bogus interpretation of history" as the focus of the novel.

25. Theroux, *Sir Vidia's Shadow*, pp. 106, 159. In the summer of 2000, Indians were threatened with expulsion from Fiji.

26. Weiss, *On the Margins*, pp. 184–93, blames Salim for his dark, pessimistic vision of Africa, fixation on decay, and cynical view of innate African problems, as if he were talking about Naipaul. Salim is a fictional character who is given certain experiences which produce a certain vision. Weiss's assumption of an "anxiety" of the "exile" (Naipaul? Salim?) is not useful.

4. Stories of Other Lives: *Among the Believers*

1. Stephen Schiff, "The Ultimate Exile/1994," in *Conversations with V. S. Naipaul*, ed. Feroza Jussawalla (Jackson: University Press of Mississippi, 1997), pp. 135–53, 149; Scott Winokur, "The Unsparing Vision of V. S. Naipaul/1991," in ibid., pp. 114–29, 128.

2. National Public Radio, *Lehrer Newshour*, 3 March 2000.

3. Salman Rushdie, *Boersenblatt des deutschen Buchhandels*, 7 December 1984. See, however, Rushdie's more realistic assessment of India's difficulties in his "Letter from India: A Dream of Glorious Return," *New Yorker*, 19/26 June 2000, pp. 94–112.

4. Charles Michener, "The Dark Visions of V. S. Naipaul/1981," in *Conversations*, pp. 63–74, 71. Naipaul also addressed here certain objections to his approach in *Among the Believers: An Islamic Journey* (London: André Deutsch, 1981): he did not rely on Islamic literature because he thought it on the whole too "missionary," and he spoke only to few Islamic leaders because their views are known.

5. Aamer Hussein, "Delivering the Truth: An Interview with V. S. Naipaul/1994," in *Conversations*, pp. 154–61, 158.

6. Schiff, "The Ultimate Exile," in *Conversations,* p. 144.

7. Ibid., p. 145; Naipaul remembers his childhood technique of saying his sentences very fast, repeating them silently to himself to check them. See also Robert Boyers in Bharati Mukherjee and Robert Boyers, "A Conversation with V. S. Naipaul/1981," in *Conversations,* pp. 75–92, 87–88, about the extraordinarily real "sense of menace" created in the "naturalistic fiction" of *In a Free State* through the "negation" of concreteness and the ordinary, and Naipaul's insistence that it was achieved through the hard work of getting the dialogue right to reflect the relations between people, the political history of the land. See Theroux on his insatiable curiosity, shooting questions at him in Africa, wanting to know everything: Paul Theroux, *Sir Vidia's Shadow: A Friendship across Five Continents* (Boston and New York: Houghton Mifflin Company, 1998), pp. 27–34.

8. Winokur, "The Unsparing Vision of V. S. Naipaul," in *Conversations,* p. 128.

9. Andrew Robinson, "An Elusive Master: V. S. Naipaul Is Still Searching/1987," in *Conversations,* pp. 106–109, 108.

10. On the "life altering" use of a small electronic typewriter for typing up his notes after the interviews for the more recent documentaries, *A Turn in South, India: A Thousand Mutinies Now,* and *Beyond Belief,* see Andrew Robinson, "Going Back for a Turn in the East/1990," in *Conversations,* pp. 110–13, 110.

11. Winokur, "The Unsparing Vision of V. S. Naipaul," in *Conversations,* p. 129.

12. On the issue of documentary objectivity see my *Critical Realism: History, Photography, and the Work of Siegfried Kracauer* (Baltimore: Johns Hopkins University Press, 1994), chapter 2, "Representation as Reclamation," and chapter 3, "The Shapes of Objectivity."

13. Paul Theroux, *V. S. Naipaul: An Introduction to His Work* (New York: Africana, 1972), p. 15.

14. Michener, "The Dark Visions of V. S. Naipaul," in *Conversations,* p. 73.

15. V. S. Naipaul, "Prologue to an Autobiography," in *Finding the Center: Two Narratives* (New York: Knopf, 1984), pp. 38–41.

16. Boyers and Mukherjee, "A Conversation with V. S. Naipaul," in *Conversations,* p. 80.

17. Naipaul's states that "the finest English minds can be found outside the purely literary enterprise" in the interview with Boyers and Mukherjee ("A Conversation with V. S. Naipaul," in *Conversations,* p. 84), qualifying Mukherjee's assertion that Darwin and Freud are great literature, not "theory." He has been most attracted to well articulated intelligence.

18. Naipaul states these fears to Schiff in "The Ultimate Exile," in *Conversations,* p. 153.

19. On the occasion of *A Way in the World:* Schiff, "The Ultimate Exile," in *Conversations,* p. 148.

20. V. S. Naipaul, *Among the Believers,* p. 12. The philosopher and physician Avicenna (980–1037) was born close to Bukhara (Uzbekistan), during the Middle Ages an important Islamic cultural and trade center, much older than the Islamic conquest with which its history began.

21. Theroux, *Sir Vidia's Shadow,* p. 346.

22. The upper-class pilgrim traffic in the holy city of Mashhad, the sacred soil of Arabia in cake form as a present for the Hyatt hotel guest, the largely secular Iranian family taking their meals in a restaurant during Ramadan where they are nominally travelers and therefore are allowed to eat during that period; the suspension of whipping in public for lighter transgressions because the person executing the punishment would

meet with social disapproval. Contemporary Judaism has very similar examples of such "negotiation" of belief.

23. Muslim groups had taken over the offices of Behzad's leftist paper and the headquarters of his communist organization, injuring and arresting the staff, destroying documents, and seizing all the arms.

24. See the description of the puzzling composite identity of an Indian from Trinidad claiming to be from Venezuela whom Naipaul meets on a flight to Venezuela from Trinidad (*A Way in the World: A Novel [1994; reprint,* New York: Viking, 1995], pp. 224–43).

25. From a mixed background of Shia and orthodox Sunni, she was introduced to the heretic messianic sect by her dead husband and embraced it fervently. These entangled beliefs and loyalties are sorted out patiently because they make the individual believer's faith concrete, if not therefore less strange.

26. "The many rules of Islam were not handed down for the sake of God, Mr Salahuddin said; they were for the good of people. Freedom came with obedience; the rules made men free" (p. 109).

27. Salim in the chaotic situation of *A Bend in the River* has something fatherly about him; he too likes solid, responsible people, and it comforts him to thinks of the men in his family as responsible, experienced merchants.

28. See the description of the plump, pious son of a wealthy industrialist just come back from a pilgrimage in style to Mecca dressed in Arab costume, the cream-colored gown and the headgear with black bands. It was his second pilgrimage, and during Ramadan, Naipaul was told by the proud parents, the child "had kept the rest of them up to the mark by his extraordinary strictness" (p. 124). The boy is an intolerable brat and also implicitly dangerous: he exhibits the evil energy of children, the terrible simplicity of the faith in totalitarian regimes.

29. Schoolbooks assert that Pakistan, in stark contrast to India with its rule of caste, is a modern democratic country, referring to the "fact" that there was no slavery under Islamic rule (p. 135). In historical actuality slaves continued to be sent from Sind to the Caliph, and the Islamization of Pakistan has not helped democratization. Naipaul's concern here is with history as the cultural foundation for modern societies.

30. See my "Political Correctness in the 1780s: Kant, Herder, Forster and the Knowledge of Diversity," in *Herder Yearbook 1994* (Stuttgart: Metzler, 1994), pp. 51–76, specifically pp. 56–58.

5. Stories of Other Lives: *Beyond Belief* (Iran)

1. V. S. Naipaul, *Beyond Belief: Islamic Excursions among the Converted Peoples* (New York: Random House, 1998), part 1, "Indonesia: The Flight of the N-250"; part 2, "Iran: The Justice of Ali"; part 3, "Pakistan: Dropping off the Map"; part 4, "Malaysian Postscript: Raising the Coconut Shell."

2. Notably *A Turn in the South* (New York: Knopf, 1989) and *India: A Million Mutinies Now* (New York: Viking, 1990). On his "discovery" of a specific emotional dimension of the documentary in *A Turn in the South,* see chapter 8 of this study.

3. Naipaul quotes the English translation of a description of a shadow play, in which many untranslatable words had to be left in Javanese because there were no comparable objects and events in English (European) culture.

4. V. S. Naipaul, "The Man of the Moment," in *Beyond Belief,* pp. 1–20. The report was also published in the *New York Review of Books,* 11 June 1998. At the height of the financial crisis, in May 1998, Margaret Scott interviewed Imaduddin, and her findings

supported Naipaul's earlier analysis of the situation (published as "Epilogue" to Naipaul's text in the same issue of *New York Review of Books*).

5. Suharto's piety, as Naipaul pointed out in 1995, is recent and political, developed under the political influence of Habibie, who, replacing Suharto, remained indebted to him and therefore could not really put him on trial as the revolutionary students demanded. But *their* politics, as Scott argued, were themselves partly shaped by fundamentalist Islam.

6. See Denis Diderot's "Supplement to Bougainville's 'Voyage,'" in *Rameau's Nephew and Other Works* (New York: Macmillan, 1986), and my "Political Correctness in the 1780s: Kant, Herder, Forster, and the Knowledge of Diversity," in *Herder Yearbook 1994* (Stuttgart: Metzler, 1994), pp. 51–76, on late-eighteenth-century debates about the meanings of race and racism.

7. Paul Theroux, *Sir Vidia's Shadow: A Friendship across Five Continents* (Boston and New York: Houghton Mifflin Company, 1998), pp. 106, 105.

8. Jeffrey Goldberg, "The Education of a Holy Warrior," *New York Times Sunday Magazine*, 25 June 2000 (references by page number to printout of online text). See also the informative accounts of fundamentalist Islam in Ahmed Rashid, *Taliban: Militant Islam, Oil, and Fundamentalism in Central Asia* (New Haven: Yale University Press, 2000), and *Jihad: The Rise of Militant Islam in Central Asia* (New Haven: Yale University Press, 2002).

9. This fact is important for Naipaul's hypothesis concerning a "convert's" altered worldview because "his holy places are in Arab lands; his sacred language is Arabic. His idea of history alters. He rejects his own; he becomes, whether he likes it or not, a part of the Arab story. The convert has to turn away from everything that is his" ("Prologue, *Beyond Belief,* p. xi). See also below, note 18.

10. Goldberg, "Education," pp. 6–8. Reminding the students that fighting the Northern Alliance meant killing other Muslims, Goldberg was told that they were "crazy" Muslims and that the parents supported the jihad.

11. See the interview "Inside the Jihad" with the Pakistani journalist Ahmed Rashid in the *Atlantic Monthly* (19 September 2000) about Omar's extremist position within the Taliban leadership and the general Taliban preference for the simplicity of an archaic religious absolutism like that in seventh-century Arabia.

12. Hence the title of that part and the analysis of the danger signs in *Beyond Belief,* part 3, "Pakistan."

13. Goldberg, "Education," pp. 8–10; the term "jihad" against India is used in the news, and the war dead are referred to as having "embraced shahadat," martyrdom. The jihad in Kashmir, seen in the past in the secular terms of Pakistan's national struggle against neocolonialist India, was an important unifying political tool for Musharraf before the events of September 11th and his reason for allowing jihadi groups to train in Pakistan. The dynamics of the Pakistan-India struggle over Kashmir, not unlike the Israel-Palestine conflict, have led to the predictable, deadly politics of terrorism: see the reports in the *New York Times* on events in the summer of 2000: "Truce Talks Lift Gloom in Troubled Kashmir" and "Massacres in Kashmir Effort to Sabotage Peace Initiative" (3 August 2000); "Kashmir Blast Kills 10 and Wounds 24, Hizbul Strikes Again" (10 August 2000). See also Isabel Hilton, "Letter from Kashmir," *New Yorker,* 11 March 2002, pp. 64–75, asking, "what do its people want?"

14. See Shahbaz's story in chapter 6 of this study.

15. Abbas seeks out war veterans, encouraging them to write about their experiences at the front, especially their friendships, and for this purpose tells them a story about two

friends at the front. Mehrdad explains his difficulties with the translation: "'it's an Iranian story, because of the affection between the two soldiers. It is hard to tell a friend about his failings. The story was about a friend who found a good way of doing that'"—the last sentence of Naipaul's retelling the story of that Iranian generation (p. 199).

16. See Simon Schama, *Citizens: A Chronicle of the French Revolution* (New York: Vintage, 1989).

17. On the similarities between Haq's Deobandism, a strongly anticolonialist position dating back to the days of the British Raj, and bin Laden's strict antimodernist Wahhabism, see Goldberg, "Education," p. 3.

18. There are different ways of going back to the past in search of a better present: Rashid's tracing in *Jihad* the genesis of recently evolving Islamic radicalism in central Asia is in a certain sense complementary to Naipaul's attempts at understanding militant Islam in *Beyond Belief*. Distinguishing between the "inward-seeking" "greater jihad" as struggle for self-improvement and the "lesser jihad" as struggle for political and social betterment, Rashid sees the global terrorism of jihadi movements like the Taliban, Al Qaeda, or the Islamic Movement of Uzbekistan as a "perversion of jihad" (p. 2). The Afghan experience of the cold war gave rise to the Taliban, "a model of extremist fundamentalism unknown in the Muslim world," who then trained Islamic militants from all over the region to spread their radicalism. But the single most important reason for the rise of militant Islam in central Asia since independence has been, in his view, the "shortsighted hard-line" policies of central Asia's rulers, continuing in the Soviet tradition of repressing religion and ethnic identity (pp. 7–10). They have denied their people a "chance to create a modern identity from their own past. By refusing to accommodate traditional Islam, democracy, and interethnic harmony, the central Asian governments have fueled the fires of extremism (p. 11). Yet there might be some lingering doubts about the viability of identity politics drawing on a symbiosis of religion and ethnicity: what do concepts like "modern identity" or "democracy" mean under these circumstances? Naipaul would agree with Rashid that central Asia's current "cultural vacuum" cannot be "filled with imitations of Western culture" (p. 11), but there *are* the real promises and problems of globalization.

6. Stories of Other Lives: *Beyond Belief* (Pakistan)

1. V. S. Naipaul, *Beyond Belief: Islamic Excursions among the Converted Peoples* (New York: Random House, 1998), p. 234.

2. See the review of *Beyond Belief* in Ian Buruma, "In the Empire of Islam," *New York Review of Books*, 16 July 1998. Buruma sees Naipaul's aversion to Pakistani Islam as "Hindu rage" against Muslims, though he himself admits that Pakistan has maneuvered itself into an impossible situation, largely with the help of re-Islamization. He also points out parallels between radical Islam and communism but not the much clearer connection to fascism.

3. In his introduction to part 3, "Pakistan Dropping off the Map," Naipaul links the different development of Hindus and Muslims in India during and after British rule with the relatively short period of Muslim power in India, pointing out that there had "never been anything like an overall or settled [Muslim] conquest, as in Iran." The British period, lasting between 200 and 100 years, depending on the area, means for him Hindu regeneration: Hindus, especially in Bengal, "welcomed" British institutions of higher learning; Muslims, "wounded by their loss of power and out of old religious scruples,

stood aside. It was the beginning of the intellectual distance between the two communities" (p. 247).

4. See Richard M. Eaton, *The Rise of Islam and the Bengal Frontier, 1204–1760* (Berkeley: University of California Press, 1993); Partha Chatterjee, *The Nation and Its Fragments: Colonial and Post Colonial Histories* (Princeton: Princeton University Press, 1993); Ashis Nandy, *The Intimate Enemy: Loss and Recovery of Self under Colonialism* (Delhi: Oxford University Press, 1983); Guha Ranajit, ed., *Subaltern Studies One: Writings on South Asian History and Society* (Delhi: Oxford University Press, 1994). For a brief, clear introductory overview of South Asian civilizations, see Karen Isaksen Leonard, *The South Asian Americans* (Westport, Conn.: Greenwood Press, 1997), 1–34.

5. See my *Visible Spaces: Hannah Arendt and the German-Jewish Experience* (Baltimore: Johns Hopkins University Press, 1990), chapter 3, "The Silence of Exile: Arendt's Critique of Political Zionism."

6. The large numbers of refugees fleeing war-torn Afghanistan, one of the many tragedies of the cold war, were a serious burden on Pakistan, to which the influx of drugs and weapons brought in by Afghans added considerably. One has to look critically at both the U.S. support and the regime that used it.

7. See here Theodore Herzl's novel *Altneuland* (Tel Aviv, 1902), the story of a paternalistic Zionist utopia with strongly theocratic aspects.

8. See Israel's argument against the right of return of Palestinian refugees as diluting the "purity" of the Jewish state.

9. Mohammed Iqbal, quoted in Naipaul, *Beyond Belief*, p. 251.

10. See the disregard for historical monuments under the Soviet regime, for example, in the former German Democratic Republic, where political Marxism had acquired distinctly religious overtones. The criminal responsibility of capitalist air raids for the large number of ruins and the country's poverty served to explain the complete neglect of sacral architecture in the postwar period. The ruling utopianist ideology made Moscow the holy place of communism and Russian the mandatory holy language. However, the redeeming dictatorship of the proletariat is the last stage of the collective progress of eschatological history, not the personal history-transcending salvation promised by Islam.

11. Clothes can be an individual's expression of self-worth, and the traditional clothes imposed by re-Islamization have also changed self-perception. See the story of the Pakistani journalist Nusrat, whom Naipaul had first met in 1979, during the reign of the "Islamizing terror" of General Zia. A devout Muslim, he had tried to accommodate the new fundamentalism but failed and left journalism. Life in Karachi with its fervent re-Islamization and bloody ethnic infighting proved difficult, and when Naipaul saw him again sixteen years later he was prematurely aged, his frailty emphasized by his short, thin white hair and loose cotton tunic. In the past he had liked to wear well-cut tweed jackets during the pleasant Karachi winter, suggesting a sense of substance important to him—and to Naipaul (p. 350).

12. One of the most haunting instances of the troubling revolutionary abstractionism is Shahbaz's response to the fate of a Christian Pakistani from Karachi, a dark, very thin, "emotional" Marxist with a loud laugh who had been close to him. Betrayed to the Pakistani army, interrogated and tortured for many weeks, he would finally be thrown out of a helicopter. Shahbaz was more "tormented" by not knowing when he was killed than by the horror of his death and never contacted his family afterward (p. 282).

13. See the ironies in Shahbaz's conclusion: the liberation war of 1971, caused by neglect of the densely populated, poorer eastern part of Pakistan while the western part was reaping the benefits of Pakistan's alignment with the U.S., resulted in a secular,

democratic, socialist constitution of the new People's Republic that should have been attractive to young revolutionaries like Shahbaz fighting Western capitalism: Bangladesh should be seen as saved, not lost. Its enduring poverty destabilized the young country to the point of accepting military rule, Muslim identity politics, and a capitalist system. Yet in the nineties, when Shahbaz laments its loss, Bangladesh, though still dependent on foreign aid, has a better educational infrastructure and public health system than the former West Pakistan, and the status of women is higher.

14. Narrative strategies intrinsic to fiction are becoming more common in documentary discourse, allowing the author an increasingly visible presence within the text. See Louis Menand's argument in "Beat the Devil," *New York Review of Books,* 22 October 1998, pp. 27–30, noting Norman Mailer's narrative presence in his "documentary" texts, whereas "objective" journalism would demand an (at least apparent) absence of the author from the text. Naipaul's concern has been *gradations* of absence and presence: the different degrees and shapes of objectivity depending on the kind of recording and reporting.

15. V. S. Naipaul, "Reading and Writing" (1), *New York Review of Books,* 18 February 1999, pp. 13–18; "The Writer and India" (2), ibid., 4 March 1999, pp. 12–16.

16. In Conrad's fiction, the climate and flora were familiar, if not the characters; more difficult was identification with writers like Huxley and Maugham, who looked at the world through their own acculturated perspective.

17. Naipaul mentions here also William Howard Russell's reporting on the Indian Mutiny for the *London Times* (1858–59): he saw the land from Calcutta to the Punjab "in old ruin, with the half-starved ('hollow-thighed') common people, blindly going about their menial work, serving the British as they had served every previous ruler" (2, p. 12).

18. The context of Naipaul's argument here is that a culture without an articulated history and knowledge of personal ancestry does not fit the genre of the novel best served by the great nineteenth-century European writers in response to the dynamics and sensibilities of industrialization and its consequences for cultural modernity. The Indian novelist R. K. Narayan, writing in English about Indian life, was a rare model for father and son because he seemed to be writing "from within his culture," "without English social associations" (2, p. 12). But writing about people in a small town in south India, "small people, big talk, small doings" (not unlike Naipaul's early novels), he isolates his characters from history and therefore simplifies their simplicity to the point of abstraction. The characters seem to have been "breathed into being"; worshipping in their ancient temples, they do not have "the confidence of those ancient builders; they themselves can build nothing that will last" (2, p. 14).

7. Uncertain Histories: *Finding the Center* and *Enigma*

1. V. S. Naipaul, "Sitor: Reconstructing the Past," in *Among the Believers: An Islamic Journey* (London: André Deutsch, 1981), pp. 286–96, 286.

2. V. S. Naipaul, "Prologue to an Autobiography," in *Finding the Center: Two Narratives* (New York: Knopf, 1984), p. vii (author's foreword).

3. In the preface to his *A Voyage Round the World in His Britannic Majesty's Sloop Resolution* (1777), Forster presented his travelogue as a "philosophical recital of facts," a "narrative" of new materials organized according to Enlightenment values, notably an active interest in and tolerance for human diversity. This diversity, he wrote, was in itself newsworthy; but he had also brought to it the effort of connecting, comparing,

and distinguishing (in *Georg Forsters Werke: Sämtliche Schriften, Tagebuecher, Briefe*, ed. Gerhard Steiner [Berlin: Akademie-Verlag, 1958], vol. 1, pp. 9–17).

4. Travel has enabled him to be "content to be myself, to be what I had always been, a looker. And I learned to look in my own way" (Naipaul, "Prologue," in *Finding the Center*, p. x). In the view of Timothy F. Weiss (*On the Margins: The Art of Exile in V. S. Naipaul* [Amherst: University of Massachusetts Press, 1992], p. 163), the traveler Naipaul is "always standing on the fault line of his split as exile" (p. 163). Naipaul's documentarist narratives reflect his own experiences but existential "exile" is not one of them.

5. David Spurr, *The Rhetoric of Empire: Colonial Discourse in Journalism, Travel Writing, and Imperial Administration* (Durham, N.C.: Duke University Press, 1993), p. 19.

6. Kwame Anthony Appiah, *In My Father's House: Africa in the Philosophy of Culture* (New York: Oxford University Press, 1992). Appiah, a professor of African-American studies at elite U.S. universities, has retained his optimism in this respect: see his "Race, Culture, Identity: Misunderstood Connections," in *Color Conscious: The Political Morality of Race*, by K. Anthony Appiah and Amy Gutman (Princeton: Princeton University Press, 1996), pp. 30–105. In conclusion he invokes the "fruitful imaginative work of constructing collective identities for a democratic nation," building on "identities . . . [that] will have to recognize *both* the centrality of difference within human identity *and* the fundamental moral unity of humanity" (p. 105)—a nice sentiment but hardly realistic in view of current polarizing politics of identity.

7. See here the story of a publisher of African journals and books on a business trip in the Ivory Coast, an attractive man in his thirties, "bright and good-humored and open." To Naipaul's dismay, he blames the great difficulties of Ghana (where his Barbardian father had worked as a British-trained physician and he had grown up) not on the racialist-socialist ideology of its megalomaniacal ruler, Nkrumah, but on the fact that his continental African vision was so much ahead of its time. In this young professional's view, Nkrumah "had done more than anyone for the dignity of black men all over the world" (115–17). See the discussion of the character of Lebrun in *A Way in the World*, chapter 8 of this study.

8. This reversal of power is a common theme in the fairy tales of many civilizations, including Europe's.

9. Amer Hussein, "Delivering the Truth: An Interview with V. S. Naipaul/1994," in *Conversations with V. S. Naipaul*, ed. Feroza Jussawalla (Jackson: University Press of Mississippi, 1997), p. 154–61, 158.

10. Alastair Niven, "V. S. Naipaul Talks to Alastair Niven/1995," in *Conversations*, pp. 162–65, 163: "The world has changed and I am aware more and more that I have lived in this last half of the century when one has been adult and active through the most prodigious change. I am very glad I had the courage to follow difficult instincts about the truth and was therefore able to capture something of the changes in the world, the changes in empire, the changes in the colonised, the changes in countries like India, which from being colonised have developed some new sense of the idea of renewal. These things seem to me immensely important."

11. Hussein, in *Conversations*, p. 158.

12. See Niven, in *Conversations*, p. 163.

13. V. S. Naipaul, *The Enigma of Arrival: A Novel in Five Sections* (New York: Viking, 1987), p. 11.

14. Niven, in *Conversations*, p. 163.

15. Schiff, "The Ultimate Exile," in *Conversations*, p. 147.

16. He notably left out encounters with the experience of racial difference. See the description of selecting "material" from his experiences on the boat from New York, going to England for the first time, for one of his earliest stories, "Gala Night." Despite the old familiarity of the topic of race, it was "too close to my disturbance, my vulnerability, the separation of my two selves. That was not the kind of personality, the writer wished to assume; that was not the material he dealt in." There is also the experience of sharing his cabin with a black American in whom he saw "aspects of myself" which he could not acknowledge: "But, with my Asiatic background, I resisted the comparison; and I was traveling to be a writer." Facing "the other thing" was too frightening; it was "to be diminished as man and writer" (*Enigma*, pp. 114–17).

17. See Bharati Mukherjee and Robert Boyers, "A Conversation with V. S. Naipaul/ 1981," in *Conversations*, pp. 75–92, 87–88. Boyers stylizes and abstracts the "sense of menace" too much. Naipaul insists repeatedly on the importance of getting the details right to create that enveloping menace: the characters' language and history and the African landscape.

18. See Keith B. Richburg, *Out of America: A Black Man Confronts Africa* (New York: Basic Books, 1997), an admirably realistic account of Richburg's experiences as a black American journalist in Kenya.

19. Naipaul has alienated many Western critics enamored of a safely abstracting "Other" with his combined insecurities about his (concrete) place in the world and belief in the significance of his work.

8. Uncertain Histories: *A Way in the World*

1. Peter Hughes, *V. S. Naipaul* (London and New York: Routledge, 1988), p. 19.

2. See Bharati Mukherjee and Robert Boyers, "A Conversation with V. S. Naipaul/ 1981," in *Conversations with V. S. Naipaul,* ed. Feroza Jussawalla (Jackson: University Press of Mississippi, 1997), pp. 75–92, 78. It did matter; particularly in that respect Theroux's and Walcott's oddly uninhibited attacks on the person and the writing of the older Naipaul are as puzzling as they are instructive.

3. Hughes, *V. S. Naipaul,* p. 21.

4. Naipaul points out in "On Being a Writer" how the nineteenth-century English writers who now give him the "most 'novelistic' pleasure" by creating richly realized life-worlds in their literary or journalistic essays—Richard Jefferies, William Hazlitt, Charles Lamb, William Cobbett—would not have been thought of as novelists in their own time. All of them, "novelistic as they are in the pleasures they offer, found their own forms" (*New York Review of Books,* 23 April 1987, p. 7).

5. In 1971 he explained to an interviewer that his trip to India had made him much more "interested in the way different cultures have different ways of seeing. Columbus, a medieval man, voyaging in a miraculous world, which causes him no surprise, Isaac Newton living in both worlds. Gandhi coming to England and leaving not a word of description, remembering only that when he arrived at Southampton, he was dressed in white" (Jan Hamilton, "Without a Place: V. S. Naipaul in Conversation with Jan Hamilton/1971," in *Conversations,* pp. 14–21, 19).

6. V. S. Naipaul, *The Enigma of Arrival: A Novel in Five Sections* (New York: Viking, 1987), p. 144. This is how Naipaul describes his work with the sources he found in the London archives while researching the history of Trinidad.

7. Aamer Hussein, "Delivering the Truth: An Interview with V. S. Naipaul/1994," in *Conversations,* pp. 154–61, 158.

8. V. S. Naipaul, *A Way in the World: A Novel* (New York: Knopf, 1994), p. 3.

9. Hussein, "Delivering the Truth," in *Conversations*, p. 155. Naipaul states here that the true novelists today, in the sense of the great realistic novels of the nineteenth century, among whom he counts a writer like Proust, are writers of popular novels: "the blockbuster—with its elements of the joke, and personal display, not unsophisticated— shows how the form has developed, and it has changed the attitude to fiction" (p. 155).

10. Naipaul has shown little interest in the many different ways in which the Western "literary novel" has responded to the experience of an expanding modern world, for instance Robert Musil's essayistic *The Man without Qualities* written in the twenties and thirties in response to a world changed by World War I. Combining elaborate fictional constructs with subtle and incisive cultural critique and unusual familiarity with scientific thought, this "novel" addressed twentieth-century modernity in ways which are still uniquely illuminating a half-century later. It is intriguing to speculate what Naipaul would make of this text.

11. Hussein, "Delivering the Truth," in *Conversations*, p. 157. "Imperial" is a term he rarely uses; he mentions here Joyce and Virginia Woolf.

12. Ibid., pp. 157–58. V. S. Naipaul, *A Turn in the South* (New York: Knopf, 1989). This "discovery" also attaches to *India: A Million Mutinies Now* (New York: Viking, 1990), a book that has often been seen as too positive, too mellow.

13. Naipaul, *A Turn in the South*, p. 268.

14. Naipaul to Hussein, "Delivering the Truth," in *Conversations*, p. 157.

15. The papers of the South American Miranda seemed to him "still warm with the life of the man" (p. 351), just as he had written them, the last volumes published in Havana in 1950 for the bicentenary of his birth, without professional editing or commentary.

16. This kind of narration is also true for the Raleigh and Miranda chapters that combine different modes of communication—interrogation, dialogues, letters, journal entries—and preserve contradictions and gaps. Remarking on the factual and fictional "denseness" of these stories that in his view contradict the attribute "unwritten," the interviewer Hussein did not react to the deliberately "open," processual quality of Naipaul's narration of these stories.

17. When the uncle asked whether it was true that the "captain of the country" at the time his grandfather came back from England was a woman, he says "yes," thinking he meant Victoria (p. 68).

18. This could be also be done by constructing a frame around his story which would enable him to comment on it. This was a solution often used in German mid-nineteenth-century realistic historical fiction concerned specifically with temporal perspective in reaction to the invention of photography.

19. Andrew Robinson, "Stranger in Fiction/1992," in *Conversations*, pp. 130–34, 133.

20. See Naipaul to Hussein, "Delivering the Truth," in *Conversations*, p. 160. He points out that one of the ironical themes of the story is also that the enemy becomes the man one loves: nothing simple in the colonizer/colonized relation. In answer to the question of cultural loss/borrowing/replacement he explains that history is an "interplay of various peoples, and it's gone on forever" and that he "can think of no culture that's been left to itself." To think that borrowing began only with the European expansion is "a very simple view" (p. 161). See here the arguments made by Alexander von Humboldt in *Kosmos: Entwurf einer physischen Weltbeschreibung* 1 (Stuttgart and Tübingen: Cottascher Verlag, 1847).

21. See Kent Worcester, *C. L. R. James: A Political Biography* (Albany: State University of New York Press, 1996), pp. 21–26.

22. This is Naipaul's expression for the "memory drill" he "instinctively" practices after every meeting in the attempt to remember "words, gestures and expressions in correct sequence," to really understand what the other person said—something he practiced already as a child to get to the truth of things in a situation of conflicting stories (pp. 96–97).

23. "You have written a very funny book. What I like about it is that I can look through its surface and see some of the things I saw all those years ago. You know the way you can train yourself to see through the surface of a trout stream, the sky, the clouds, the reflections" (p. 97).

24. Many readers, myself included at the first reading, thought Morris real and tried to look up his book.

25. C. L. R. James, *The Life of Captain Cipriani: An Account of British Government in the West Indies* (Nelson, Lancs: n.p., 1932), excerpted in Paget Henry and Paul Buhle, eds., *C. L. R. James' Caribbean* (Durham, N.C.: Duke University Press, 1992), pp. 269–70.

26. Worcester, *C. L. R. James,* p. 22.

27. Robert Hill, "In England, 1932–38," in *C. L. R. James: His Life and Work,* ed. Paul Buhle (London: Allison and Busby, 1986), p. 64.

28. C. L. R. James, *The Black Jacobins: Toussaint L'Ouverture and the San Domingo Revolution* (London: Secker and Warburg, 1938).

29. C. L. R. James, interview by Alan MacKenzie, October 1975, quoted in Worcester, *C. L. R. James,* p. 36.

30. Quoted in ibid.

31. Cedric J. Robinson, *Black Marxism: The Making of the Black Radical Tradition* (London: Zed Press, 1983), p. 384. See here also Worcester, *C. L. R. James,* pp. 37–40, on the book's goal "to demonstrate the applicability and Marxist analysis to social change in what later became known as the Third World." On the influence of *The Black Jacobins,* see *C. L. R. James: His Intellectual Legacies,* ed. Seldwyn R. Cudjoe and William E. Cain (Amherst: University of Massachusetts Press, 1995), pp. 79–211 (part 3, "*The Black Jacobins:* An Assessment").

32. C. L. R. James, "Discovering Literature in Trinidad: The 1930s" (1969), in *Spheres of Existence* (Westport, Conn.: Lawrence Hill, 1980), pp. 237–44, 237.

33. Naipaul makes Lebrun more orthodoxly communist; see, however, James's critique of the Soviet Union in *World Revolution, 1917–1936: The Rise and Fall of the Communist International* (London: Secker and Warburg, 1937) and his political utopianism in the 1948 *Notes on Dialectics: Hegel, Marx, Lenin* (Westport, Conn.: Lawrence Hill, 1980).

34. Worcester thinks "On the Run" a "painful dissection of the C. L. R. James story," containing many similarities between Lebrun and James "too striking to be overlooked." Lebrun's "political mischief" in West Africa seems to him a "slam at James' politics," but he likes Naipaul's witty observations of the older regal revolutionary among his reverent disciples in London and New York, where James lived from 1938 to 1953 (pp. 173–74).

35. This may be a reference to James's conclusions in *Notes on Dialectics* and perhaps *Facing Reality* (Detroit: Bewick Editions, 1958), a study based on the Hungarian Revolution of 1956, the historically determined "withering away of the party" and the "*disappearance of the state*" (*Notes,* pp. 175–76) enabling the unmediated rule of the proletariat, a utopian grassroots democracy understandably loved by the kinder sort of communist intellectual but not a concrete political option in Naipaul's view. For a brief and useful analysis of James's political belief system, see Martin Glaberman, "The Marxism of C. L. R. James," in *Intellectual Legacies,* pp. 304–13.

36. James's early novel *Minty Alley,* written in Trinidad during the summer of 1928 and published in London by Secker and Warburg in 1936, portrayed the poor black residents of Trinidad's barrack yards not so much in political but social-psychological terms: individuals concerned with class differences, poverty, violence, and sexuality. It was one of the first indigenous novels of the West Indies, and Worcester finds "traces of the earlier generation's modernist and cautiously experimental influence" on later writers, including the early Naipaul (Worcester, *C. L. R. James,* pp. 20–21).

37. Naipaul reviewed James's 1963 *Beyond a Boundary,* an autobiographical exploration of the larger cultural and political meanings of cricket. James quoted from a letter from Naipaul: "I have only read half of the book so far but I want to let you know at once I am extremely glad because it lets these English people know who and what we West Indians are" ("Discovering Literature," in *Spheres,* p. 243). In "A Tribute to C. L. R. James" for the *Washington Post,* Derek Walcott praises the "grace of his English" that he finds in "the syntactical balance of James' sentences. The only writer who comes immediately to mind who has done this is V. S. Naipaul" (in *Intellectual Legacies,* pp. 34–48, 35). Walcott praises Naipaul's review of *Beyond a Boundary* (p. 36)—fittingly, since the mediating grace of the team sport cricket is central to the book's argument.

38. C. L. R. James, *Nkrumah and the Ghana Revolution* (Westport, Conn.: Lawrence Hill and Company, 1977); quoted in Worcester, *C. L. R. James,* p. 198.

39. In Worcester's view Naipaul did not understand James's achievement and character; he is especially disturbed by Lebrun's "raw sensibility" and underlying lack of balance, where James had a "cool maturity that expressed itself primarily through irony and measured historical observation"; a "proud and dignified rhetorician" (*C. L. R. James,* p. 175). Judging from some of James's later texts, Naipaul had reasons not to see him that way. Worcester's portrait of the old James is too smoothly reconciling: see here other portraits like Anna Grimshaw's in her "C. L. R. James, 1901–1989: A Personal Memoir," in *Intellectual Legacies,* 23–33. Above all, Lebrun is not James; if Naipaul "used" James for his own purposes, the character of Lebrun does not diminish James.

40. Quoted Robinson, in *Conversations,* p. 132.

Index

Khomeini, Ayatollah Ruholla, 79–80, 85–86, 91
Kincaid, Jamaica, 11

Lenin, Vladimir I., 146–47

MacGowan, Gault, 3–4, 31–33
MacKenzie, John M., 152n12, 157n27
Malaysia, 64–65, 68; Malaysian Muslim youth movement, 64
Mao Tse-tung, 101
Marx, 57, 146; Marxist revolutionaries, 57–59, 100–104, 146–47
Memory, ix, 127; instability of, 78, 118, 120, 122, 126, 133
Michener, Charles, 51, 160n4
Miranda, Francisco, 125, 131–32, 134, 147
Modernity: and change, 117, 135, 149, 167n10; and curiosity, xiv, 23; and mobility, xiii, 4, 23; and orientation, 4, 9; and responsibility to know, 149; and secularity, 58; social-political, 107; technological, 1, 58, 67, 116; and temporality, 24, 67, 148–49; and transformation, ix, 4, 6. *See also* Cultural complexity; European Enlightenment; Incompleteness
More, Thomas, 61
Mukherjee, Bharati, 10, 154n52
Multiculturalism, xii, 10, 11, 14, 18–19, 63
Musharraf, Pervez, 75
Musil, Robert, 53, 169n10
Muslim League, 94
Mustafa, Fawzia, 14–17
Muttawakil, Wakil Ahmed, 75–77. *See also* Taliban
Mysore (Hindu kingdom), 107

Naipaul, Patricia, 159n4
Naipaul, V. S.: as colonial, 7, 16, 18, 111, 114; as documentarist (*see also* Documentary discourse; Incompleteness), ix, xiii, 6, 12, 17, 33, 51–52, 55, 68, 82–85, 99, 104, 108, 117–18, 126, 131, 133–34, 136–40, 144, 148; factual-fictional discourse, 133–48; as inquiline, 148; and observational position (perception, perspective), 1–2, 9, 55–56, 68, 81–82, 118, 120, 122, 126, 129, 131, 133, 139, 143; self-perception, 126–27; untouchability, 8; as writer and traveler (*see also* Documentary discourse; Incompleteness), ix, xiv, 6, 9, 14, 23–24, 50–53, 66, 110–12, 114, 122, 125–26, 131, 135–41, 143, 149
——and accusations against: betrayal of Third World solidarity, 21–23, 56; Eurocen-
trism, 12; misogynism, 12; nihilism, 3, 7; pessimism, 3, 10, 12, 51; racism, 12, 21, 38
——family of: death of his sister Sati and brother Shiva, 129; Hinduism, 3–4; Kali worship, 32
——father of: correspondence with, 30, 159n13; relationship with 3, 30–31, 62, 128; writings of, 3, 30–33
——and fear: of extinction, 2–3, 9; of human superfluousness, 2, 53, 110; of invisibility, 53
——and Hinduism, 7–8, 129; importance of guides, 54, 56, 59, 62–65, 81–84, 114
——and strangeness (*see also* Understanding), ix, xii, 17–18, 43, 48–49, 56, 61, 63, 65, 73, 81, 85, 97, 104, 114, 118–21, 132–44; of the past, 132–33, 135, 138–40, 144, 147–49; strangers (*see also* Understanding), xiii, 38–41, 54, 56, 59–60, 83, 116, 118, 121, 123, 125–26, 128–32, 135–37, 140–41, 143, 148–49; temporal distance, 132, 138, 148; time travel, 133
——and Trinidad, 2, 24, 29–32, 50, 54, 62, 70, 105, 119, 122, 125–26, 128, 131–32, 138, 141–45; memories of, 127–28; Trinidad Guardian, 3–4, 31–32
——and Wiltshire: cottage, 118–19; valley, 121, 123–24, 129
——and writing: as profession (vocation), ix, 2, 9, 11, 30–31; as transformation, 8, 33, 50, 53, 68–69, 118
——writings of: *Among the Believers,* x, 3, 5, 33, 52, 54–67, 94, 108, 130–31; *An Area of Darkness,* 2, 5, 125, 128; *A Bend in the River,* ix, 7, 9, 20, 33, 41–49, 53–54, 59, 63, 108, 112, 124, 147; *Beyond Belief,* x, 12, 33, 54, 68–105, 130, 133, 137; "Conrad's Darkness," 14–16; on *The Enigma of Arrival,* ix, 12, 20–21, 23–24, 53, 55, 58, 68, 78, 109, 117–31, 148; *Finding the Center,* ix, 24, 58, 109, 112–17; *Guerrillas,* ix, 13, 33–41, 59, 63, 124, 147, 160n20; *A House for Mr Biswas,* ix, 30–33, 52, 125, 130, 142–43; "In a Free State," 33, 123–24; *India: A Million Mutinies Now,* 12; *India: A Wounded Civilization,* 2–3, 6; *The Loss of Eldorado,* 130, 134, 139; *The Middle Passage,* 11, 125; *Miguel Street,* 142; "Reading and Writing," 105–107; Review of C. L. R. James' *Beyond a Boundary,* 171n37; "Trinidad," 14; *A Turn in the South,* ix, 133; *A Way in the World,* ix, 7, 12, 17, 55, 58, 68, 78, 84, 109, 130–47; "What's Wrong with Being a Snob?" 10; "The Writer and India," 105–107

Nehru, Jawaharlal, 94, 146
Neo-Romanticism, 9, 23, 117
Nixon, Rob, 154n69
Nkrumah, Kwame, 147, 167n7

Orientalism, 15, 27

Pakistan, 61–64, 74–80, 92–105; theocracy, 62,
   75, 95; re-Islamization (see also Islam), 95;
   political regression, 96, 99; reinstitution of
   Koranic punishments, 96; retribalization
   (see also Zionism), 96; similarity to Israel, 94
Pathans, 74, 102, 104
Perception, acculturation of, xii–xiv. See also
   Forster, Georg
Political activism, 37, 39–41, 135–37, 142–47
Political institutions, cultural importance of,
   60, 90, 95–98
Politics of identity, 51, 59
Postcolonial, xiv, 7, 11–12, 33, 37, 39, 103, 110
Postcolonialism: certainties of, 143; diasporic
   self-perception of, 27, 29; grievances of,
   25; postcoloniality, 27–29, 158n29; post-
   modernist postcolonialism, 25–26, 50; theo-
   ries and theorists of, ix, xi, xiii–xiv, 1, 10,
   12, 14–16, 18, 21–22, 25–29, 52, 55, 59, 147
Precolonial, 27–28, 106
Pre-Islamic Persia, 57, 91
Price, Richard, 157n27

Rachlin, Nahid, 58
Raleigh, Sir Walter, 85, 125, 131, 134, 138–41
Ramayana, 105–106
Ramlila, 106
Rashid, Ahmed, 163nn8,13, 164n18
Reed, Ishmael, 11
Rembrandt van Rijn, self-portraits of, 128
Revolutions: African, 144–47; American, 125;
   French, 67, 85, 125; Haitian, 125; South
   American, 125, 131
Reza, Mohammad (Shah of Iran), 57–58, 79–
   81, 85, 90–92
Rousseau, Jean Jacques, and concept of noble
   savage, xii–xiii, 23

Said, Edward, xiv, 5, 15, 27–28; Orientalism,
   10, 27–29, 152n12
Schiff, Stephen, 161n7
Sharia (Islamic law), 74–75
Sharif, Nawaz, 75
Spirituality, modalities of, 80, 83–85

Spivak, Gayatri, 25–26
Spurr, David, 112
Stalin, Joseph, 67, 85
Subaltern Studies (Guha), 25–26
Suharto, Kemusu Argamulja, 71–72
Sukarno, Achmad, 108, 110
Suleri, Sara, 154n51

Taliban, 73–77; foreign minister Wakil Ahmed
   Muttawakil, 75–77; leader Mullah Omar,
   74–75; Talibanization, 75
Technocracy, 1, 51, 68, 71, 79, 85, 92, 95–96;
   combined with theocracy, 71–72, 74–75;
   combined with tribalism (see also Africa),
   85, 96
Tehran Times, 79, 82
Theroux, Paul, 5–6, 20–21, 42, 53, 55–56, 73;
   The Great Railway Bazaar, 5; My Other Life,
   56; Sir Vidia's Shadow, 20, 55, 159n4, 161n7
Thirty Years' War, 107
Toussaint L'Ouverture, Francois Dominique,
   144, 147

Understanding: circularity of, xi–xii, 50, 63;
   desire for, 121; historicity of, xiv, 121; incompleteness of, ix–xiv, 45, 82–84, 110, 116,
   126, 133, 135, 137–40, 144, 147–48; of the
   past, 132–33, 135, 138–40, 144, 147–49;
   strangeness (see also Naipaul, V. S., and
   strangeness), ix, xii, 17–18, 43, 48–49, 56,
   61, 63, 65, 73, 81, 85, 97, 104, 114, 118–21,
   132–44; strangers (see also Naipaul, V. S.,
   and strangeness, strangers), xiii, 38–41, 54,
   56, 59–60, 83, 116, 118, 121, 123, 125–26,
   128–29, 132, 135–37, 140–41, 148–49

Walcott, Derek, xiv, 20–25, 56; African heri-
   tage, 21; "The Antilles," 22; "Café Mar-
   tinique: A Story," 21; Caribbean writers,
   21; celebration of the provincial, 23–24;
   "The Garden Path: V. S. Naipaul," 20;
   Omeros, 22; politics of identity, 21; and
   solidarity, 22–23; "Tribute to C. L. R.
   James," 171n37; and Trinidad, 21–23
Weiss, Timothy, 34, 151n7, 160n26
Worcester, Kent, 170n34, 171n39

Zia ul-Haq, 94
Zionism: politics of water and weapons, 96;
   retribalization, 96. See also Pakistan

Dagmar Barnouw is Professor of German and Comparative Literature, University of Southern California, and author of *Weimar Intellectuals and the Threat of Modernity* (Indiana University Press, 1988) and *Germany 1945* (Indiana University Press, 1997), among other books of cultural criticism.